"This is no mere memoir, but a handbook on how to date the adult way. By reading Arnold's entertaining and upbeat story of voracious exploration, Generation X, Y, and Z can learn everything no one ever taught them about effective communication, self-care, emotional responsibility, and joyful sexual freedom. If dating is in your future, this inspirational book is for you."

—Robin Rinaldi, author of *The Wild Oats Project: One Woman's Midlife Quest for Passion at Any Cost*

"This book will have great appeal to other seekers—men and women—especially those who are older or long for a deep sensual connection to others. Carolyn is such a role model for other middle-aged women—unafraid, unabashedly sensual and assertive. I love how brave and brazen she is!"

—Julia Scheeres, author of the *New York Times* best-selling memoir *Jesus Land*

"Carolyn's goal of fifty dates was a brilliant way to find a partner, and her communication skills, honesty, and appreciative regard for her dates would help anyone - not only in dating, but in all one's relationships."

—Chas August, Relationship & Intimacy Coach

"Carolyn Arnold's dating stories in *Fifty First Dates After Fifty* will be inspiring for any woman who worries that life has passed her by and that it's too late to attract a life partner. There will be bad dates, broken hearts and dashed expectations—and some hot fun along the way. Carolyn's stories of dating resilience and persistence show us that finding a deep love is possible at every age."

—Sasha Cagen, feminist life coach and author of *Quirkyalone: A Manifesto for Uncompromising Romantics*

"*Fifty First Dates after Fifty* is not your typical dating book. Carolyn boldly shares the raw vulnerabilities of being a person truly living life on her own terms. You'll be rooting for Carolyn all the way through as she tries, fails, feels, picks herself up, dusts herself off, and courageously moves forward into her next new adventure . . . funny and engaging . . . I was hooked at the prologue. You will be too."

—Wendy Newman, author of *121 First Dates: How to Succeed at Online Dating, Fall in Love, and Live Happily Ever After (Really!)*

FIFTY
FIRST
DATES
AFTER
FIFTY

FIFTY FIRST DATES AFTER FIFTY

A MEMOIR

CAROLYN LEE ARNOLD

SHE WRITES PRESS

Published 2021
Printed in the United States of America
Print ISBN: 978-1-64742-211-0
E-ISBN: 978-1-64742-212-7
Library of Congress Control Number: 2021914649

For information, address:
She Writes Press
1569 Solano Ave #546
Berkeley, CA 94707

Interior design by Tabitha Lahr

She Writes Press is a division of SparkPoint Studio, LLC.

To all the brave older women who are looking for the right partner, may you find him or her; to Jim, for being the right partner for me; and to my fifty dates, for being the right path to Jim.

AUTHOR'S NOTE

All the events in this story are real, told from my own perspective, with my own name. To protect the privacy of the other people in this story, all of their names and many geographic, chronological, and identifying characteristics have been changed.

CONTENTS

~~~~~~~~~

PART III: HOPE

PART IV: LONGING

PART V: VISIONS

PART VI: DISCOURAGEMENT

PART VII: REVELATIONS

Prologue

MONOGAMOUS DATING

〜〜〜〜〜〜〜〜〜〜〜〜

"You're still sleeping with other guys?"

George asked this in a voice shrill enough for the other diners in the cozy Ethiopian restaurant to hear. Several looked over at us—a middle-aged white couple—with expressions ranging from annoyance to amusement.

I had suggested this romantic Berkeley spot for our fifth date because I thought that George, who performed with an African dance troupe, would like Ethiopian food. It was a bad place to have this discussion.

"But I told you that on our third date," I whispered in a low voice, trying to discourage eavesdropping by diners who were still looking our way. "Before we slept together."

"You said you had other lovers then," he said. "But why would you keep seeing them?"

"'Cause they're my lovers," I said. "They support me while I look for a partner."

George leaned back in his chair and shook his head in disgust. Wispy strands of long brown hair had come loose from his ponytail and swayed on either side of his thin face.

"How could you do that to me?" he asked with sorrowful brown eyes.

Inside, I was sighing. I didn't want to hurt him. George had his own, traditional dating rules, and I had violated the one that said "stop sleeping with all other men after you spend a night with me." It was monogamous dating. And while I eventually wanted a monogamous partner, I was not interested in committing to one man while I was still dating.

I wondered how much time and how many apologies I owed this sweet man before I gently extricated myself from what he thought had become a relationship. My experiment of dating men who were outside of my usual circle was not going well. Could I only relate to men who, like me, had attended personal growth workshops on relationships?

I was fifty-eight years old, and I had a goal of finding my life partner by going on dates with fifty men. George was date number 31. I'd started the project with great optimism, but now that it was more than halfway done, I wondered if I would find a partner of any type by the fiftieth date.

It had been over a year since I'd said good-bye to Peter, and I was determined to go on, no matter how long it took. Date 32 was scheduled for Saturday—a walk around the Berkeley Marina. This guy looked promising . . . a fifty-six-year-old therapist from Marin County.

PART I
LETTING GO

LETTING GO ONE (2008)

~~~~~~~~~~~~~~~~~~~~~~~~~~

"Peter, I love you, I honor your journey, I set you free."
I gazed into Peter's blue eyes, twins to my own blue irises. Even in the low candlelight in my living room, his eyes twinkled over his tan cheeks; his wild white hair still looked like a blond halo to me. Peter and I had been together for seven years—five years longer than the two he had said he was good for and five years longer than my longest relationship. Tears pressed into my eyes as I imagined letting go of this man, who I still believed was the best partner for me.

"Carolyn, I love you, I honor your journey, I set you free," Peter said kindly, but free of tears. I believed that he loved me—but not enough to stay with me. He was ready for seven months of traveling in Europe and India, ready to be single again.

How could I let go of someone who had been my perfect match for seven years? Peter was a happy Buddhist beach boy in his late fifties, living a mellow retired life in Hawaii. His upbeat attitude and peaceful home had provided an oasis for me, a new age California girl in her late fifties living a hectic professional life in the Bay Area. Good friends for a year before becoming lovers, we could talk about anything and end up laughing. He would say, "Great!" and mean it, after anything I said. He

3

bought me gifts—an iPod Nano to have music when I ran, a snorkel and fins for my visits to Hawaii, pillows when mine had lost their fluff, and "clitoral cream" to help me have better orgasms. How could I let go of someone who bought me clitoral cream? Even though I was making plans to date other men, it was hard to imagine being with anyone other than Peter. I would need more than a letting-go ceremony for that. Luckily, I had a plan.

THE PLAN

~~~~~~~~

I'd come up with the idea a month before Peter left for Europe. My friend Kate and I were sitting on the grass beside the crowded Oakland Grand Lake Farmer's Market on a sunny September Saturday, catching up while we took a break from buying flowers and organic vegetables. Kate was in my women's group, and we loved talking about relationships. Younger than me by fourteen years, she was transitioning from a career as a pole-dance teacher to a therapist and was not afraid of asking direct questions.

"Are you looking forward to dating when Peter leaves?" Kate asked.

"Kind of," I said. "But I'm going to miss Peter a lot." I sighed. "I'll probably look for someone just like him!"

"You were getting pretty bored with him, though, remember?"

She was right. My latest trips to see him on the Big Island had left me feeling more restless than relaxed.

"But my heart still loves him," I whined, "and believes we're the ideal match." I watched a happy young couple float gracefully through the market like a pair of swans.

"He *was* ideal for you all those years, but now someone else might be better," said Kate. She perused the crowd, as if the better guy might be in sight. I had confessed in our women's group that I was starting to want a real partner, not a part-time temporary one—someone who would do what Peter could not: live nearby, do something besides relax, and commit to a long-term relationship. But they would have to be as joyful and loving as Peter—a Peter-plus person.

"Maybe I need to go on a lot of dates to find someone," I said, following Kate's gaze to a gangly man walking by. "It might help me get over Peter and see what other types of men are out there."

"That's not a bad idea," Kate said, turning back to me. "How many dates do you think it would take?"

"There was that movie," I said, laughing. "*Fifty First Dates.*"

"Didn't she go on fifty first dates with the same man . . . because she had amnesia?"

"Yeah," I said, "But *I* could go on fifty first dates with fifty *different* men."

"That's a lot of dates!" She looked at me with an admiring smile.

I liked the sound of fifty. When I bought my home, I'd looked at over a hundred houses until I found the perfect one. As a statistician, I knew that samples of only fifty were needed for significant results. Fifty dates sounded like plenty to get over Peter and check out different types.

"Maybe I could make a research project out of it," I said. My heart beat faster. That was it! I worked as a researcher at a college. I gathered data on the students and determined which groups needed support. By dating a lot of men, I could determine if there was a better man for me than Peter. The whole idea cheered me up. It wasn't just dating—it was a dating research project!

"I think I'm going to do that," I said. "I'll set a goal of going out on fifty first dates."

"Sounds like a great plan," said Kate. "And you know a ton of men."

Kate and I had both attended workshops put on by the Human Awareness Institute (HAI), a Bay Area nonprofit that offers classes on love, intimacy, and sexuality.[1] In my ten years of participating in and then volunteering to assist with HAI workshops, I had met hundreds of people seeking better relationships. Many of my fellow volunteers were single men, and some had told me, with a twinkle in their eye, "Carolyn, if you're ever available again, let me know." What better group of men to date than those plucked from the HAI pool?

"Yeah, I'll start with men from HAI. But there are other places I can go to meet men, like Sierra Singles hikes, or the meditation nights for singles at Spirit Rock. Also professional singles events and online dating sites. And I don't have to limit myself to men who'd make ideal partners—I can explore different types of men!" I was getting excited.

"I can't wait to hear how this goes," Kate said, smiling in amusement.

But then I felt a pang of doubt. "What if I don't find anyone better than Peter?"

"I doubt that'll happen," Kate said, looking more serious. "It's natural to think that the last guy you were with was the best—especially since he was your first long relationship. But you're breaking up for a reason. After you start dating, I don't see you being able to go back."

I pondered her words silently as I watched a tall, suntanned man in blue nylon running shorts walk by carrying a mesh bag of oranges. He looked about my age—and definitely a type I wanted to explore.

Kate caught me staring and grinned, and I grinned back.

I hoped she was right.

FLASHBACK

~~~~~~~~~~

The Human Awareness Institute had prepared me well for this project. I had turned to HAI in my forties, when I became serious about finding a life partner and realized that my dating choices had led only to short-term relationships. After twenty years working through a progression of jobs and graduate school degrees in women's studies, statistics, and education, I had finally settled into a community college research job that I loved. Now I had time for a personal life, but I was afraid I would never find a lasting partnership if I didn't change what I was doing. So I was relieved to learn that HAI (pronounced "Hi") offered weekend workshops on love, intimacy, and sexuality just two hours north of my house, on the grounds of Harbin Hot Springs, a new age retreat center that I frequented often.

It was natural for me to turn to nontraditional personal growth workshops to learn how to improve my relationships. I had never wanted a traditional life, despite being primed for it by my middle-class upbringing in the Los Angeles suburbs of the early 1960s. My conservative parents, who were transplanted New Englanders, thought they were raising me to be an educated housewife like my mother, and had similar conventional ideas for my younger brother and sister.

When I was fifteen, they sent me to a girls' boarding school back East, far from the permissive California of the '60s. Flying back and forth across the country, however, planted seeds of independence. And by the time I started college, the '60s had reached the East Coast. As a student at a women's college in Massachusetts in the early 1970s, I tried marijuana, protested the Vietnam War, and abandoned my parents' conservative views for more liberal ones. I also woke up to feminism. My father had not let my mother work until their youngest was in grade school, and she'd resented it. I vowed to never become economically dependent on a man. My parents' traditional suburban life looked boring to me—I wanted my life to be a grand adventure.

After college, I moved back to the West Coast, where I settled in Berkeley and spent the next twenty-five years exploring alternative lifestyles. I moved into a vegetarian cooperative house, waitressed, and volunteered at the Berkeley Free Clinic, which offered free health services to demonstrate that health care was for people, not profits. I went to spiritual ceremonies, tried LSD, and started backpacking by myself.

While working in a feminist women's clinic, where we demonstrated women's control of our own bodies, I lost interest in men, who seemed stuck in outdated gender roles, and declared myself a lesbian. For eighteen years I thrived on being at the forefront of social change. I moved into an all-women's house and embraced all the emblems of a lesbian feminist in the 1970s—wearing overalls, cutting my long blond hair short, going to women's music concerts and festivals with lovers, and leading women's backpacking trips. We were redefining what it meant to be women.

Identifying as a lesbian enabled me to separate financially and emotionally from men—I earned two master's degrees and a PhD during this time and loved many women—but I never found the partner I dreamed of. In 1993, when men were emerging from first marriages, therapy, and men's groups with a feminist awareness, I grew interested in them again.

Dating men in my forties after an eighteen-year hiatus was like being a teenager without the restrictions. My lesbian years had given me a healthy self-confidence, and I knew I didn't need a man for financial security. I was attracted to their bodies and wanted to try out all kinds of male-female sex. My feminine side came out, and I started wearing dresses and heels again. After experiencing the full range of personalities among lesbians, I could see men as the complex people they were, trying to relate to women as best they could. I was still not interested in getting married—it felt too close to the housewife role—but I did want a long-term equal partner.

But five years later, I was still alone. So turning to an organization like HAI—which had a nontraditional approach to relationships, welcomed people of all sexual preferences, and held their workshops at a new age retreat center that reflected my own alternative lifestyle—seemed completely normal.

THE WORKSHOPS

~~~~~~~~~~~~

When I arrived at the spacious, high-ceilinged wood-and-stone conference center for my first HAI weekend retreat in 1998, I could see that the workshops would be the perfect training for me. I was ready to learn how to have a successful relationship, and that is exactly what these workshops taught. HAI's philosophy about relationships was that loving others started with loving yourself. One-on-one and small-group exercises promised to give me and the sixty other people there, half women and half men, the experience of loving ourselves and appreciating others.

My first workshop started right off with learning to look for the goodness in each person and was led by two facilitators, a man and a woman. "Find a partner and form a big circle," said the male facilitator. "In this ceremony you'll get to greet everyone."

As I wondered whom to ask, a tall, thin man moved closer and said, "Would you be my partner?"

"Sure," I said, relieved, and we moved into the circle.

"Now face your partner and put your hand on your heart." Angelic, harmonious music played softly over the speakers. The female leader said, "Gaze into the eyes of this person, and say with your eyes, 'I'm glad you're here.'" I gazed up into the man's eyes, saw the gladness coming from him, and sent my own gladness back. I felt a surge of joy. After a few seconds, she said, "Open your heart, kiss the hand, and step to the left." I followed the gesture they had taught us—I took my hand off my heart, opened it as if for a hug, and then took the man's hand and kissed the back of it while gazing into his eyes before I moved on, feeling tender toward him. My next partner was a plump woman my height who smiled serenely at me. "With this partner," the leader said, "look into their eyes and silently send the message, 'I accept you just as you are.'" We both beamed. I felt a deep peacefulness, like a coming home. We carried out the same heart and hand gesture, a gentle leaving. This ceremony was just what I had been looking for—a way to connect with men and women closely, without having to think of what to say—just experiencing and appreciating each person. We rotated around the circle until we had been with each person there. The facilitators' caring words helped us focus kindly on each one. There were so many different types—in height, size, age, skin tone, gender—and they each communicated differently with their eyes. Some could not look me in the eye for the whole time, but others had sparkling eyes that looked eager for connection. I wondered if that meant they liked me. I tried to project acceptance to each person.

Later that evening, we got to pick a buddy for the weekend. They said that we would do a few exercises with them, but mainly this would be our support person. When we were asked to select a buddy, I looked around at the sixty people and froze. Do I pick a woman I feel safe with, or a man I'm attracted to? Everyone was being picked, and a short, balding, smiling, Buddha-like guy was looking at me with a goofy grin.

"Would you like to be buddies?" he said. "My name's Andrew."

I wasn't attracted to him, but I didn't see any other options. "Sure," I said, feeling skeptical that we could relate to each other.

But when Andrew said he was a chiropractor who led fire walks—where people walk over hot coals to overcome their fears—and that he'd come from Santa Cruz with his men's group, I realized he was from a similar alternative, feminist background. Soon I would learn that most people who came to HAI were seekers of some sort. Although not everyone walked on hot coals, all were looking for new ways to find love, self-acceptance, and life purpose. Ranging in age from twenty to eighty years old, with economic situations from low income to very prosperous, most were, like me, middle-aged and middle income. For everyone, personal growth was a high priority.

In our first paired exercise, Andrew and I sat against backrests on the floor facing each other, talking about our past relationships and why we came to the workshop.

"I've been wanting a male partner for a long time," I said, feeling my tears begin. "I'm forty-seven, and I've never had a relationship last for more than two years." Andrew nodded, following the instructions to just listen rather than respond and try to fix me. I sank into my own sadness, and my tears flowed down my cheeks. I felt Andrew's kindness and compassion in the way he listened so fully to me, nodding with empathy.

When it was his turn, Andrew said, "Well, my men's group thought this would be a good experience. I've been divorced for a year, have joint custody of two young kids, and things are good. I'm not necessarily looking for a relationship, but I'm open." I nodded, smiling at him.

"And now," the male facilitator said gently from the front of the room, "one of you, take your hands and cup your buddy's face, look into their eyes, and see if you have permission to gently stroke their face." Peaceful music enhanced the tenderness of the moment. Andrew asked if he could go first, and as I nodded yes, he held my face and smiled into my eyes. As his fingers started stroking my face, my heart melted. His touch was delicate and sure. I realized I'd never been touched so reverently, even in sexual situations, and the facilitators had made it clear that we were not going to be sexual. Again, I felt filled with peace. I had come home. My face relaxed, and more tears flowed.

When it was time to switch roles, I tentatively brushed my fingers over Andrew's little round face, and he started looking beautiful to me, this funny-looking man with such a kind heart.

Andrew turned out to be the perfect buddy for me. The next morning, I was cursing myself for not getting up early enough to go running before breakfast. "Don't you see what you're doing to yourself?" he said to me. "You can't love yourself when you keep seeing yourself as wrong. Hey, you needed the sleep."

"But it's too late to go running!" I wailed.

"No, it's not. Let's go."

While we ran along the sun-dappled canyon road, surrounded by tall pines covering the steep grassy hillsides and leafy branches waving over us, Andrew taught me to laugh out loud in gratitude for the beauty of the California hills. I felt a glimmer of enjoyment in the moment and loved myself a little bit more. Andrew would be a friend for years to come.

⊸————⊶

Besides a buddy, we also chose a small group for the weekend to be our support team. My small-group leader was Bruce, a HAI volunteer. "I'm fierce at loving myself," he said in our first meeting. "And because of that, I finally found my wife—my life partner—and I'm staying in love with her. Even though she loves me, I still tell myself how much I love and appreciate myself every day." I hoped to get to that loving place with myself and a partner.

As our group of four sat in a circle on the floor, Bruce asked us to notice any negative thoughts we had about ourselves and share them. I had plenty of negative thoughts about myself, many of them from my mother. As her firstborn, my teenage rebellion had challenged her, and she had criticized me harshly—for my hairstyle, my clothes, my interest in sexuality, and the liberal attitudes I'd picked up back East. Because I left home at age fifteen, we never got to resolve our differences, and her disapproval continued whenever I visited her. Although she told me often that she loved me and was proud of my achievements, her critical voice had settled into my head. When it was my turn, I started listing my faults, echoing my mother's words.

"I'm so critical," I said. "I notice what people, including myself, are doing wrong, and I focus on that. I try not to say anything to others, but I often curse myself out loud for what I do." I could barely look at the other group members, but I felt them looking at me sympathetically, so I went on. "Also, I'm selfish," I said. "I think I've taken this whole taking-care-of-myself thing too far. I put myself first in most situations." I felt a flush of shame at even admitting that. "I also worry a lot—about everything. It's part of focusing on what could go wrong rather than what could go right." I was feeling worse and worse, but I glimpsed some of the group nodding as if they understood. Then I remembered why I was there. "I'm afraid that I'm not lovable—that because I'm critical and selfish and worry so much, no one will want to stay with me and be my partner." Lost in my tears, I slowly looked up at the group.

They were smiling at me warmly. "Send this person some love and appreciation for what they shared," Bruce said. My little group sent me love with their eyes or bowed with their hands together. I still felt glum, but I sensed their support. Then we went on to the next person. By the time everyone had shared, we were all slumped in our seats.

"Now," said Bruce, "shake out your body, sit up straight like you are proud, and share what you love about yourself." *Oh, good*, I thought, *this will be easier.* My parents had given me positive messages as well. Their investment in my education had made me believe in myself. My mother had encouraged me to love my small breasts and wide hips. My father had always supported me in nontraditional pursuits. He'd bought me a tool-kit to fix my bike and VW Bug.

"I love my high energy," I started, "which I got from my parents. It makes everything possible. I love that I found a career I love that supports me, and I'm proud that I was able to buy my own house." I hoped this didn't sound like I was bragging. I had never imagined I could buy a house in the Bay Area as a single woman, but I'd been lucky—and privileged. The interest rates had gone down and my income had gone up at just the right time, and my grandmother had left me enough for a small down payment on a modest bungalow in an old Oakland neigh-borhood with a crime rate that ebbed and flowed. "I love that I'm adventurous—I went to Peru by myself, I go salsa dancing, I backpack by myself, and I lead women's backpacking trips. I also write songs." I was proud of my daring and creative sides. "And," I said, deciding to go for it, "I love my body—I love its shape and how I can keep it lean by running, and I love how my hair frames my face." I shook my light brown hair back and looked up. Now I was embarrassed, thinking I'd been too positive. But my group all looked at me the same way—nodding with warmth. As the others shared their intimate thoughts, I sent them encouraging looks. But as I sat there, a critical voice returned. *If I'm so great, why haven't I found a partner?*

Bruce, however, had been listening well. Afterward, he gave me three affirmations to say to myself every day—I am beautiful. I am lovable. I deserve a loving relationship. I felt a flicker of hope that I could overcome my critical internal monologue with these positive thoughts.

In the ten years after that first workshop, I returned many times to that conference center, going through the series of workshops that HAI offered, and then assisting at them. During those weekends, the tenets of HAI sank into me—I gradually learned to love myself, focus on the good in others, communicate in an honest and loving way, and trust my own relationship choices. My connections with both men and women deepened. Although my first relationship with a guy I met at a HAI workshop lasted only the usual two years, I was now part of a large community of people who would become my friends, lovers, and partners. Then, at a HAI party in 2000, as I was gazing into the eyes of each person, a pair of twinkling blue eyes smiled and blinked back.

LETTING GO TWO (2001-2008)

P eter was living in San Francisco when we first became lovers in 2001, but after three years, with a nest egg from a real estate career, he retired to Hilo, Hawaii. For four years we commuted between Oakland and Hilo, where I loved to visit but had no desire to live. We saw each other about once a month and talked every night—for me a nourishing blend of support, pleasure, and independence. My life was full with a demanding college research position, an old home and large garden, several groups of friends, songwriting, running, and weekends spent volunteering at HAI workshops. A boyfriend in Hawaii whom I saw once a month had been just right.

Since early on, Peter and I had committed to staying together monogamously for six months at a time. The short-term promises had worked well—they gave us some security while calming our mutual fears of being trapped. Six months after six months had added up to seven years, but as we reached our late fifties, I was ready to risk a longer commitment, and he was not. I was trying to be attached to a Buddhist, who cultivated non-attachment.

By spring of 2008, Peter and I were both feeling restless. He wanted to travel in Europe and India for months, move to Bali, and never commit. I wanted to stay in the Bay Area and find a committed relationship with someone who did more than meditate. We decided to separate when he left for Europe in the fall. I had suggested the letting-go ceremony for the night before his trip in October 2008. I needed to hear out loud that we were moving on. As much as I wanted a Peter-plus person, I knew that once he left, I would have a hard time letting go of my longing for a simple Buddhist beach boy.

PART II
TOUCH

CHOICE

~~~~~~

One Sunday a month later, I was jogging on my usual route, a residential street on the crest of the Oakland hill I live on, feeling a lightness finally returning to my heart as I gazed out over the shining San Francisco Bay. The view still thrilled me after thirty years of living in the Bay Area, although I hadn't noticed it lately—the aching in my heart had weighed down my spirit in the month since Peter had left for Europe. But now the sharp missing of him had subsided enough for me to once again notice the world around me. It was time to begin my dating project.

I was not surprised by how much I'd pined for Peter that first month. Despite the letting-go ceremony, I had not completely let go. After he left, I joined a songwriting class and wrote several sad songs about my lover leaving. However, in early November, I found myself writing a joyful tune about Barack Obama winning the presidency. I was ready to date.

I reminded myself that one purpose of the project was to get over my longing for Peter, so it was fine to start even if I was still missing him. As I ran past the familiar houses in my neighborhood, I was thinking of the men from the HAI workshops who had said they wanted to date me when I was available. *I should let them know I'm ready*, I thought, with a shiver of excitement running through my heart and down my body.

As I lost myself in these delicious feelings, Randy, a handsome neighbor, smiled and waved. I'd known Randy from several years of jogging by and occasionally chatting with him or his wife. She had invited me to his backyard fiftieth birthday bash a year earlier, where, to my dismay, she had criticized him in front of everyone. "Why did you barbecue the chicken before the corn?" she yelled as he carried a full plate of chicken into the house. Cringing, I'd wondered why this gentle man with such a warm smile stayed with someone like that.

I hadn't seen his wife for quite a while, and since he smiled, I stopped and asked how he was. He paused from clipping the vines back from the stone wall in front of his brown-shingled Craftsman bungalow. His gardening clothes looked a bit crumpled.

"Well," he said with a sigh, "it's a long story, but Diana and I split up, and she moved out." For a second, the brow on his youthful face furrowed, his voice wavered, and he looked like a sad little boy. But then he looked into my eyes, smiled, and sighed, sounding relieved.

Although I imagined it was complicated, I was relieved for him.

"Oh, I'm so sorry!" I said, though inside I wasn't feeling sorry at all, and couldn't help but think that this might be a fortuitous beginning to my dating project. I had always been attracted to Randy's kind eyes and lanky body that looked relaxed and strong under his weekend work shirts and baggy pants.

"Would you like to come in for a cappuccino?" he asked.

I told him I'd love to as soon as I finished my run. Running made me feel fit and happy, and I wouldn't give that up, even for a man I suddenly wanted to date.

After my run, I quickly showered and changed. When I returned, we talked for almost two hours at his kitchen table. He made me a tea latte from his cappuccino machine after I confessed that I didn't drink coffee. As we sipped our drinks, he told me the long, involved story of his marriage, as well as the equally long story of buying the cappuccino machine in Italy decades earlier.

I empathized with the difficulties in his marriage and oohed and aahed over his adventures in Italy, but I noticed that he wasn't asking me any questions, a dating red flag. During a rare pause, I said, "Your stories are helping me with my sadness. I just broke up with a guy I was with for seven years. We're still close friends, but now he's traveling in Europe."

"Oh, that's got to be hard, breaking up when you're still feeling close," he said.

His words went right to the place in my heart that felt how hard it was, surprising me that he understood. Maybe Randy could do more than just tell stories. Maybe he could also reach inside my heart and hold me, and my feelings, tenderly.

I got up from the table to start my day, but offered to make him lunch at my house. To my surprise, he accepted. We ended up spending the afternoon talking at my kitchen table.

He did most of the talking, and most of his stories were long, but he also asked me questions. "So how is it for you when someone leaves?" he asked, gazing at me earnestly with his kind brown eyes. But as soon as I started to answer, he was off talking about himself again. Still, Peter had never asked about difficult feelings. I wasn't sure how close I wanted to be to Randy, but those questions drew me in.

We finally broke away to continue our own Sundays, as the sun curved toward the horizon across the bay.

◦————◦

Later that night, he called. "Carolyn," he said. "I really enjoyed talking with you today."

"Me too," I said. "Thanks for inviting me in." I was smiling to myself. I figured we could work on balancing out the talking.

"I was wondering," he said, "if you'd like to come over tonight and use the sauna?"

Well, what new age sensual Northern California girl does not accept an invitation to a sauna at ten o'clock on a Sunday night?

Over my years in the Bay Area, I had spent many a late night naked in friends' hot tubs or saunas. I had also spent enough time in clothing-optional situations to know that being naked didn't necessarily imply being sexual. And yet, the thought of being naked with Randy in a sauna thrilled me. It was an innocent excitement—I was enjoying feeling turned on without assuming it would lead anywhere. I was good at letting men know how physically close—or distant—I wanted to be. Ten years of workshops on relationships had taught me the concept of being "at choice"—that in every moment, I can choose differently. I didn't know what Randy was expecting, but I assumed that he would respect whatever my choices were.

I went over in a T-shirt and jeans, with a towel and a purple sarong. Randy greeted me at the door and guided me to his cozy family room, where a sauna was built into the wall. On a coffee table in front of a big mission-style couch, he had laid out a cutting board of crackers, cheese, pieces of oranges, apples, and figs, and wine glasses. A saxophone played peaceful, meandering jazz.

I took a deep breath. "Oh, this is so nice!"

He beamed.

After a few bites of cheese and crackers, we took off our clothes, nonchalantly, as if we did this all the time. In fact, it was completely normal for me—I'd been going to nude beaches since my college days, and Harbin Hot Springs, my favorite retreat center, was a clothing-optional resort. At Harbin, nudity was nonchalant and nonsexual, and I enjoyed the sensuality of sun and water by soaking in the springs and sunning on a wide deck by the swimming pool. Still, it was exciting to be alone and naked with someone I was attracted to. I wondered how Randy was feeling about being naked with a woman different from his wife.

As we stepped into the sauna, we peeked surreptitiously at each other's bodies. He looked as lean as I had imagined. I was glad that running and yoga had kept me toned.

The sauna had two full-length wooden benches on different levels. He let me have the higher, warmer bench, and we each stretched out and relaxed into the growing heat. We didn't talk much. We didn't touch, although I wanted to. He sprinkled water on the coals from his perch on the lower bench. I was breathing in the steamy hot wood-scented air, wondering what would come next, savoring the nearness of him.

In the past, this type of private naked situation would have inevitably led to sex. I loved touch, and I loved sex, and one would lead naturally to the other. But I had learned in the last ten years that there was a whole range of touching between an affectionate brush of the hand and passionate lovemaking. And that I loved all of it and could choose where I wanted to be on that continuum at any given moment. As I lay in the sauna next to Randy, I wondered what choice I would make.

When we got out, we wrapped up in Randy's fluffy white robes and sat on the couch. I was feeling cozy and warm with the robe around my shoulders. My purple sarong, draped on the couch behind us, provided a ceremonial backdrop. We sipped some wine and nibbled on the cheese and figs. We eased nearer, eyes soft, smiling, murmuring, "It's nice to be here with you," and "I'm glad you're here." Our lips got closer until they met in a long, gentle kiss, which was just what I wanted. When it ended, I gazed into his eyes and started slowly caressing his face. I realized I was not ready to make love—I still missed Peter and was not certain where I was going with Randy—but I was enjoying this sensual touch. My robe loosened, and he started stroking my now bare shoulder and my chest, heading toward my breast. I redirected his hand with mine and brought it up to my face, whispering, "I'd like to wait to go further."

He whispered back, "I really want to make love with you."

"Did you expect we would do that tonight?" I asked, truly surprised. But this was unfair. I had just decided against that myself. Randy could easily have misinterpreted my eagerness in coming here late at night. He probably had the same assumption I used to have—that a naked woman and man in a sauna late at night equaled sex. I couldn't blame him, but I was hopeful he might enjoy simple skin-to-skin touch. I was thinking of all the face stroking I had done in HAI workshops, where the facilitator narrated how to touch each other reverently and see the unique beauty of each person. I was offering this experience to Randy as a way to get to know each other.

"I didn't necessarily expect to make love," he was saying, "but now that you're here, and feel so good, yeah. And once I start, I don't want to stop." He smiled like a little boy who was used to getting what he wanted.

"Well, I'd rather just kiss and caress your face for now, and see if we want to do more another time. Would that be OK?"

"Yeah," he said, still smiling, "but I can't just kiss. If we do that, I'll want to do more."

I realized that I couldn't convey the pleasure of nonsexual touch in ten minutes, when it had taken me ten years to learn it.

"I'm sorry," I said. "I'm not ready to do more. I should go anyway. It's a work night."

His smile drooped a bit. "I understand," he said, sighing heavily like Eeyore, the sad donkey in *Winnie-the-Pooh*.

"Thanks for a sweet evening," I said as I dressed, gathered my things, and left, disappointed that he could not just hang out in the sweet place of sensual, lightly erotic touch.

* * *

The next day, while I showered and got ready for work, I savored the deliciousness of this first of fifty first dates—his warm welcome into a peaceful room, the heated sensuousness of the sauna, the first gentle kiss. As I registered disappointment in how it ended, I realized that this date with Randy had done exactly what I'd hoped dating would do—help me gather information about what I wanted in a partner. I was attracted to Randy, and his questions touched me on a deep level—deeper than conversations with Peter. However, I wanted a man with better listening skills, a man who could appreciate the moment and nonsexual ways of touching. Would I have to stick with workshop-trained men for that? I was glad I had learned to trust my own choices, minute to minute, and that I had not made love with Randy.

Better for neighbors to be friends than lovers anyway, I thought as I got into my car. *Thank you, Randy, for opening the door to my dating project. I wonder who else is out there.*

WAVES

~~~

By the following weekend, I had lapsed back into grief about Peter. On Friday, I called Luke, a friend and past lover. I trusted him, a wild-haired spiritual guy and self-trained counselor and body worker, to support me through big emotions.

"Luke, it's about Peter. I still miss him so much. I'm afraid I've lost the best relationship I'll ever have." My voice was trembling.

He came right over. We sat on my big soft purple couch, the one Peter had left me when he moved to Hawaii. I cried and cried while Luke held me. A soothing song that repeated the words, "Waves are comin' in, waves are comin' in,"[1] played over and over on my CD player. It was a song I had listened to with Peter, and it made me miss him even more.

Luke picked up on the recurring words. "Healing's comin' in, healing's comin' in," sang Luke into my ear. "Going into the feelings makes you lighter," he whispered.

He was right—as I let myself feel the waves of sadness deeply, I could feel it lifting. I thought it would hurt more to be so sad, but the more I felt it, the more it seeped out in my tears.

Luke tucked me into bed and left; I cried off and on until I finally drifted off to sleep. When I woke on Saturday morning, most of my tears were gone—which was good, because I planned to attend my first social event that evening.

⋄———⋇

I had decided to jump-start my dating project at a social gathering in Sonoma, the wine country north of San Francisco. Put on for women and men who had attended the HAI workshops, the gathering offered an evening of planned activities with old friends and new acquaintances. Like the workshops, it was led by a facilitator and included time to socialize, share in pairs, and exchange reverent face stroking. Most of the people attending would be those I knew from workshops, but I was also hoping to meet someone new.

The event was held in a big farmhouse and included an optional sleepover, which meant that the next day I would be close to my favorite beach at Point Reyes National Seashore. I wanted to go walking along this wide-open shoreline—it was the perfect place to feel the "waves comin' in"—and cry out the sadness I still had for Peter. This plan comforted me. Knowing that I had a time and place for my grief made me able to put it aside and focus on meeting new people, especially men, at this party.

I felt brave but shaky going alone. My favorite women friends were not going. Neither were most of my men friends. My married friend Jules surprised me at the entrance gate with a bouquet of pink and yellow flowers. "I knew you were sad about Peter, so I got you these," he said, smiling like a little boy who wanted his mother to be happy. A friendly Latino with tan skin and white curly hair, Jules was known in HAI for his generosity. A Vietnam vet who'd served in a MASH-like unit, he'd retired from successful careers as a radiation technician and a building contractor and often used his time to make his friends' lives better. The big hug he gave me before he left to go home for an evening with his Russian wife, Tatiana, left me feeling less alone.

The room was crowded with more than fifty people settled against backrests on the floor, listening to the leader explain the evening's activities. In a sea of mostly jeans and T-shirts, I felt self-conscious in my long lavender skirt and shimmery matching purple top. I'd been out of the party scene for a while and had missed the memo on going more casual. Not seeing many people I knew or felt comfortable with, I quickly sat down and leaned against Ben, a sturdy, affectionate, dark-haired, thirtysomething man I knew from workshops. He immediately put his strong, sculpted arms around me and held me close on his lap. I leaned into him, soaking it in. I hadn't realized how starved I was for touch.

As we moved into the sharing in pairs, I reluctantly let go of Ben. My first partner was Susan, an acquaintance I had seen in workshops but rarely spoken with. She shared her struggles with her teenage daughter, and I shared my hopes for my dating project, and we parted feeling closer than before. My partner for face stroking was Alan, an older man who had recently married my friend Beth. As I stroked his weathered face, I appreciated the years of experience and love he brought to Beth. When he stroked me, I took in every little caress.

By the end of the evening, I was curled in Ben's lap and receiving a foot massage from someone else. I had gone from feeling shaky and alone to feeling soothed and connected. The sleepover in the open room was like a big modest slumber party, with people sleeping alone or side by side on futons, all clothed. Ben and I agreed to share a futon, planning to cuddle each other all night. Feeling his close presence through our clothes was exactly the touch I wanted. We admitted that we felt attracted to each other, but unlike Randy, Ben was trained to appreciate nonsexual touch, so we did not need to act on the attraction that night. We knew we would see each other again. I was feeling alive in my body and grateful for this group of people.

The following morning, I kissed Ben lightly, thanked him for a sweet night, and declined his offer to come with me to Point Reyes. I was determined to go there by myself to cry. We made a dinner date for the following Friday. It would be the second "first date" of my project.

⊷————⊷

By early afternoon, I was perched in my favorite spot on the dunes of Limantour Beach in Point Reyes, having passed only a handful of people in the one-mile walk along the sandy shore from the parking lot. Small waves were coming in, and they kept coming in, although not in the regular rhythm I expected. Some hurtled themselves high onto the shore, dissolving into the dry sand. Others, the same size, only made it partway to the dry sand before retreating back into the water. Some didn't even try to get to the shore—they plopped their wave water right beneath them on the wet sand. And yet they were also waves, a movement of some type. The waves felt like the swirling thoughts I had about Peter's leaving: he had left and was far away from me forever; he had left only temporarily, soon to return; he had not really left. After each wave retreated, wriggling sand crabs buried themselves in the wet sand like I used to bury myself in Peter's chest. Shorebirds scampered into the surf to dig them out, just like I had scurried to dig them up on L.A. beaches as a child during carefree summer days.

Watching the waves and birds and sand crabs, I got ready to cry and shout to myself in sorrow about Peter. But I found myself longing for a gorgeous dark-haired guy who was meditating farther back on the shore. I'd passed him during my walk along the beach.

Hmmm, I thought to myself, *I'm feeling turned on, wanting to touch and be touched. I thought I missed Peter. But what I really want is that stranger to make love to me.*

Another wave rolled in. I got up and shouted out loud, "I'm feeling *fine* here by myself! I'm going to be *fine!*" I stomped on the sand and opened my arms to embrace the ocean in the late autumn sun. What had started as a yearning in my groin for the stranger became a rush of energy pulsating through my torso and heart and out through my head and limbs. My whole body was vibrating, and my chest felt open and light. I felt solidly on the sand yet also expanded over the waves into the vast sky and sea. Waves kept coming in, adding the energy of the ocean to mine.

During four years of commuting to Hawaii to see Peter, I had shut down my sexual feelings except when I was with him, and even then, menopause had diminished my lust. I had feared that feeling sexual was behind me, but now those feelings, the key to my own vitality, were rushing back.

Peter was gone. I was trying to feel sad but instead felt excited. I laughed out loud. Soon I would start dating and being lovers with other men. I was celebrating my new freedom. Would it lead to a partner? I didn't know, but my friends, potential lovers, the dates to come, and these feelings in my body would sustain me on this journey.

<hr />

Ben arrived for our Friday night date looking irresistibly handsome, his rounded face, golden bronze skin, and black hair all groomed and glowing, set off by a neat paisley shirt and ironed slacks. His firm, stocky body was practically bursting out of his clothes with sexual vibrations, but he acted the part of the perfect gentleman. He smiled shyly when I answered the door.

Seeing him on my front porch, my whole body lit up. Although Ben was younger than me by twenty years, his comforting embrace at the party had lifted me out of my lingering sadness about Peter. Having this date was part of reclaiming my sexual self, separate from Peter.

When I welcomed him in, he hugged me and whispered in my ear, "It's so good to see you. You look great." An anticipatory jolt of excitement ran through my body under my flowery dress.

Leaving my house, he held his car door open for me, saying, "Please, my chariot!" I smiled as we drove off to my favorite sushi restaurant.

"You are such a sexy woman," he said as we sat side by side in a booth. He put an arm around me and murmured into my ear, "And you're so easy to talk to." I smiled again. Peter had told me these things too, but hearing them from a younger man boosted my confidence.

Ben listened with interest to my story about Peter. "It sounds like you two really loved each other, but you both needed to do other things with your lives," he said.

For a thirtysomething guy, he was wise about these issues. He told me about his open relationship with his longtime lover Rochelle, who was my age. She was hanging out with him while she looked for her "real" partner. They loved each other, but Ben also wanted a partner his age. I was relieved to hear this. This meant that Ben knew and loved older women, so I did not need to feel self-conscious about being twenty years older. And it meant that he would not be looking for me to be his partner. Which was good, since I also wanted a partner closer to my age.

As I sat there with Ben's arm around me, I could relate to Rochelle's desire to have Ben in her life while looking for her partner. Ten years before, during my search for a partner in my forties, I'd decided that I liked touch and sex too much to be sleeping alone, waiting for the perfect man. While I looked for him, I allowed myself to be close to men I enjoyed. Peter had been one of those lovers before we became serious. Maybe having someone to sleep with during this project would provide the touch and sex I thrived on instead of expecting it from my dates. Maybe Ben could play that role.

Ben and I were both anticipating the rest of the evening. I had invited him over for the night, and I knew I wanted to be sexual. I assumed that Ben wanted that too, or would tell me if he didn't. He had attended the same workshops—I trusted that we would each say what we wanted, respect any differences, and appreciate whatever we did.

When we returned home, I put on some peaceful new age music by Patrick Bernard and led him into my softly lit bedroom. Looking into his eyes for permission and finding an expression of delight, I unbuttoned and took off his shirt, unbuckled his belt, unzipped his pants, and pulled them down. His smile, subdued so far, burst out.

I started lifting my dress.

"Let me do that. Wow, I love your body!" he said as he pulled my dress over my head. His hardness confirmed his admiration as he slid the rest of my clothes off. We kissed softly, and I pulled him over to the open bed.

To meandering otherworldly music, we gently kissed and caressed each other, from head to toe. My yoni[2] opened to his fingers, while my hands spread his sexual energy throughout his body. Finally, he turned me onto my back and expertly stroked my now-wet yoni until I came. Then he donned a condom and entered me and quickly came himself. Afterward, we were both grinning wildly, like we had won some sort of grand prize. We kissed, wrapped our arms around each other, and slept peacefully.

◦————◦

When I woke the next morning, Ben was still grinning. "Ready for round two?" he asked. Startled, I thought, *Oh, the sexual energy of a younger man!* I didn't feel ready and was about to tell him. But then I decided to touch him and see where that led. To my surprise, I felt turned on. We made love again. My orgasm spread and hummed through my whole body.

Oh yeah! I remembered. *I love sex! It energizes and mellows me out at the same time.* I was lucky that I had never been hurt or coerced into sex by either men or women, so my association with sex was all pleasure. I'd gotten a late start, losing my virginity to a man at twenty before taking a delicious detour into relationships with women from twenty-four to forty-two, only to rediscover men in my forties. Now, I unabashedly enjoyed sex with men with the exuberance of an innocent teenager and the confidence of an unscathed adult.

When Ben left later that morning, we agreed to see each other again. I looked forward to more nights with him while I focused on finding a partner.

TOUCH

~~~

The following Saturday, I went to a "sensual party," where I
hoped to find men to date and/or to touch. Marco, a regal,
long-haired Italian friend, had been putting on these parties for
the last year in his suburban ranch house, and as a woman who
loved touch and sex, I gravitated toward this type of event.

Although I was new to Marco's parties, I was not new to
the activities in them. The invitation enticed me with dancing,
eating, cozy rooms with fireplaces and futons for sensuous
touching, and something called a warm pool water ceremony.
Ceremonies had been part of my life since the '70s, when I had
bowed during Native American rites in Berkeley and howled
at the moon during goddess rituals on the banks of Northern
California rivers. Now, I led my own pagan ceremony each
winter solstice at my house. A sensual party with a water ceremony combined three of my favorite things—ceremony, warm
pools, and touch.

Marco's party would be a safe place to experience those
things, since most of the people who attended his parties had
attended similar workshops as I had about communicating and
respecting choices. Whether or not I found men for my dating

project, I was hoping that parties like these, along with men like Ben, would meet my need for touch and sex along the way.

I spent most of Saturday getting my nails polished, my body toned, and my clothes carefully selected—a lacy black tank top and slinky black skirt. As part of feeling more sensual, I wanted to feel sexy and attractive to myself. This couldn't hurt for finding dates either.

When I got to the party, Marco gave me a big warm bear hug. "Good to see you! This is my girlfriend, Dawn," he said with a broad smile. She had wispy hair and bright eyes and moved to hug me in a soft flowing dress. "Welcome," Dawn said. "Let us know if you need anything." Their greeting helped me feel brave, and I pushed myself to mingle.

My wild-haired counselor friend Luke, in whose arms I had cried about Peter weeks before, was there to encourage me. "You look great. Go find someone new," he said.

Luckily, I was feeling gregarious. We needed partners for the water ceremony, and I looked around at my options. A young, vaguely familiar guy with dreamy-looking eyes under wavy locks had said, "You look very kissable!" when I had first arrived. He moved toward me, so I asked him. I had seen Kelly at workshops, so I knew his communication about boundaries would match my own. I could trust him to say and do what he wanted and respect my desires.

At Marco's request, we moved down a hall with forty other people in respectful silence toward his enclosed backyard pool. He kept the water at ninety-nine degrees, comfortable for various therapies he offered, such as water breathwork, Tantra, and meditation. As we passed through a changing area, we shed clothes—bathing suit bottoms were required, but we all got to be topless. In the unheated pool area, we stood in line for showers, murmuring and shivering in the November air. Kelly rubbed my shoulders to keep me comfortable, and soon we were walking down the steps into the warm water, which embraced us in a wet hug.

The water was chest-high at each end of the full-length pool where the steps were, but in the middle it was almost over my five-foot-six-inch head, so I had to float and bob there. Kelly was about my height, so we tried to stay afloat together. The light was low, with candles flickering along the walls and little colored lights strung over the pool like friendly stars.

As we bobbed in the water, Marco stood above us like an ancient sorcerer, flowing dark curls spilling over a shimmering blue robe. His soothing Italian voice floated over the water slowly, caressing each word. "As you come into the pool in silence with your partner, feel the water all around you, enveloping you, surrounding both of you with warmth, with healing, with reassurance that you are safe." As the murmuring died down, a sense of peace filled me.

"Welcome to this sacred ceremony of spirit, of body, of heart, of soul. Tonight, we ask the spirits of the water to heal us and help us connect with ourselves, and with each other.

"And now, let there be spaces in your togetherness. Stand on your own and feel the water all around you. Close your eyes, and feel every inch of your skin, every inch of your body being touched by the water. Feel your skin dissolving into the water that is outside you. You are water on the inside. Merge with the water. Move with the water." I started swaying gently, imagining the water flowing in and out of me, feeling like I was the water, connected to all the others there, including Kelly, who was swaying nearby.

"Now open your eyes, turn to your partner, and look into their eyes." Kelly and I found each other's hands and moved to face each other with a strong and welcome grip. "The eyes are the landing strip of the soul, so look right into their soul." I tried looking into Kelly's pupils, down the landing strip into his soul, but all I could see were his dreamy eyes, and all I could feel was the electricity of our hands touching.

"Now close your eyes and feel your partner's fingers, tracing each one gently with yours. Feel how each finger is different from each other, so different from yours, but also the same." The electricity of our hands was now causing sparks in my fingers, and elsewhere.

Marco continued with a series of meditations, focusing on different nonsexual parts of our body, as we all bobbed in the warm water. However, I barely heard what he said, because Kelly, discreetly and with my permission and delight, was lightly stroking my breasts in a way that made me want more. I floated through the water ceremony in a blissful erotic dream.

Afterward, Kelly and I slid out of our wet suits, dried off, wrapped ourselves in sarongs, and drifted into the warm fireplace room, which was filled with futons and pillows of colorful fabrics. We lay down in a corner, wanting the touch to continue. As I lay on my side, Kelly reached over and slowly ran his fingers lightly over my face and through the sarong. He stroked my breasts and back, tracing his fingers along my side curves, down my legs to my feet, in a way that made my body hum. I reached over to stroke him lightly along his back from his head to his toes, lingering on his backside and darting in front to lightly tease his thighs. His stroking made me want more, and I moved aside our sarongs. Kelly slowly and gently explored me with his fingers. I melted. I fondled him with my fingers. He *mmmed*. We went back and forth like that for a long time, neither of us moving toward anything more sexual.

Although I was feeling exquisitely turned on by his caresses, neither of us was making any attempt to talk, so my heart, unlike my body, was not opening to him or wanting to date him. This simple touch was just what I wanted. It must have been enough for him too, because he didn't speak or act like he wanted more.

Neither of us spoke at all. We dozed there on the pillows for a while, and then I went home, feeling satisfied. Though no date came out of it, the party had given me what I needed—sensual touch and the feeling of being desired. Besides, I had a date coming over the next morning.

HOT TUB DATE

At a little after ten the next day, I welcomed my friend Ron at the front door for first date number 3: breakfast and a hot tub. We were friends from HAI, and he always made me laugh. I loved his blond surfer hair and mischievous smile, but I wasn't that attracted to him because he was shorter and smaller than me. I wanted to see if I would see him differently on a date.

When Ron walked into my house, he said, "This feels like my place in Mexico." A 1929 stucco California bungalow painted peach and turquoise, my home holds an informal jumble of original wood built-ins, bright Mexican paint, and comfortable furniture, all adorned with vibrant fabrics and Peruvian tapestries. I beamed. "That's what I was aiming for," I said, feeling proud that it compared favorably to Ron's open-air winter house on the coast of Mexico.

After breakfast, we moved into my backyard garden, where Ron exclaimed over the bright purple, blue, and turquoise benches, steps, and plant trellises amid the trees, bushes, cactuses, and ground covers spilling down my sloped yard.

"More reminders of Mexico!" he said, grinning like we had a sexy secret.

Under the boughs of the gingko tree and the Canary Island date palm, we slipped naked into the hot tub. Gazing around the yard, he pointed out all the cactuses that he also had in Mexico. I sank into the warm water, feeling connected to him through our love of Mexican colors and plants.

After asking permission, he stroked my feet lightly and then firmly, exquisitely, melting me inside and out. After a while, I dug into the sore knots in his back, and he moaned happily. I could see that we gave each other great pleasure. However, I wasn't more attracted to him, and neither of us moved to take it further. After an hour of soaking and stroking, we ended the hot tub with affectionate hugs and light kisses all over our faces. Ron didn't seem to expect more.

I realized that a friendship with someone who made me laugh and gave me great foot rubs was perfect just as it was. I wanted those qualities in a partner, but that partner didn't have to be my friend Ron.

HAI SINGLES / PETER

The following Saturday night, I went to a HAI singles event in San Francisco and met two potential dates. However, it left me longing for touch, and I didn't have anything else planned that weekend. Sitting at my computer in my kitchen nook, I emailed Peter, who was living in Rome for a month, and told him how much I missed him. I was thinking of all the weekend evenings we'd spent snuggling on his couch or mine, watching *The Daily Show* or *Friends* episodes, before falling asleep wrapped in each other's arms.

The next morning, he responded:

Hi, sweetie, thanks for the email. . . . Sorry you had a lonely weekend. . . . Soon you will find men to date, and they will appreciate your charms. I'm so glad I'm here in Rome. I think it is good for my spirit to be out in the world. Have fun out in the wilds of the dating world. I keep you in my heart. love you lots, peter

I inhaled his words, leaned back in the chair in my kitchen nook, and breathed out. Through the window, the gingko tree's bright yellow leaves shone in the sun, like Peter's optimism for my dating prospects. Those leaves had been soft green when Peter was here, and I could still feel that lushness in my heart.

TANTRA

~~~~~~

A week later, I attended a weekend workshop on Tantra—the practice of weaving together spiritual and sexual energy. I wanted sex to be part of this dating project, and this weekend promised people who not only liked sex but who might be interested in exciting, soul-shaking sex. Plus, my psychic friend Blake had predicted that I'd meet my partner at a workshop this fall, so I was hopeful.

It was held at a place I'd never been—a retreat center near the town of Calistoga at the top of the Napa Valley—so I assumed there would be men I didn't know. I thought I'd also see some familiar faces, since many of my friends were drawn to Tantra. However, when I arrived at the retreat, I realized I knew most of the men from other workshops and parties. Reluctantly letting go of the expectation for a new partner, I focused on enjoying the experience.

By the end of the weekend, many things had transpired to bring my forty fellow participants and me to a safe, sacred, sexual, and adventurous moment. A belief in sexuality as sacred permeated the entire workshop. In guided one-on-one exercises, we opened our hearts and spirits, savored spiritual and sexual energy between each other without acting on it, and stroked each other's naked bodies in sexual and nonsexual ways, seeing all contact with another as sacred. The leaders had created safety by helping us locate our personal sexual boundaries—how much touch did we want from strangers, friends, lovers?—and showing how to respect our own as well as others' boundaries. Through sexual history discussions, we had practiced choosing the safe sex supplies we would use with each person, just in case we were sexual with them.

Now at the end of the workshop, a culminating exercise gave us a chance to honor and celebrate our own sacred sexual energy. We'd been asked to form groups of four of the same gender and discuss how we wanted to interact with a group of four of another gender. My group of four women were in agreement—we wanted to be sexual with the four men we had selected, one man at a time, deciding our own level of sexuality moment to moment. Tantra workshops like these created such a safe and open atmosphere that having sex in front of others was a natural extension of the sacred view of sexuality. I had enjoyed group sex with a few friends before, so it wasn't new to me.

The first man we brought into our circle was Homer, a tall smiling guy with salt-and-pepper hair. As he lay on his back, we were honoring him by kissing and stroking him all over his body. We were also taking requests.

"This is awesome," he said. "Could someone fuck me?"

We looked at each other. Although we were all fairly sexual women, none of us knew him well, and suddenly everyone seemed shy, and no one volunteered. I remembered from our safe sex discussion that he had just been tested and had no diseases to worry about. Making love to a stranger was one of my fantasies, and this seemed like a safe opportunity.

"I will!" I said, slipping on a condom, mounting him, and performing enthusiastically.

I had not really noticed Homer until this moment. I had avoided him for the whole workshop without realizing it. He'd been pursuing other women in the room and playing his drum whenever he could. I dislike drums and I dislike being one of many, so I had not paid any attention to him. Since he was the one man in the workshop that I didn't know, one would think I would have spotted him right off. But I had literally not noticed him. And he had not noticed me. Now, in this suddenly intimate encounter, we had finally gotten each other's attention. We looked into each other's eyes with surprised amusement.

"Well, hello!" he said, with a warm Midwestern drawl, his eyes smiling and widening.

"Hello!" I said, giggling at how much I was enjoying this outrageous situation.

His time was soon up, and we moved on to the other men, who had more modest requests.

After the workshop ended, everyone was moving rapidly through the retreat center, eating dinner and packing up to leave. Homer rushed by me as I was packing my gear and tossed out, with a confident drawl, "Hey, who are you? I want to get to know you!"

When he said that, I realized I'd been thinking the same thing. I smiled and called after him, "I want to get to know you too!"

"How long are you here for tonight?" he asked, pausing his forward motion.

"I'm leaving after I'm packed up," I said. "I have to get home soon."

"Me too. How about if we get together for a bit before we leave?"

I agreed.

"It's a date!" he crowed, and rushed on.

After dinner, we looked around for a place to "talk," knowing we wanted to do more than talk. My futon was still set up with sheets and blankets and sleeping bag in the sleeping room, which was cleared out by now. We got under the covers and started kissing. Soon, we were taking off clothes and finding a condom and he was fucking me energetically. I matched his energy with equal thrusts back, and we were both grinning and moaning like two cats who had found all the canaries they wanted. I had met my playful sexual match. I wanted more, but after a half hour, we reluctantly agreed that it was time to get dressed and go home.

We headed out for the one-and-a-half-hour trip at the same time, I in my perky Toyota Corolla and he in his loping Lincoln Continental. As we drove, we talked by cell phone. He revealed that he had a girlfriend, Janice, and he only had permission to "play" at workshops. Like many couples, they regarded workshops as safe, self-contained playgrounds that did not affect their relationship. I was disappointed, but I was not thinking of him as a partner. I just wanted more sex with him. I pressed on. What were the limits?

"Was what we just did part of the workshop?" I asked.

"Yes!" he said.

We were driving through the Napa Valley on the Silverado Trail, the wine-tasting route that winds along the edge of the valley. It has no traffic lights and no street lamps, and it was almost deserted this Sunday evening after dark. I had another idea. It was a clear cold night.

"How far does the workshop extend?" I asked.

"As long as I'm still on the road!" he said. Homer was definitely stretching the workshop container, possibly for my benefit. Although I felt a twinge of complicity in the stretch, I accepted the gift. I figured it was not up to me to interpret their agreements.

"Well, let's pull over and look at the stars!" I said, hoping for romantic starlit kisses.

"Sure!"

I found a long unlit stretch of road with a wide shoulder up against dark vineyards and parked my car. He pulled up behind me, leaving several feet between our cars. We met outside between his car and the fields, and I reached up to kiss him. He reached down and pulled out his cock. My shock turned quickly to longing—my belly trembled; my yoni moistened.

"Hmmm," I said in a low voice. "If you have a condom for that, I'll suck it."

He did and I did, kneeling down on my jeans in the gravel behind his car. Looking up at him under a wide expanse of starlit sky, I sucked his cock in and out of my mouth, the gravel digging into my knees. My submissive position, the location on the side of the road in the dark, my mouth full of this almost stranger's cock, and the slight pain in my knees were all deeply arousing. I had wanted this—pure sex. The stars twinkled in approval.

Suddenly he pulled me up to standing, walked me over to the front hood of his car, and said, "Pull down your jeans and panties and bend over."

I was thrilled. This was a scene out of another fantasy—a man forcing me to take off my clothes and get in a vulnerable position. Even if he just gazed at me, my yoni would be wet, and I would be quivering. But Homer had more in mind. When I was bent over and exposed enough, he told me to keep my arms above my head, while he held on to my hair and entered me from behind, thrusting me into the car hood. I felt utterly and satisfyingly taken. Suddenly he pulled out and stood me back up.

"Back on your knees!" he commanded. I knelt down again, this time with my jeans down to my knees, and sucked his cock some more. Then he pulled me back up, and bent me over the car again for some more fucking. We went back and forth many times.

Occasionally a car would drive by on the road, giving us ample warning with its lights. I'd pull up my jeans and we would lean against the far side of his car like we were simply making out. When the car had gone by, I would pull down my jeans and get back on my knees and suck him until he pulled me up and over the car hood. I surrendered to the rhythm, not wanting it to end, but eventually he came, with one last thrust. We shared a deep kiss after I pulled up my jeans, feeling very well fucked.

On the drive home, we continued our cell phone discussion, and he explained that except for workshops, he had made a commitment to Janice to be monogamous for four months—until mid-January. I was disappointed, but I respected short-term commitments. The six-month periods that Peter and I had pledged had added up to seven years together. There was a security in the commitment, and a freedom in the end-in-sight aspect. Whatever Homer and Janice's future, this arrangement was working for them.

Sadly, I said good-bye to him in my body and heart. I had let myself want him as a sexual playmate—an occasional lover who would delight me as I searched for my real partner. Mid-January seemed a long time away. At least I knew what I wanted—an adventurous sexual partner like Homer.

INTUITION

~~~~~~

But my next date barely wanted to touch me, let alone have sex with me. Timothy came by my house one evening for tea, on his way home from a communications consulting job.

⊳———⊲

We had met a week or so earlier in San Francisco at the HAI singles event, in an exercise in which we were asked to share what we least wanted others to know.

"What I *least* want you to know?" Timothy said, crinkling up his long straight nose and high forehead under neatly trimmed brown hair.

"I could start," I offered, making my face as soft and warm as possible. I wanted to rescue this conservative-looking man from this touchy-feely question.

"I refinanced my house to buy investment property," I said, "and I jumped into the Phoenix real estate market at the peak. Now the costs are draining my savings, and I'm scared about my financial security. I can't sell it, because it's worth less than I bought it for, and I'm afraid no one will want to be partners with me with such a heavy debt." I looked down, a wave of shame washing over me, afraid he would judge me like I was judging myself. I'd been so stupid to think I knew what I was doing when I bought the overpriced, dilapidated duplex right before the housing crash on the advice of a real estate club. Here I was a researcher, and I hadn't done enough research.

When I looked up, he was nodding with a serious but sympathetic expression. The instructions were for the listener not to respond, and to just look lovingly at the speaker, which he did. His eyes were soft, concerned. I was relieved.

"Well, for me," he said, "it's that I have no social life. I work all the time to keep my business going. I'm too tired to go out with friends, let alone date. I'm lonely. It's why I'm here."

As I nodded, trying to look sympathetic and loving, my heart nodded too. *He can admit he's lonely, and he can listen to my feelings.*

The leader suggested that we stroke each other's faces. As I tenderly stroked his soft, handsome cheeks, I felt a surge of attraction. I wondered if a man who was successful in the business world would be interested in me, a feminist steeped in personal and spiritual growth, sensuality, and sexuality. When he gave me his card and asked for mine, I felt like I'd just been given an E ticket at Disneyland, the expensive one that used to get you on the best rides.

⸱───────⸱

At my house, we sat on the purple couch drinking tea, and he told me about the time he had worked in a meditation center.

"It was a spiritual organization," he said, "so we trained ourselves to trust our inner awareness. We were on a much larger path than we could know, so we learned to trust how spirit was guiding us."

It was refreshing to talk with someone who worked in the professional world and also felt directed by spirit. I kept my world of work so separate from my world of personal and spiritual growth. "How do you know when you're being guided?" I asked.

"You just have to learn to trust your intuition," he said. "I use it in my consulting work all the time. I can see that you have a lot of intuition that you don't trust."

He was right. I had taken classes to develop my intuition in my twenties but had never gotten attuned enough to trust it. His casual observation felt like he could see into that part of me and had the key to help me recognize it. I longed for him and what he knew.

As we talked, I crept my fingers along the back of the couch and landed them lightly on his shoulder and neck. No response. I put my hand out for him to grab. No response. I petted him on his arm. No response.

He left without touching me at all, and without that, I didn't want to pursue it, regardless of his insights. Since I didn't hear from him, I assumed he was equally uninterested.

I was not concerned. It was only the fourth date.

WORKING LATE

~~~~~~~~~~~

I was looking forward to my fifth date—a Friday night dinner and movie with Cesar, a handsome Peruvian who worked in a high-tech start-up, whom I'd met at the HAI singles night. I was drawn to Peruvian men based on three memorable visits to Peru, and I was looking forward to getting to know Cesar. He seemed like the perfect mix of South American charm, Silicon Valley tech savvy, and Bay Area personal growth awareness.

However, here it was Friday, the night of the date, and I was still at work after a long workweek. I loved my job. As the "institutional researcher" for a large, diverse community college, I evaluated students' academic progress and the college support services to ensure that all groups of students were moving toward their educational goals. Before finding this position, I had worked at a research firm that wrote statistical reports for the US Office of Education, which sounded perfect for me since I had graduate degrees in statistics and sociology of education. In that job, however, I never saw a teacher or a student, never knew who was using my reports.

Here in my college office, my student data walked right by my window, and instructors dropped in to talk about their successes and failures in the classroom. My little department, consisting of me, one research analyst, and a few students, churned out tons of tables, graphs, pie charts, and commentary about how well the students and the college were doing in terms of success rates, graduation rates, transfer rates, and whether our support services—such as tutoring and study groups—were working. Faculty and staff used our research, and I felt it made a difference.

That afternoon, after a day of meetings and many emails, I had finally gotten some quiet time to draft the "need justification" section of a grant proposal for federal funds to encourage more first-college-generation African American, Latinx, and Southeast Asian students to enter and succeed in our STEM (science, technology, engineering, and math) programs. As a perpetually underfunded community college, with students who had more academic, economic, and emotional needs than those at the better-funded state and private universities, we were always looking for ways to help our students succeed. My justification had to be strong in order to get funded—we were competing with colleges across the country. I had to finish it tonight so Alyssa, the grant writer, could weave it into the rest of the proposal over the weekend and get it out by Monday.

I considered turning in my first draft so I could leave sooner for my date, but then thought, *What's more important: being with my date, a Latino who was already successful in high tech, or making sure that other first-generation African American, Latinx, and Southeast Asian students have a fair chance to enter and succeed in these lucrative fields?*

The obvious answer was why I worked late hours almost every night. No matter what research I was doing, it felt like it contributed to the larger goal that all of us who worked at the college had—to help students who would not otherwise even be in college to succeed. With the time getting later and later for me to go home and change for my date, I finally got to the end of my best argument, saved it, put it in an email, and hit send. I hoped Alyssa could work with it. And I hoped my date would forgive me for being late.

PERU AND LESBIAN NATION

~~~~~~~~~~~~~~~~~~~~~~~~~~~~~~~~

When I'd met Cesar at the HAI singles evening in San Francisco, I was first drawn to him simply because he was from Peru. Tall and thin, with dark curls falling onto his face, he reminded me of a man I'd met there. My three trips to Peru had included romantic encounters with Peruvian men, and I thought I might feel the same way about Cesar. However, the more we talked, the more I realized how much we also had in common, given his high-tech job, housemates, and attendance at this new age singles event. I'd done research on gender and racial segregation in high-tech jobs in Silicon Valley, lived in cooperative houses for fifteen years in Berkeley and Palo Alto, and was steeped in these types of personal growth experiences. We shared the same world. Plus, he seemed to have good relating skills.

"What brings you here?" he asked gently, and really listened when I told him why I was dating again.

"What kind of work do you do?" he asked. Again, he listened well.

I told him, in rusty Spanish, that Peru was my favorite country and that I had visited three times. However, he was from the sprawling, industrial metropolis of Lima, not the quaint Andean city of Cusco, the gateway to Machu Picchu high in the mountains that I had returned to each time. So we didn't have much to share about Peru beyond a mutual admiration for Machu Picchu. I let him know that I really liked Peruvians—but I didn't tell him the details of my trips or that Peru had played a big role in my relationship with Peter.

⟜───────⟞

For my first visit to Cusco in July 1996, I'd joined a US-based spiritual tour but had flown there ten days early to experience Peru on my own. I'd been drawn to Peru ever since my twenties, when those exuberant and haunting flute tunes touched an ancient longing in me, and the trip was my forty-fifth birthday present to myself. During those first ten days, I walked through Incan ruins of perfectly cut stones stacked into intentionally shaped walls, and I felt echoes of my own past lives there—confirming my own spiritual connection to Peru.

I'd befriended a local couple, Maria and Ricardo, and had shared a flirtatious overnight adventure with them and a tall curly-haired single guy during a fiesta in Pisac, a village over the hill from Cusco. We had taken the bus to the fiesta but found ourselves stranded because we'd danced until after the last bus and taxi left. We ended up staying with Susana's friends in a two-story house with no windowpanes, heat, or electricity and only a cement double bed upstairs that we had to sleep four across with no blanket. Shivering in the winter chill, we cuddled close for the rest of the night, erotic attraction between me and my date seeping through our layers of clothes. The next day, we rushed back to Cusco and made it in time for our morning classes—theirs in tourism, mine in Spanish—but I never saw the single guy again.

I had become enamored of Diego, a Peruvian shaman-in-training whom I'd met at Saksaywaman, the ruins above Cusco. A skinny man with a disheveled ponytail, he drew me in with his focus on the spiritual energy of the ruins. In the dazzling thin atmosphere of a two-mile-high city, we had become lovers, and in the days before my spiritual group arrived, when I was not hanging out with Maria and Ricardo, I was making love or sleeping with Diego. I didn't know if it was the altitude, the drugs I was taking for the altitude, or my own excitement about finally experiencing Peru that made Cusco—and the men there—so sexually charged for me.

For my second trip, a year and a half later, I returned to be the photographer for Maria and Ricardo's wedding and resumed being lovers with Diego. On a trip with him to Machu Picchu, I had ignored my own safe sex practices and made love without a condom.

"I want you to have my baby," he whispered in Spanish. "This is your last chance to conceive." He was right, since I was forty-six by then. And in that moment, I actually did want to have his baby and live in Peru. I had never wanted to have a child in the States, yet here I was drawn to having one. We even worked out how his mother would help us raise the baby. I was relieved when I got neither pregnant nor any sexually transmitted diseases (STDs), and vowed not to take that chance again.

So for my third trip three years later, when a male friend invited me and a few others to go to Machu Picchu for the full moon, I said I would go on the condition that he and I sleep together, because I did not trust myself to resist handsome strangers in sexually charged Cusco. That friend was Peter, and that January 2001 trip to Peru was the beginning of our seven years as lovers. True to my experience in Cusco, we made love as soon as we arrived.

<hr />

But now that I had said good-bye to Peter, I did not want to resist this handsome Peruvian. Cesar picked me up for our date in an old Toyota Corolla. He'd been understanding about my running late, and I was excited to see him. In the email in which he'd invited me out, he had flirted. "I'm sure I'll enjoy seeing you, in any way I can!" he had written, and I shivered with anticipation. I had cast Peruvian men in an erotic role in my life, and he seemed to be playing the part.

However, now that we were together, he showed no signs of wanting to engage with me, either verbally or physically. He seemed to have run out of questions, and after a few more informational items about how he liked living in the suburbs, I had run out as well.

"What do you like about working in high tech?" I said.

"It's interesting," he said, and I did not feel encouraged to ask more.

Looking back, I wish I had asked about his growing up in Peru. I knew some of the possibilities, having talked with Maria and Ricardo about living in Lima and Cusco, and read Mario Vargas Llosa's *Aunt Julia and the Scriptwriter*, a sexy coming-of-age story about a boy growing up in the Peruvian countryside. But that story only reinforced my sexual stereotype about Peruvian men and probably had little relation to Cesar's background.

I figured he was focusing on driving to the theater and that he would talk when we got settled. He parked and we rushed over to the food court, but we only had fifteen minutes to eat before the movie, thanks to my being late. To start a conversation, I launched into what I thought would be a short account of my week, which was, by any measure, one of the most successful ones I'd ever had. Besides finishing the grant proposal, I had facilitated training groups for instructors, developed a way to evaluate campus departments that everyone praised, and hosted our federal grant evaluator, who left a glowing report. At home, I'd started a song for my sister's birthday and celebrated her, helped with a mediation between friends, and comforted a neighbor after she was held up on our street. Throughout all this, I had been calm, prepared, and supportive, more than I had ever been. I wanted him to know not just what I'd done but why it meant so much to me, as a way for him to know me. But there was no way I could cram all those events and the background leading up to them into the five minutes we had left, and my talking faster was not helping. I longed to be telling Peter or one of my women friends, who would know why all this was important. Instead, I felt like I was talking nonstop to a cardboard statue, as the combination of my speed and intensity appeared to overwhelm him. He did not respond, except for some nodding. And then we had to leave for the movie.

"Oh no, I've talked the whole time without asking you a thing!" I was feeling guilty that I'd done so, as well as disappointed that he had not spoken and that it felt so unsatisfying.

"It's fine," he said, looking at me with a weak smile.

⁂————⁂

The movie was *Milk*, about Harvey Milk, the gay San Francisco supervisor who, along with the liberal Mayor George Moscone, had been shot to death on November 27, 1978, by Supervisor Dan White, a conservative. For the liberal and gay and lesbian communities, a time of heady and growing hope had been shattered by these murders. Since I was living alone in San Francisco at the time, the movie brought back vivid memories of that era.

It was early in my lesbian period, just two years into what would become eighteen years of identifying as a lesbian. I had not had much success in finding the woman of my dreams, but I was still hopeful, reveling in the financial and emotional independence, heartfelt music, and freedom from gender roles. Although I was in San Francisco, the center of Lesbian Nation, and attending graduate school in women's studies along with other lesbians, I was feeling inexplicably lonely and writing sad songs. The night of the murders, I'd attended the candlelight vigil at city hall alone, feeling full of grief not only for Moscone and Milk but for myself. One month later, Joan Baez gave a free Christmas Eve concert at city hall as a gift of healing for San Franciscans after these murders and the Jonestown massacre the week before. I attended, full of sadness, alone once again.

After the movie, memories of the hope and sadness of that time were spilling out of me, and once again, Cesar was not able to respond to any of my thoughts or feelings. I wished I were with someone who either knew me better or had lived in San Francisco then.

We didn't have much to say on the drive home. I didn't invite him in for tea. Neither of us emailed afterward. He must have thought I was terribly self-centered, which I had been on this date. I hadn't given him the chance to be either my image of a sexy Peruvian man or the man he actually was, and I knew it was both my failure and my loss. I vowed to do better on future dates.

PETER'S BIRTHDAY

~~~~~~~~~~

However, by December, after only five dates, one sexy party, one sexy workshop, and a singles night, I was discouraged and tired of dating. Would dates or occasional touch at parties or workshops really get me closer to a partner who was better than Peter? I just missed him more.

I missed Peter's optimistic Buddhist wisdom—how he listened so well and gave me wise, compassionate advice for solving problems ranging from house repair to issues at work to how to talk to my critical mother. I missed how we listened to Van Morrison and Bob Dylan songs and sang the words as if we were singing to each other. I missed how we touched most of the time, and how he held me close all night and made love to me to romantic sexy music.

Peter's birthday was coming up, and I wanted contact. I figured I was still his friend, so I spent over an hour at a bookstore and picked out five spiritual and travel books that I thought he'd like and sent them to his hotel in Rome. Even if they weren't right, I hoped he would feel my caring. The day of his birthday, I called him. I was feeling sexy and close to him.

"Hi, sweetie! It's me! Happy birthday!"

"Carolyn. What a surprise." His voice was flat.

"I wanted to let you know I was thinking of you on your birthday."

"Oh, that's nice," he said, evenly. "I have these books from you."

"Oh, you got them—do you like them?"

"They are very nice. Thank you."

I had expected a more enthusiastic response, but I didn't let that deter me from my next tack. "I've been imagining you here in my bed," I said.

"OK," he said, slowly.

"Can you imagine what I'd like you to do to me?"

"Not really," he said, sounding put-upon.

"OK, do you not want to talk about that?" It was finally sinking in that he was not feeling the same way that I was.

"I guess not." My heart contracted in embarrassment and hurt.

"Do you want to talk at all?"

"I guess not. Thanks for calling though."

After we hung up, I flopped onto my bed and lay there, listless, loveless, and friendless. I had forgotten how cold he could be at times, and we were in new territory, trying to be friends. I knew I was no longer his lover, but now I felt rejected as both a lover and a friend. Was that the end of what I thought had been our connection? My hurt heart tightened.

<hr />

I had to get up and go on. It was the weekend of holiday parties. That night, my friends Chandler and Carrie held their annual dance party in their big house in the hills, and I danced until late. The next day, the annual HAI holiday party took place in a hotel by the SFO airport.

At the HAI party, I chatted with Kate and other women's group friends, Ron (my hot tub friend date), and Ben (my young, sexy lover). I also planned a date with tall, willowy Tom, whom I'd met the previous summer, and danced with other potential dates.

The following day, I called Peter in the morning, hoping against hope for a better talk.

"Carolyn! How good to hear your voice!" That was how he used to answer. My heart flooded with relief.

"How are you?"

"Much better, thanks," he said. "I was feeling pretty down yesterday."

"Yeah, you were kind of short with me."

"I know, and I'm sorry. I just froze up."

"What was going on?"

"I was lonely and wanted to be left alone. But I'm better now!"

"Did you enjoy your birthday?"

"Not really, but I love these books you sent! I'm already reading this Buddhist one."

"Oh good. I'm glad I called."

"So am I. I love you, sweetie!"

"I love you too."

When I hung up, I savored the return of our closeness. I'd been afraid we had lost it, but this call was enough to reassure me. He was there, doing his thing, and I was here, doing mine. But we still loved each other.

⊶────⊷

And in my life, I had things to feel good about. Homer, my Tantra guy of roadside sex, had called, just when I'd put him out of my mind.

"Hi, darlin'," he said. "I'm available one month early! And I want to see *you*!"

"Great!" I said, delighted. "What changed?" He said he'd negotiated an early release from monogamy because he had been so good, and because Janice was going out of town, a situation that always canceled their monogamous agreements. As long as Janice was OK with it, it was good enough for me. Hearing his voice and his availability made me tremble inside.

"When are you free?" he said.

We made a date for a week later—the Saturday before winter solstice—and planned a sexy, romantic evening. I would dress up, and he would take me for dinner at the Claremont Hotel, the most elegant restaurant in the East Bay. Before and after dinner, we would have wild sex. I started having fantasies about him, all variations on our roadside scene.

Three days before our date, Homer called in the middle of the day at work. I smiled when I heard his voice and leaned back in my chair.

But he sounded more serious than usual and said, "I'm afraid I'm going to have to cancel our date. I'm not so available that night after all. Janice needs me."

A wave of hot disappointment and tears swept through me. I had wanted this date so much. I didn't feel angry—just extremely sorry for myself, as if my father had lost his job and didn't have money for Christmas presents. I knew that he was not purposely hurting me. I understood that his girlfriend, his primary partner, had priority. Knowing that truth protected my heart from men who had partners. It had nothing to do with me, so my innermost heart wasn't hurt. But I still ached.

"I'm *so* disappointed," I said, trying not to sound pathetic, but wanting to let him know how I felt.

"I know, it really hurts," he said, pausing. I felt him holding me and my feelings. "And you know how much I wanted to see you."

"Yeah," I said, feeling comforted by that thought. "I'll get over it." I knew that I would. He had a primary partner, and I hadn't even had a real date with him yet.

"I'll make it up to you when I can see you," he promised. When we hung up, I felt more lonely than ever. His empathy had helped a bit—I'd told him how I felt, and he had heard it, something I wanted in any relationship. But I still didn't have him.

As I hung up the phone in my office, I said out loud to myself, "I want a lover who is very loving and connected to me. I will have that."

———————

The next day, Peter called me.

"Carolyn!"

"Peter! How great to hear your voice!"

"I just wanted to call and tell you how much I appreciate you."

"Really? For what?"

"For calling me on my birthday and sending me those books. You're a true friend and sweetie." He was back to the same old Peter. This was erasing that one horrible phone call.

"I'm glad you called. I'm feeling really sad right now."

"What's wrong, babe?"

"Oh, this guy. I was really looking forward to our first date, and he just canceled it."

"That bum! Well, you just tell him he doesn't deserve to go out with you. You tell him Peter said so!"

We both laughed. Peter would not hurt a fly, but I loved it when he stuck up for me.

"You just go right on to the next guy!"

"OK, I will!" This was new, and nice, having him support my dating project.

He was chatty—he told me about his favorite parts of Rome and wanted to know who had been at the HAI holiday party. It was like our nightly phone calls, only he was farther away.

I hung up smiling. Maybe he would always be there, cheering me on, no matter what happened to us. I was glad I had this dating project so I could go right on to the next guy, without dwelling on what had, in fact, happened to us.

WINTER SOLSTICE ONE (2008)

The next guy—the sixth date—would be tall, willowy Tom, whom I'd met the summer before at a memorial service for Verne, an older HAI friend.

Tom had introduced himself with a proposition. "Would you mind if I caress you from behind?" It was a pretty audacious thing for a guy to say to a woman he didn't know at a memorial service, but it was a hot summer day in a vineyard in Sonoma, we were all in scanty little summer dresses, and the gathering was made up of those of us who had known Verne, an eighty-five-year-old former engineer, through the HAI workshops. This was back in July, after Peter and I had decided to break up but before he had left for Europe.

Although we were there to mourn Verne's passing, he had led such a long, successful, and loving life that the gathering was more like a celebration. I knew that not only would Verne have approved—he would have wanted me to indulge in a simple caress in honor of him.

"I don't mind at all," I answered. I considered it a polite request from the dark-haired stranger with a smile that matched my own. I knew that he would only touch me as much as I allowed. I also knew that I could change my "yes" to a "no" at any point, and back again to a "yes" a minute later. "Every second you get a second chance," Stan Dale, HAI's founder, constantly reminded us. In this warm air that was already caressing me, I wanted this handsome man to touch me as much as possible, the more sensually the better. As Tom gently kissed my neck and let his hand glide over my bare shoulders and skim my breasts, bare under the dress, delicious tingles went through my body.

"You are so pretty," he whispered. My heart melted.

But I was not planning to date until after Peter left. Tom and I agreed that we wanted to get to know each other, and trusted that a date would happen in time.

⚬———⚬

The date finally happened in December, the night before my annual winter solstice gathering. Tom and I sat on the purple couch, and he grilled me.

"So weren't you getting into real estate when we talked?" he began. "How did that go?"

"Not so well. I don't even want to talk about it." I looked down, too embarrassed to look at him. I'd hoped that buying rental property in Phoenix would give me supplemental retirement income, but instead it was draining my current income and threatening my future. I didn't want to tell him I'd made such a foolish investment and had increased my own mortgage to fund it. "And weren't you seeing someone in Hawaii?"

The thought of those sweet days in Hilo still pinged my heart. "Yeah . . . Peter . . . we broke up two months ago. He's traveling in Europe for seven months."

"Do you miss him?"

Of course I miss him! my heart shouted. "Well, yeah . . . that's why I'm dating. . . ."

"Have you been dating a lot?"

"I'm slowly starting on it." I didn't feel like a meta-analysis of how dating was going.

I tried to focus on him. "How's your relationship with your friend in the Valley?" I knew that his heart was taken by a longtime lover in the Central Valley who was married. He spent many of his vacations with her. I wondered how well this worked. Some of my friends were in longtime marriages and supported each other to have other lovers, and other friends maintained several important relationships at a time, all known to everyone. They were all happy, but I didn't see that working for me. I barely had time for one relationship, let alone two. Besides, I was looking for my own partner/lover and didn't want to share.

"She's amazing," he said. "I love how I feel when I'm with her." That was why I had stayed with Peter for so long—it felt so good. However, now I knew that feeling good was not enough if you couldn't be together and wanted different types of lives. Tom's response about his lover left a lot of unanswered questions. How close could they be in that situation? Was Tom available to be close to me? However, he was being about as open as I was, so I didn't press.

"How long have you been in your house?" he asked.

It went on and on, these queries, until I was feeling numb. I knew he was trying to connect, but I felt unable to respond on a more heart-to-heart level, despite our years in HAI.

Our date livened up when we started touching, picking up where we had left off at the memorial service the summer before. I knew enough to be wary about getting to know someone only through touch—I had kissed many princes and princesses who turned out to be frogs—but I trusted my instincts now after ten years of workshops and seven years of a sweet relationship.

On the couch, our hands playfully explored each other's bodies, with lots of commentary about how this or that felt and giggles about doing it. Eventually, we made it to my bed, where he initiated making love. He had great talent with his tongue and fingers. We kept talking and giggling about every touch, right through condom donning, gentle lovemaking, and orgasms for each of us. Then we slept about six hours, interspersed with more laughing and giggling. I draped my leg over him, and he held me close.

⚬———⚬

The next day was the winter solstice, the shortest day—and the longest night—of the year. Tom left, promising to return that evening to help me with my annual solstice gathering. Ancient pagan ceremonies that honored the winter solstice predate the Christian and Jewish celebrations of light observed on Christmas and Hanukah. To honor the darkness of that night and celebrate the return of the light, I'd created my own ritual for my friends.

My version of the ceremony, based on elements of pagan rituals I knew, had been refined over twenty years of offering it for my friends in my various homes. It always started with a feast of hot appetizers, light dinner, and mulled cider and wine, and ended around the fireplace with a ceremony in which we wrote down and then stated what we wanted to let go of into the darkness and what we wanted to bring into the light.

I spent the day cleaning the house, arranging a ceremonial altar and writing supplies in the living room, shopping, heating mulled cider, and meditating in preparation for the evening. My body and heart were humming happily from the night with Tom.

When Tom returned that evening, he acted the part of a longtime partner—he kissed me when he arrived, helped me prepare and arrange appetizers, and made the fire. The cinnamon scent of the mulled cider and the warmth of the fire filled the house.

"Would you like me to put this dip in the dining room, or should I smear it over your body and lick it off?" he asked me as I was chopping up celery.

He was making me laugh at a time I was usually feeling harried. I reveled in that feeling of partnership—a glimpse of what I was looking for. My ten other guests started arriving, and I greeted each one with a hug. These were my closest friends— three couples and four singles, including Chandler and Carrie, my friends who gave the holiday party; Kate; and others from my women's group. Most came every year. They all welcomed Tom, whether they knew him or not.

This year, as usual, most people gathered in the kitchen, where Tom and I passed out hot spanakopita and chicken pot stickers and kept everyone's cider mugs or wine glasses filled. Thanks to Tom's help preparing and passing out food, I was able to have conversations with most friends. Some I saw often, others only this one evening a year, so it was a rare treat to talk with them. Most of these women and men knew each other, and they were animatedly chatting and eating while standing in the kitchen, sitting on dining room chairs next to the buffet table, or lounging in the living room on the purple couch and easy chairs.

Although I allowed two hours for socializing, we always wanted more. However, when I announced it was time to start the ceremony, everyone brought their dishes into the kitchen and refilled their wine or cider. They chose chairs arranged in a long semicircle with the altar table in the middle and the fireplace at the open end. Covered with a purple cloth shining with gold spirals, the altar table held five candles, along with symbols of the elements of the four directions at each corner—burning sage for the air of the east, salt for the earth of the north, a burning candle for the fire of the south, and water for the west. The table also contained objects we had brought to symbolize what each of us intended to let go of or bring into the light.

To set the spiritual tone for the ceremony, we started by welcoming the four directions and their associated spirits. I had asked four people to lead us in calling the directions. Holding the symbol of that direction, each one stood and called out the qualities of that direction.

"Spirit of the east!" called Chandler. "Spirit of new beginnings! The air we breathe! The new light of day!" He and his partner Carrie had been there every year for over ten years.

Then the rest of us added other qualities: "Warmth! Inspiration! Openness!" Chandler walked around the circle, smudging us with the sage smoke.

He concluded, "Spirit of the east! We welcome you to our winter solstice circle!" Then the next person stood up, called the next direction, welcomed the qualities, and touched us with its symbol—either sprinkling us with water, hovering over us with flame, or dashing us with a pinch of salt. As each direction was welcomed, someone lit the corresponding candle. At the end, I lit the center candle, symbolizing going into our inner selves. A sacred space had been created.

Then it was time for our declarations. First, in silence, we each pondered the qualities or aspects of ourselves or our lives that we wanted to let go of into the dark night, and wrote them down on a purple piece of paper. I had randomly passed out my self-help and spiritual books as writing tablets, and they became additional symbols for those who received them.

In my meditation that day, I had realized what I wanted to let go into the darkness—fear of the future and looking back on the past with regret, specifically regrets about my failed real estate investments and my failed relationship with Peter. If I could let those fears and regrets go, maybe I could love and trust myself more, and be able to love someone else in the future.

One at a time, each person stood at the edge of the circle in front of the fire and read out loud the qualities they had written.

Everyone said, "Ho!" or some other exclamation, and then the person placed their paper in the fire. As it burned, the smoke of the qualities disappeared up through the chimney to be released into the universe. We watched each paper burn differently— some went right away, others took longer; some were a bright blaze, others a slow smolder.

After everyone's qualities had been burned and released, we turned out all the lights and candles and sat in stillness and darkness for several long minutes, feeling that empty place— imagining ourselves without those aspects. I could detect a new spaciousness inside me.

Then, in a burst of music, I put on a song that celebrated the return of the light, and we relit the candles and turned on the lights. This time, we wrote and declared the qualities or aspects of ourselves or our lives we wanted to bring in, nurture, and grow in the returning light, on the way to the longest day of the year on the summer solstice. We would burn these papers in the fire as well—this time imagining their smoke as a message to the universe.

In my meditation I had come up with what I wanted to bring into the light. I would bring in a bright future—filled with love, sex, joy, peace, creativity, and abundance. This seemed like a lot to ask for, and much of it seemed far from where I was right then, but the solstice was the night to imagine the most I could. As I stood in front of my friends and declared these things, I tried to feel as if I had them already. I thought of how many declarations by my guests and myself had come true over the years, and I hoped this was one of those years for me.

After the ceremony, we all lounged in front of the fire, chatting, eating fruit, drinking more cider, and feeling lighter and happier from our declarations and those of our friends. Tom acted like a proud boyfriend—he lifted up my newly painted silver sparkly toenails and said, "Look at Carolyn's beautiful toes!" And after everyone left, he kissed me.

He had to go home that evening, but his presence lingered—I loved the lightheartedness we shared, whether or not we were touching. I wanted that easy comfort in a relationship, and I thought it showed potential for us. Although the sexual energy that Tom and I exchanged was more playful than compelling, we had so much fun that I was sure he'd call back.

But he didn't. Not that week or the week after. At first I felt hurt—*hadn't he enjoyed our evening?* Then I noticed that I was not inclined to call him either. We had both held up protective shields around our hearts when we talked. That was *not* how I wanted to be in a relationship. I would have asked about that had he called. But he did not. Maybe he didn't want anything more than one date since he was already in a relationship. Maybe for him, like me, our connection had not been compelling enough.

<hr />

Soon I was busy with other dates, and Tom faded from my mind. Date number 7 was a dinner and sleepover with an affectionate teddy bear of a HAI friend who was in an open marriage. He offered a gentle night of lovemaking; I enjoyed it thoroughly without needing more. Date number 8 was with an arrogant guy I had dated ten years before. I'd hoped he'd grown out of his pompous attitude. He hadn't, but we'd kissed a lot and enjoyed a Christmas Eve dinner and party with his men's group. Against my better judgment, I agreed to meet him the next day for a Christmas excursion to San Francisco to feed the homeless, which I had always wanted to do. However, he couldn't find the place, so we ended up talking in my car at Ocean Beach, watching the turbulent ocean on a dazzling clear, cold day. Our words crashed against each other like angry waves, and the date ended frostily, but I was glad I had given him another chance.

My dating project was starting to gather momentum, and I didn't need to dwell on dates that did not work out. I had many dates to look forward to. The project was helping me focus on that bright future of love, sex, joy, peace, creativity, and abundance rather than my regrets over failing at real estate, my relationship with Peter, and even date number 6 for not calling back.

PART III
HOPE

SEX

~~~

A few days after solstice, Homer called, but not to reschedule our date. He invited me to another event—a New Year's Eve party in the Santa Cruz mountains.

"It's a drumming party, with some Burning Man friends," he explained. "We can stay there overnight. Let me know if you want to join me. Janice is out of town that weekend."

I was not crazy about drumming, and I had not been to Burning Man, the wild weeklong art festival in the Nevada desert, but I wanted to be with him. Although I could not imagine him as a partner—I didn't want to be in Janice's position—I felt far from finding my match, and I could definitely enjoy a sexy lover like him while I looked for one. I had visions of being his paramour, and spending New Year's Eve with him fit that fantasy.

I told him I'd consider it. But I didn't want to do it without having our original date.

"Of course not," he purred. "Let's see. New Year's Eve is Wednesday night. How about if we go out to dinner on Monday night?"

"Great, it's a date," I said, hoping he wouldn't cancel again. It would be date number 9.

I was insisting on this "real" date because if I was spending all this time with him, I wanted to count him as one of my fifty dates. And if I was having all this sex with him, I wanted to know more about him. It was a way of containing my feelings, or so I thought.

A few nights later, Homer and I entered the Fat Lady Restaurant, stepping into the intimacy of a former brothel with its low lights, red tapestry walls, paintings of naked women, small low-ceilinged rooms, and tables in private nooks and corners. I felt as sexy as the restaurant, enjoying the smooth tightness of my leather corset under my velvet strapless top and the slinky surface of my satin skirt hugging my knees close together above my high black strappy heels. My gartered silk stockings and crotchless panties made me feel deliciously naked underneath, giving me the exhilarating thrill of sexual vulnerability that I can only experience with the right combination of risk and safety. Wearing my long black wool coat over it all on this cold winter night, I was reveling in the outward appearance of a proper date with a handsome gentleman who had picked me up at my house, escorted me to his classic Lincoln Continental, opened the door for me, and walked me proudly on his arm into the restaurant. Inwardly, I was anticipating a deliciously sexual evening with this cowboy. With his broad shoulders and friendly face; his shock of salt-and-pepper hair showing under his black suede cowboy hat; his strong chest and long legs outlined by his expensive black leather jacket, crisp black jeans, and shiny cowboy boots; and his swaggering walk that matched his confident smile, he exuded a playful as well as powerful sexuality that made me quiver.

⊱————⊰

I'd spent all day in sexual anticipation and preparation for this date—having my toenails polished, getting acrylic nails to make my fingernails beautiful and indestructible, and choosing just the right clothes and earrings. I'd been waiting for him on my living room couch, drinking wine, thinking of what I wanted to do with him. When I let him in, his eyes widened, then squinted, and his smile lines rippled upward from his mouth to his cowboy hat.

"Wow," he exclaimed in his cowboy drawl. "You look good enough to eat."

I smiled and said, "Good idea. I'd like your cock in my mouth and my pussy right now."

"Well," he drawled, with his eyes crinkling in delight and appreciation. "I'd be happy to oblige a lady." He took off his belt, unbuttoned his jeans, and slipped his cock out.

I dropped to my knees on the carpet and took him into my mouth, sucking with my lips and cheeks and circling with my tongue, as his cock quickly grew. I looked up at a blissed-out cowboy and started moving my head toward him and away, so his cock would stimulate my throat. He started thrusting to match my rhythm, and soon I was following his, letting him pound the back of my throat, making me feel deliciously filled, opened, taken. After a few minutes, I gave his cock a deep throaty kiss and got up and led him to the couch, where I leaned back and, without taking off my top or skirt, showed him that I had crotchless panties on. "I like this!" he said, and happily fucked me for a few minutes. I enjoyed every condomed plunge.

❧

At the Fat Lady, they gave us a table tucked in a corner, so we were by ourselves. Our waitress looked the part of a brothel worker, with voluptuous cleavage peeking out of her long velvet dress. Homer ordered wine, and we picked out appetizers and dinner. I relaxed into enjoying this handsome man in the same way he was enjoying me.

"You look gorgeous," he said, looking into my eyes. I smiled, inside and out.

"What can I tell you about myself so you know who I am?" he asked. He knew that this date was basically for building trust. Our sexual encounters had been thrilling romps with a stranger, but if we were going to be ongoing lovers, I wanted to know whom I was loving. He told me about his years in Oregon, raising his sons in the country with a wife who became more and more of a fervent religious fanatic. He gave me glimpses of his years as a Boy Scout leader as his sons were growing up, and his time on the rescue squad, which he was still on when he was there. He recounted what it was like to start a successful insurance company, then to lose it all in the divorce. He was now building his business back up. He asked me enough questions about my life to show me that he wanted to know me.

As we talked, I could feel his sincerity and honesty, as well as the intimacy and sensuality of the restaurant, the food, the conversation, the touch, and the eye gazing. I not only trusted him; I wanted him—in my bed and in my heart.

Back home in my living room, he took off my layers, one by one, delighted to find the leather corset underneath.

"Let me show you something," he said. "Lie down on the couch facing up, with your head leaning over the edge and your mouth open."

I was already turned on, wearing only my corset around my waist and breasts, and I'd enjoyed the other sexual places he'd led me, so I did what he asked. When I was in place, he bent over my face, pushed his cock into my mouth, and thrust deep into my throat. I had conquered my gag reflex a long time ago, and now I loved the feeling of my throat being totally opened. This angle allowed me to take him deeper than I'd ever done, and as his cock filled me, I felt completely surrendered to him, which turned me on even more.

I was filled with delicious anticipation that we would continue to go deeper, at least into my throat. We moved to my bed, where we used my vibrator against my clitoris, with his cock moving slowly inside me. Then he pulled out of my yoni and plunged his cock down my throat, triggering my coming, like a switch. Wow. Yum. Wow.

We slept peacefully together, cuddling easily, and he was sweet and tender in the night and morning, until he left at eight for work.

———————

It took me two hours of writing, yoga, and meditating to figure out what I was feeling that day.

I was afraid of my feelings. The sex was what I had dreamed of. I was enough of a strong feminist to feel chagrined that I liked being submissive, but enough of a sex-positive feminist to let myself enjoy what I liked without judgment. I could feel myself come alive with this sex, and I was longing for more. But I was afraid that I'd lose my heart to him—that helpless feeling that is delicious when reciprocated but painful when there is no chance of being his partner. I was not the only woman besides Janice he was seeing. While I could possibly accept his partnership with Janice, I might not be able to handle him being with others. I was starting to want him too much. I was afraid my heart would be broken if I kept seeing him.

Maybe I don't have to worry, I told myself. *Maybe there's a natural limit to my feelings. For all the hot moments, I feel untouched deep in my heart.* Or was that just me being self-protective? We were leading with sex. I could wait and see if my heart caught up.

But the sex was making my heart race ahead. Could I stop it? Did I want to? With just the right fantasies and scenes, he had awakened my deepest sexual energy. I didn't want to turn away from that life energy in myself. I wanted to use the dating project to learn about it.

I gave my fearful heart a hug.

85

"*I want to experience this*," I said to my heart. "*And I'll protect you, OK?*"

"*OK*," she said, "*if you promise.*"

"*I do*," I said, saying yes to her and to my own sexual energy, no matter where it took me.

IDEAL

~~~~~

Homer and I drove south to the drumming party that sunny New Year's Eve afternoon in his big red-and-white Lincoln Continental, cruising along the highway like it was the 1950s. The cool December air shimmered in the muted light of midwinter.

"Look in the glove compartment," Homer said. "There's a gift for you!" Finding a little toy vibrator, I shivered in anticipation.

Homer had more in mind than our twosome for the evening. He had introduced another idea gently on the phone the day before. "A couple's going to be there that I really like—I've played with them in the past."

I was pretty sure that "played with them" meant he'd been sexual with them. Was he asking me to "play" with them too? I wasn't sure I could do that with strangers. I needed to be attracted to anyone I was sexual with. What if I wasn't attracted to these friends of his?

"I think you'll like 'em, and I think they might be interested in getting together with us. You could meet 'em at the party and see if you're comfortable. They're high-quality people."

Homer used "high quality" to mean people who had responsible jobs and were also good-looking, intelligent, sexy, and smart about being sexual. The way he described this couple, his confidence that I would like them, and his offer as an option, not a requirement, made me curious.

"I'd be open to getting together with them if I liked them," I said, still feeling wary.

"I think you will!" he replied, and we left it at that.

We arrived at the hilltop location in time to help set up and were welcomed by the hosts, Maria and Niko. Maria's ranch-style stone house straddled the top of a hill above Santa Cruz, with high ceilings and big open spaces in the central living room and kitchen, flanked in each direction by hallways of bedrooms. The front windows suggested a view of the ocean, but the clouds and fog obscured it and created a gray bubble around this spacious house and stone-stepped grounds.

As the party got going, the kitchen and living room filled with women and men who all seemed to know each other. Homer introduced me to his Burning Man friends—mostly couples and a few single women. Some of the women had been his lovers and some were just friends, but they were all friendly toward me. They told me funny stories of intense work and play amid giant art structures and bonfires on Burning Man's immense dry lakebed. "You should join our camp!" said one soft-curled woman with a wide smile. I started to feel part of the group.

Homer's main role in the party was to organize and lead the drummers, percussionists, and anyone else in a drumming session—the main musical offering of the party. He had a knack for leading drummers through different rhythms that were in tune with the mood of the party, and he had people swaying and dancing to the beat in the living room from early on. The party got more crowded, and I squeezed into a couch among my new acquaintances, but the drumming was too loud to allow much talking, and I was craving connection with Homer.

Extricating myself from the couch, I slipped in behind Homer on his chair with my arms around him while he drummed. It was an uncharacteristic gesture. If I had seen another woman do this, I would have assumed she was not a feminist, was hopelessly dependent on her guy, and was too shy to venture out into the party. No one but I knew that as a former lesbian and longtime independent hetero, I had spent many parties moving as a strong-willed free spirit and was now letting myself enjoy the comfort of closeness to a man I was wildly attracted to.

It was while I was looking out into the living room over Homer's shoulder that I saw the most dramatic couple sweep into the house. He was very tall with well-trimmed gray-blond hair, a goatee, and a long black cape that opened to reveal red satin. She was petite with a friendly face under a cap of wavy brown hair, dressed in just the right amount of leopard skin to cover major body parts, and just enough lace on her legs and arms to be sexy and alluring. They were glowing with a happiness and confidence that shone across the whole party. I assumed that they were yet another part of the crowd I didn't know, and they disappeared into the other room. However, when they reappeared nearby, I realized that I knew the woman, Olivia, from various workshops. We had never been close, but I had admired her from a distance for her confident sexuality and poise. To my surprise, they made their way over to our group by the couch, stopping in front of Homer, who grinned and gestured that Olivia and this guy were the couple he had been talking about.

I pried myself out from behind Homer to greet them. Olivia smiled and shouted, "This is Reed!" I could feel my apprehensions calming and my hopes rising when I realized that I could be "playing" with a woman I was totally comfortable with and a man I was immediately attracted to.

Homer, still directing the party, announced that everyone should take a percussion piece and sit in the drumming circle.

I found a string of bells and a comfortable seat. To my delight, Reed folded his lanky body into the next seat, turned toward me, and started a conversation.

"So Homer says you're a songwriter," he said, pinpointing the area of my life I was most proud of. He leaned close to my ear like he was imparting a great secret. "Do you hear the chords in these drum rhythms?" It felt like an intimate question.

I listened to the tones underneath the drums for the first time, and heard them. This started a lighthearted but absorbing conversation about music—how we had learned it, what kind of songs we each wrote, the instruments we played, and his delights in one of his jobs—promoting young bands. While we talked, I laughed easily and felt appreciated by him. He understood the joys and challenges I had working in a community college, and praised me for assisting with the HAI workshops, noting that he and Olivia had attended quite a few. He added that they'd been together for two years and had gradually incorporated sex with others into their relationship, to their great enjoyment. Throughout our conversation, he managed to demonstrate a sincere interest in me while affirming his relationship with Olivia.

I was captivated—this was the type of man I was looking for. I was attracted to him on many levels—besides his pleasing face, hair, and body, he had a quick and curious mind, a kind gregariousness, a passionate involvement in his work, a sincere interest in mine, a positive view of sex, and a sensitivity to his primary partner when reaching out to other women. I had a twinge of feeling sorry that he was already "taken" by Olivia. However, I was mainly glad to know that men like him were in the world—it gave me hope for my project. After all, I only needed one. If Reed existed, there must be more. Homer was a sexual cowboy and I still wanted to explore my desire for him, but I longed to end up with a more well-rounded partner like Reed.

It was way after midnight when the party wound down. Most guests left for home; others disappeared into bedrooms. Mellow music played. Those of us who were still awake, including Reed, Olivia, Homer, and me, spent an hour cuddling on the big living room cushions, lazily caressing each other over our clothes. I suspected that Reed had been interviewing me earlier and that I passed, for he spent most of this time next to me, lightly running his fingers through my hair, stroking my arms, and gazing into my eyes. After a while, he leaned over and kissed me on the lips, soft enough to be sensual and hard enough to bring up sexual longing for him. I barely registered that Homer was kissing Olivia on the next pillow.

Just as I was wondering where we would be sleeping and playing with Reed and Olivia, Niko appeared and led us to a basement room that was filled with mattresses, sheets, and pillows. We found places for our clothes and overnight supplies and carved out a bed for four in the corner, making it up with new sheets and pillowcases. We brushed our teeth and lay down, ready to continue the sensual touching we had started upstairs. It was very late. I wondered how we would proceed and how this would work. Who would touch whom? What about safe sex?

To my relief, Reed suddenly declared: "Carolyn, first we'll have a safe sex discussion—for your benefit since you're new to the group—to share our health status and sex practices." He had obviously done this before. With gentle humor and lots of information, he and Olivia walked me through their sexual health: any STD history, recent tests, types of sexual practices they liked, barriers they used with new women or men (condoms), and the type of lube they preferred (coconut oil). It was both entertaining and comforting, as they were both completely healthy. I trusted them—we had all participated in workshops that emphasized honesty and openness—and I knew I could count on Olivia's integrity. Homer then gave his report, which I knew, but it now included what he usually did sexually with Olivia and when they used barriers. Apparently, they had quite a history. I didn't feel threatened, however, because I knew how solid Olivia and Reed's relationship was. When Homer had finished, I shared my health status, the barriers I'd been using with Homer (condoms for intercourse), and what I would feel comfortable doing and using with Reed (anything, with condoms) and Olivia (kissing and stroking). Although everyone was healthy, I wanted to use condoms just to be safe, and they were completely supportive. Finally, we were ready to start. I was looking forward to making love with Reed as well as Homer.

However, it had taken an hour to confirm that we were all healthy. By now we were too tired to do anything. The best we could do was fall asleep, wrapped in our own partners' arms.

We all woke up several hours later. Slowly, in a relaxed and unhurried way, we reached out for each other's naked bodies. We started by kissing our own partners and progressed to kissing and stroking each other's partners. Every touch by Reed was heightened by his kind gaze, tracking my reactions with a warm smile. He seemed to be responding to every small quiver of my body. I knew it seemed strange, but in this very unconventional way of getting to know someone, I could feel his caring for me. At one point, Reed was inside me and Homer was moving inside Olivia while he was kissing me—a total connection to my current lover, my new lover, and his partner, my friend. Eventually we made love in as many combinations of male-female sex that we could with two cocks, two yonis, four mouths, and lots of fingers. I didn't have an orgasm—that required more one-on-one focus for me—but it didn't matter. The shared turn-on was excitement enough.

I was falling for Reed—his confident and generous sexuality

and focus on me made me feel wanted, sexy, and sexual. I was also enjoying Homer's pleasuring of Olivia—they were both so delighted with each other. It didn't make me jealous—I felt secure and satisfied by all the sex and attention from both Reed and Homer.

The next morning, we had brunch outside on the sunny patio with Maria, Niko, and some other guests. I was feeling happy and in love with Homer and Reed, but beginning to feel insecure—would this connection with Homer, as well as Reed and Olivia, continue?

As if to answer that, when Homer and I got back to my house, he made love to me again until I had a wonderful orgasm with his cock deep in my throat. Sitting in my hot tub afterward, he said, looking right into my eyes, "So you liked playing with Olivia and Reed?"

"I loved it!" I said, looking right back. "I'm thinking of getting together with Reed."

"Go for it!" Homer said. "I knew you'd enjoy them. We'll do it again. By the way, my Burning Man friends really liked you—they even invited you into our camp."

"Did they mean that?" I asked.

"Of course they did! They got to it before I could—yeah, come camp with us!"

"Won't Janice be there?" I hoped not.

"Yeah, she'll be there, but she's used to my other lovers being there too."

I had always wanted to go to Burning Man. But with my own man, not sharing him.

"I'll see," I said. "But that's August. It's only January—when's the next party?"

He laughed. "That's my kinda gal! I'll find out!" Although I cringed at the "gal" reference, our easy banter about seeing others and the hint of future plans assured me that besides the sex being so satisfying, we might even be growing a friendship.

But Reed was my ideal partner type, and I wanted to experience him on a one-on-one date. It sounded like he and Olivia were used to "playing with" others. Would Olivia feel OK about my having a date with Reed? There was only one way to find out. I emailed them both.

DRIFTING

~~~~~~

On Friday, the day after New Year's, I was still waiting to
hear from Reed and Olivia about getting together. I went
to a friend's birthday party, but I was missing Homer and disappointed that neither Olivia nor Reed had responded to my email.
My coupled friends at the party embraced me and danced with
me, but I felt sad amid these people in relationships.

When I got home, I asked myself, *Will I ever have a primary
partner?* It was scary to ask. What if the answer was no?

Of course *I will!* I told myself, talking back to the *no*. I
wanted to believe that I would find a partner eventually. That
night I took a bath and fell asleep to peaceful music. I knew that
I needed to tell *me* that I loved me, and I was doing that in these
small comforting ways.

⊷————⊶

Reed and Olivia's emails arrived on Monday—they did want
to get together.

"Looking forward to exploring our connection," said Reed.

"Let's get to know each other," said Olivia. "Can you meet
me at Ann's café tomorrow?"

At the café the next day, I asked Olivia how she felt about my seeing Reed.

"I feel fine about you dating him," she told me. Her eyes crinkled with joy and some concern. "But Reed is really busy. With his crazy work schedule, we can barely find time to get together. I'd just want you to work around that."

"Of course," I said. "I see your relationship as a model—I certainly don't want to get in the way of it."

She chuckled. Now her eyes held only joy, and we went on to share about our jobs.

❧━━━━━❧

Reed and I made a date for a Thursday when Olivia was out with someone herself. It would be date number 10. He arrived at my house around ten thirty—a good time for Reed and me since we were both late-night people and lived only fifteen minutes apart. Earlier in the evening, I had attended a goals workshop, and that group told me I was sabotaging my goals by staying up late and getting up late in the morning. They had been full of suggestions about how and why to go to bed earlier. Now I was glad for my late schedule.

After such a sexy meeting on New Year's Eve, I had expected a sexually charged night. We started out talking animatedly on the purple couch in the living room about my songwriting and his work managing and songwriting with a band that had a chance of being signed by a big label. I felt his interest in my songs and his passion for his own work.

Eventually, we moved into my bedroom, and to peaceful new age music, we slowly undressed each other, savoring each familiar body part as it was revealed. Reed stroked me lightly and leisurely and intently like he had before, and I could see his caring again. When he got to my yoni, he explored me expertly with his tongue and fingers, and I could feel myself getting wet.

However, I was not as excited as before—his touch seemed more affectionate than sexual. We started laughing and kissing. We started falling asleep. When we noticed our attention drifting, we made up stories about drifting dreamily down a river and landing softly on a beach. His ability to weave words was one thing I loved about him.

He didn't spend the night—he had to be home in the morning—and I didn't mind him leaving. My body had pulled back from being passionate lovers and drifted into being affectionate friends. I was still in serious like with his face, his focused attention, and his words, but I was no longer smitten. I hadn't let him capture my heart. After all, he was Olivia's guy. I had to find one of my own.

GIFT

~~

It would be nice if I could find someone to sleep with while I'm here, I thought. It was my first day at a real estate seminar in Cabo San Lucas, Mexico, and I was already less interested in buying property and more interested in enjoying the romantic atmosphere of this beach hotel. *A passionate Mexican*, I thought. *Or a stranger from home.* I'd just found out that I was losing even more money on my Phoenix property, so I couldn't afford to buy anything, but the seminar was free, and I was already in Cabo.

It was a week after my New Year's dates with Homer and Reed. I'd come to Mexico not only for the seminar but to celebrate my friend Jules's birthday with his wife, Tatiana, and to visit Ron, my hot tub friend from date number 3, at his open-air home in a nearby coastal village. Ron's walls and furniture were splashed with Mexican colors even more exuberant than mine. I was starting to like the freedom of being single, now that I was three months into it. Although I was looking for a partner, I was enjoying going places with friends and dating different types of men.

At the seminar I met someone *very* different—an animated businessman from Mobile, Alabama, named Norman who liked to tell self-deprecating jokes. "Growing up on the bayou," he drawled, "I never knew you could *buy* property—we just built a shack and put up a 'No Trespassing' sign!" He was grinning like a little boy. Younger than me by about ten years, his thin face was attractive when he smiled, but his superficial friendliness kept me at a distance.

Yet he fascinated me—he was *so* different from anyone I knew. That evening, on a chilly sunset sailboat ride, I huddled next to him on the deck. With very little prompting, he opened up about his life. He'd been a successful social worker, model, and corporate manager. He'd had one early and short-lived marriage. "I'm saving myself for my future wife," he drawled. He had broken his back in a car accident seventeen years earlier and been in pain ever since, despite surgery. This had cut short his modeling and management careers. Now he was a financial consultant, working on an MBA, but his real passion was volunteering as a mentor for handicapped children.

Throughout the next day's seminars of how to buy property in Mexico and tours of possible properties, I kept standing or sitting next to him. I asked a million questions about how he'd succeeded in such varied careers and sustained himself emotionally. "I just worked as hard as I could, night 'n' day," he said. I admired his discipline.

He did not ask me one question. *I guess he's not interested*, I thought.

I couldn't quite see him as a model—his face and short wavy black hair were not *that* good-looking—until he showed up at dinner that night in a very hip and fitted black shirt and pants that set off his face, hair, and body perfectly. My heart leapt—I wanted him.

We met at the bar, by the tables set up for our group next to the beach. My loose black sleeveless top and long pants flowed softly over my body, and by the smile in his eyes, he thought I looked pretty good too.

"Would you like to sit together for dinner?" I asked.

"Yes!" he said, like he had assumed it.

We didn't talk to anyone else. I asked more questions, and he pondered each one. He got out his computer and played me some songs he'd written—about relationships (insightful despite his lack of experience) and his ideals for a wife (Christian, modest, and ready for children—not me!). He didn't ask me a thing. Afterward, I suggested we take a walk along the beach.

"This is purty romantic!" he exclaimed, as we walked barefoot along the sand under a sky brilliant with stars.

Yes it is, I thought. But I wondered, *If he feels so romantic, why doesn't he take my hand or move toward me in any way?*

"The stars, the warm air, the little ocean waves lapping at our feet, wow!" he went on.

"Yes!" I agreed. I took his hand. He kept it there.

"So why don't you ask me any questions?" I finally asked as we walked along.

"I don't want to pry," he explained. "Questions drive a person where they may not want to go."

"Is that what my questions have done?" I asked.

"No," he said, "I like your questions."

"Well, I wish you would ask me some."

On a lounge chair in front of another hotel, he sat down facing the sea and stars. I slipped behind him, supporting him and gently caressing his hair.

"OK," he said. "I'll ask you some questions."

"Great!" I replied, anticipating some curiosity about my life.

"Would you rather make love on a beach or in an ice house?" he asked.

"Hunh?" I started. "Well, of course on a beach!" I said. *Is this his way of saying he wants to make love?*

"Do you sleep in pajamas or naked?" he continued.

"Well, it depends," I replied. "If I'm alone, I wear a nightgown or PJs, but if I'm sleeping with someone, I'm usually naked. How 'bout you?" *This is quite a leap*, I thought, *to be talking about sleeping together already.*

He ignored my question. "Why did God make the stars?" *OK, something spiritual*, I thought. "Well . . ." I began.

"Are there more stars than grains of sand?"

My hope fell. These questions were not an invitation to connect, and he didn't seem very interested in my answers. We walked back to our hotel. I assumed the date was over.

"I'll read you a story in my room," he said. He didn't ask. He just declared it.

"OK," I said. *Hmmm*, I thought, *maybe he does want to sleep together.* I was still attracted to his handsomeness and the differences between us. I still wanted him.

We sprawled on his bed. He read an excerpt from a short story collection by the politician John McCain about a football hero who served his country as a soldier and died doing so— inspiring, but hardly romantic.

Is this what he reads to keep himself motivated? I wondered.

He brought up another story, about Mother Teresa, and we began teasing each other, laughing, and playing with words. I was lying on my back, and he was on his stomach next to me, but not moving toward me. I reached over and started giving him a gentle backrub. He seemed to like it. At one thirty he started reading another story. If I wanted to sleep with him, I could see that it was up to me.

I summoned up my courage and said, "Hey, it's late. I'm going to give you a choice." He looked at me quizzically. "I can either leave now, or leave and return with my PJs, or take my clothes off and get in your bed. All three choices involve kisses."

Narrowing his eyes into a worried frown, he took a few minutes to reply. I was sure he'd just say good night. Finally he said, practically whispering, "I want you to stay with no clothes on."

"OK," I whispered. I kissed him tentatively. He kissed back. "I'll be right back," I said, and went to my room for my safe sex supplies before he could change his mind.

Wow, I thought, *I really am getting to sleep with him.*

Returning, I slipped out of my clothes and into bed beside him. He had put sweat pants on. We kissed softly, then deeply.

"Norman, could I massage you lightly from head to toe?"

"Yes," he said immediately.

I stroked him gently all over, including his groin and his legs. He had the body of a model—sculpted torso, strong toned arms, and a firm butt and thighs I could feel through his sweats. He smiled without looking at me and took off his pants so he could feel more.

When he looked at me expectantly, I said, "Do you want me to make love to you?"

"Kind of," he said. "Umm, would you mind touching me until I had an orgasm?"

"I'd be glad to," I said. "How should I touch you? With my mouth or my hands?"

"I don't really know what works. It's been so long."

"How long?"

"Since before the accident," he whispered.

My heart melted. I would be the first one touching him in seventeen years. My desire to sleep with him for my own needs disappeared. I wanted to give him whatever he needed.

We decided my hands would be best, so I got out my lube and caressed him strongly and steadily, varying my strokes.

"Ooh, that feels good!" he exclaimed. "I've not had any feeling there since the accident."

I stroked him fast, slow, lightly and strongly for a long time. I had never felt so satisfied just purely giving to someone else. Eventually he got soft without coming. It was three o'clock, and we curled up to sleep. Due to his back pain, he could only sleep on his side for two hours at a time. So we slept spooning, first with my arm curled around him, and then, most touching to me, his arm curled around me.

———◦——————◦———

In the morning, wincing from pain, he didn't want to talk about the evening.

"How do you want to be in the group today?" I said, starting to kiss him. "Can we stay close and still be discreet?"

"When you get close and have to separate," he said, pulling away, "there's a break, a tear. I'd like to keep it light."

"OK," I said, aching as he backed away. He was going back into his disciplined mind that I'd marveled at the day before. It kept him moving forward without messy feelings.

I knew I was losing him, but I knew what I'd done. I'd given him a safe place to let down his armor, if only for one night. I'd given him the pleasure of his own body. And I had learned what a gift it was to simply give. For date number 11, that was enough.

In the week after returning from Mexico, I still felt a longing for Norman that I didn't quite understand, given our differences. I had reached across the gulf between us and touched his body, and it had been fulfilling to be the giver for once. But he had given me something too. To find out what it was, I wrote a song, and this chorus came to me: "*You pondered all my gentle questions, you did not turn away, you laid your armor down so sweetly, once along the Cabo Bay.*"

I was longing for a man who did not turn away—who would stay with me and be that vulnerable.

PETER'S SKYPE FROM INDIA

S oon after I returned from Mexico, Peter emailed me from a
beach town in southern India. I'd written him about how
satisfying the Mexico trip had been, how much pressure I was
under at the college, and how badly my real estate investment in
Phoenix was going, adding: *It sounds like your travels are giving
you what you wanted—that feeling of following what your spirit
and heart want and learning who you really are.*

He replied:

Dear Carolyn,
*Thank you for the wonderful email. I love how you
are so full of heart and perspective. Mexico sounds like
it was great. . . .*

*So sorry that Phx is going so badly. . . . The US econ-
omy is affecting things here too—usually there are
thousands of tourists here, but now, hardly any—I'm
in a major pickup area, but nobody has picked me up.
I'm using all my best HAI training but to no avail.*

Thank you for the Deepak Chopra book that has been spot-on in its perspective.

Sorry you can't be here, but it sounds like you have your hands full at the college. Sorry you don't get the support you want (why can't life be like a HAI workshop?). Write soon, love you, peter

I felt his support and love for me. I was sorry no one was picking him up, since he must be lonely, but I also knew it would be hard for me if someone did. I didn't really want anyone to take my place. If the books I'd sent him in Rome for his birthday were perfect for him, maybe I was perfect for him. Maybe we'd get back together after our adventures. Then I reminded myself: *He wanted to travel and live in Bali, and I didn't.* I had to keep telling myself that.

But when he suggested that we Skype, I jumped at the chance—I'd been wanting contact since I'd called him in Rome. After struggling a bit, we finally got Skype to work, and all of a sudden, there he was, looking tanned and relaxed in a little café on the cliffs above Varkala Beach. My heart thumped in recognition. He turned his iPad so I could see the café, the cliffs, the beach, and the craft booths along the cliffs.

"Isn't this sweet?" he said. "Over there is the booth where I bought a sarong for a dollar!"

My heart leapt into the café with him. "It looks great!"

"It is!" he said. "You would love it!"

Does he wish I were there with him? I wondered.

He smiled widely. The beach was wide and sandy, and I could imagine being there with him, although for days, not months.

"Oh, Carolyn! It's so good to see you!"

Does that mean he misses me? "It's so good to see you, Peter!" *It means that to me.* "I miss you so much!"

"I miss you too, Carolyn."

All we could do was smile. He went on to tell me what he did there and how much he was enjoying it. I was savoring the fact that he missed me—it gave me hope that he might return to me if this dating project didn't work. Even though I was enjoying the project.

"I'm enjoying dating," I said. "It's keeping me busy while you're away."

"Those guys are so lucky!" he said. "I hope they appreciate you."

"I hope you get picked up," I said, feeling more generous now that I knew he missed me.

"Me too," he said. He kept smiling. We were both dating.

After our Skype call, I spent the rest of the evening cooking and listening to Van Morrison, remembering how happy I'd been with Peter. Van had been our soundtrack. I gazed at my favorite pictures of Peter and me, still up on my fridge.

How lucky I was, I thought. *How could I care for myself like that right now?*

The only thing I could think of was to write myself a note, since Peter wasn't here to say it.

I love you, Carolyn! Love, me

And I felt the flickering of feeling loved.

VIEW

~~~

The next weekend, I woke up in the honeymoon cabin of the West Point Inn near the top of Mount Tamalpais, the highest peak in Marin County, just north of the Golden Gate Bridge. My friend Samantha had filled the inn with her friends for her sixtieth birthday party from Saturday noon to Sunday noon. I lingered in bed in this romantic room with a view across the bay.

I'd spent the early morning kissing and being held by Larry, my assigned roommate for the night. Samantha had guessed that her beach buddy Larry, a wiry and energetic fiftysomething, and I would like each other; she'd also figured that with all my sensual and sexual experience, it would be no big deal to share a six-bed cabin with a man. She was right. Larry and I had hit it off at the birthday party and that night had started out sleeping in separate beds in opposite corners of the room. However, by dawn we were in the same bed after we'd finally admitted we were longing for each other. He apparently had the same need for touch that I did.

He kissed me like he had nowhere else to go. "May I stroke your breasts?" he said, and he stroked them slowly and reverently, leaving me wet. "Your body is so beautiful," he whispered, kissing me deeply. That kiss, his enthusiasm for my body, and his eagerness to get together made my heart reach toward him. With his youthful appearance, I saw him as a loving puppy.

Samantha had given us all a gift by bringing us to this spectacular perch in the sky overlooking the bay. The night before, sitting around the living room by the fire, we had given her gifts. Mine was a long list of things I loved about her—how artsy and stylish she is, how she hikes on Mount Tam three times a week and finds wonder in it every time, how her optimism about life is contagious, how she, a therapist, still loves to talk about relationships with her friends.

Just three weeks earlier, walking on the beach in Mexico under the stars with a handsome guy, I'd thought, *It doesn't get any better than this.* But on the night of Samantha's birthday party, I'd gazed out at the lights of the San Francisco Bay Area under a bright moon on a twinkling sea, from a warm house with friends, food, and talk. And now I was in the honeymoon cabin with an adorable guy. It *does* get better.

But as adorable as Larry was, I knew he was just a potential date I had yet to explore, not a partner yet.

The next time I return here, I said to myself, *it will be with my real partner.*

<hr />

Larry called me on Tuesday, and he told me how amazing I was and how glad he was to have met me. His words poured out like a waterfall, and I barely noticed that he didn't ask or listen much. It was as if being with Peter had trained me to be loved by someone, and here was someone who was gushing with love. I slurped it all up and wanted more.

"Are you free this weekend?" I asked.

"Oh yes," he said. "Whenever you want—I want to see you and really be with you."

I knew what that meant—we would probably be sexual on

our first real date. Just the thought of it made me wet. I wrote an erotic email to Larry and canceled a date with Homer.

The next night, Larry called. "I'm sorry, I can't get together after all," he said.

"What? Why?" I breathed deeply, trying to calm my body and voice. His ex-girlfriend had decided to come to town, he said. He had told me he was free of that relationship. I felt like screaming. I'd believed he was single and allowed myself to want him.

Instead of screaming, I burrowed into the soft purple couch, cradled my cat, watched *Friends* episodes, emailed sad notes to my therapist friend Kate and to Peter, and went to bed, holding my crumpled self.

The next day I called Homer. "You know that guy I canceled our date for?" I said. "He just broke the date *and* my heart. Any chance you can spend the night tonight?"

He had a massage date, but he shortened it and came over. "That guy didn't deserve you," he said. "You can always depend on Homer to love you up." He took me to bed and did just that.

Emails from Kate and Peter trickled in with encouraging words. "I love how open you are to different people," said Kate.

"You will be fine. Keep dating!" wrote Peter.

By Friday, my yoga poses stretched to the sky again. I went to San Francisco to attend a lecture on the future with Samantha, the stylish birthday girl. The reception was filled with interesting men, and we actively mingled from group to group, hoping for dates. We found none, but had fun trying.

As I drove home from San Francisco, I thought about my attractions to Norman in Mexico and Larry in the honeymoon cabin. I had to admit that I loved getting to know men through touch and sex, even though it often led my heart into some painful places. However, it was never more than I could handle, especially with the support of my friends, my lovers, even Peter. *I'm taking good care of my heart*, I thought.

VALENTINE

~~~~~~~~

Soon it was Valentine's Day, and the only card I received was from my mother. I tried not to think about the many Valentine's Day evenings I had shared with Peter—the romantic presents, dinners, sexy clothes, and sex that always made me feel loved. My mother's card was comforting—at least someone loved me. Making individualized cards was a major way that Mom showed her love, and I usually took it for granted that she'd send a card on every occasion, but this time I gazed at the card and felt the love she'd put into it. It partially made up for not having a special man in my life, despite having several lovers.

A sensual Valentine's party at Marco's house that night, with many people I did not know, offered the possibility of new men, romance, touch, and spiritual connections. It felt scary to go alone, but I had to get on with this dating project. Four months into the project, I had dated only eleven men. It had been a month since the intimate encounter with Norman at the beachside hotel resort in Mexico. Now that I was home, parties and my lovers—handsome young Ben and sexy cowboy Homer—had been sustaining me. However, I knew I needed to reach out to new men to attain my goal of fifty first dates. I was hoping to get there before Peter returned in May.

By now I had been to a few of Marco's parties, so I knew what to expect. There were always separate areas for eating, schmoozing, dancing, talking quietly, and sensual touch, plus a separate "Tantra room" for sexual activities, so I could choose my level of sensuality. And I felt safe with people there. What drew me to this Valentine's event was that Marco had planned a group meditation ceremony in the pool that sounded so mystical—music, mists, laser lights, spiritual ritual—that the romantic psychedelic pagan in me did not want to miss it.

I arrived at the party feeling lonely as well as self-conscious about coming alone on Valentine's Day. My slinky black top and twirly diaphanous skirt gave me some confidence, while my Mexican adventure still reverberated inside me like magic rocks in my pocket, making me feel brave and determined to meet more dates. However, as I walked into the entrance hall and kitchen, everyone seemed to be in pairs. How could I meet anyone new? Knowing only Marco and his sweetie Dawn, I talked with them, soaking up their welcome. *I'm OK*, I told myself, *even if I am alone. My other lovers love me and want me. They just aren't available.*

Soon Marco was gathering everyone to start the pool ceremony. As we all changed into our bathing suits, showered, and distributed ourselves around the edge of the enclosed warm pool in a circle, I looked around for someone to stand with, but everyone seemed to have a partner.

Marco stood majestically above us by the side of the pool like a magician, his wide chest wrapped in a silky blue robe and his full head of wavy brown hair flowing down his back.

"Welcome to this magical night of love and light," he said, his gentle Italian accent warming and caressing the words as the water caressed our bodies. "To begin, I ask you to stand separately from each other . . . find your own space separate from the others, close your eyes, and breathe. Feel your own spirit in your body, expanding and joining with all the spirits in this room." I was grateful that my solitary state was the starting point for the ceremony. I closed my eyes and felt the sensual pleasure of the warm water on my body, I felt myself as a loving, longing spirit who was both self-contained and wanting to connect.

"Now open your eyes," Marco said after a few moments. "Find a partner, and form a double circle around the edge of the pool." I opened my eyes to the steamy pool room filled with laser lights shooting through the mist like stars, and peaceful music wafting through the murmuring voices. People were quickly pairing off, but there were some extra people who needed partners. I settled in front of a pale balding younger man who stared at me blankly.

"Look into the eyes of this angel," Marco directed, "and see the beautiful spirit of this person." Fresh from HAI workshops that always started with eye gazing, I imagined a lovely spirit in this man, but he was frowning, maybe having trouble seeing the angel in me. "Give this person a hug or namaste to complete, and move one person to the left," Marco continued. With relief to be moving on, I realized that I would have a chance to connect with people even if they had a partner. Since both women and men were standing on the inner and outer circles, I might be paired with either. "With this partner, breathe together," Marco suggested, and the young, dreamy-faced woman in front of me smiled. We breathed in sync, enjoying the easy camaraderie of being with another woman at a party where most people were focused on the opposite gender.

I floated around the circle in this peaceful, openhearted atmosphere. After about ten partners, Marco said, "Now, bring your partner and join with everyone in the middle of the pool." We all bounced and floated toward each other through the water until we were all in a clump, arms around each other, looking into the center. Marco started a low hum—"Oooooooooooooohhhhhhhh"—that we all picked up, and it built up to a full multitoned hum and tone. "Aaaoooooooooaaaaaahhhhhhh" filled the room, vibrated the water, and filled our hearts. I felt connected with everyone, despite still being alone, and I opened my heart to take in as much of that connection as possible. "Aaaooooooooaaaah." The hum rose and fell as people added their breaths and voices, and for a while we just swayed and hummed. Eventually, the tone died down. Marco called gently, "May your spirits be filled with the love and light of this night."

I took that in, feeling the love and the light. The group loosened their arms, and couples and singles drifted either to the pool steps or to the sides of the pool. Not wanting to leave, I floated dreamily over to steps at one end of the pool, where I noticed a man who had been one of my partners sitting alone. He had a handsome thin face with a welcoming smile. His long hair was pulled back into a ponytail, as if his stallion aspects were controlled. His face looked like it was sculpted from the same English cast as my family. He held out his arms to me, and I floated into them, grateful for someone whom I could hug. The hug was gentle, as well as tingly and alive. I lifted my face from the hug to look at him, and it seemed natural to kiss him. The kiss also felt gentle yet exciting, warm lips pressed against mine, responding to my pressing into him. I sank into the kissing moment, which lasted a long time.

When we came up for air, he murmured, "I'm Ray. What's your name?" When I told him, he asked, "So how come a beautiful woman like you is alone on Valentine's Day?"

"I'm dating different men right now, and no one was free tonight," I whispered. "I wanted to be here at Marco's and was hoping I'd meet someone new. How 'bout you?" I felt open and confident since both the kiss and the question had felt so sincere.

"My wife is here with her boyfriend," he whispered back. "I was just expecting to hang out by myself. I'm really glad you appeared." He smiled, a mix of adorable sad boy and hopeful adult. His unassuming smile and the apparent abandonment by his wife on this night made my heart open up to him. The warm water, the ceremony, the kiss, the laser lights in the mist, and the deeply peaceful music increased my desire to meld with him right there.

Marco had asked us to refrain from talking in the pool, so we just continued kissing until we both felt a little waterlogged.

"Would you like to snuggle in the fire room?" he said, referring to the cozy living room covered with futons and warmed by the fireplace.

"Yes," I said, looking forward to more sensual, not necessarily sexual, touch.

In the fire room, other couples lounged on colorful futons and pillows, either against the wall or in front of the blazing fire. Wearing our sarongs, we found space near the fireplace and lay down in an embrace that was close enough to feel touched but separate enough to talk.

"What were you going to do here if you hadn't met me?" I asked.

"Nothing, I guess," he said. "Just wait for Ruth and Sam to be ready to leave."

"Oh, you're Ruth's husband!" I said. "I had a nice connection with her at a party here last weekend. Were you there? I didn't notice you." Ruth had seemed very in love with Sam.

"No, I missed that party. I was visiting my daughter that day."

"How is it for you to have Sam here?" I asked.

"I'm used to it," he replied. "When Sam visits from L.A., Ruth just wants to be with him. We've been together for fifteen years, and we each have other boyfriends or girlfriends."

I wondered how available he was if he already had a wife and other girlfriends.

"But I'm not seeing anyone else locally right now," he finished with a smile. "Would you like to get together sometime?"

"How about tonight?" I asked softly in his ear. I trusted him enough to ask this because I knew Ruth and felt like we were all part of the same large friendship circle.

"I'd love that," he murmured in my ear, and kissed me some more.

"Great," I said, and kissed him back. I was glad to not sleep alone on Valentine's night. On the way out, I checked with Ruth. As expected, it was fine with her for me to take Ray home.

Gee, I thought, *I seem to be good at finding men who are already in relationships to date . . . um, I mean sleep with.* So far on my first dates, I had been more likely to sleep with the men who had partners, like Ben, my young lover with the older woman partner; Tom, my willowy winter solstice date with the partner in the Central Valley; and Homer, my cowboy with the on-again, off-again girlfriend. I was more likely to have non-sexual dates with men who were single. Why was I dating and sleeping with married men?

I reminded myself that until I got Peter's "perfect boyfriend" image out of my mind, I would not be open to any other types. It didn't really matter if any particular man was available to be my mate. If I liked him at all, I wanted to have at least one date with him, to replace Peter's image with the energy of different types of men. And if he delighted me and I felt safe, sleeping with him was the best way to fill my heart, mind, and body with his energy. Partnered men were safer emotionally to sleep with than single men—my heart already knew they could not be my partner, so she did not get her hopes up, at least not as much. Kissing Ray had felt magical. He seemed a good candidate for this dating project, and for sleeping together.

⸻

He appeared on my doorstep later that night, after driving Ruth and Sam home. His shy smile looked like he was trying to contain his delight. I let him in and we hugged, then pulled back to look at each other.

"Thanks for inviting me," he said. "I can't quite believe I'm here."

"I can't quite believe it either," I said. I was feeling a little shy too. As much as I love sleeping with men, it was quite a leap from meeting to sleeping together the same night. Driving home from the party had taken away some of the magic. Now, here was an actual man in my house, not just a type, and I needed to interact with him.

"Well, I'm glad I'm here," he said. "And we don't have to do anything more than kiss."

"I know," I said.

Naked in my bed, we started cuddling as we had at the party, preparing to kiss. He was awfully skinny, and his bones bumped up against mine.

"Guess I'm a little bony!" he said, sounding embarrassed.

"Well, it's good I'm a little padded," I said, laughing.

And then he laughed too, relieved, and we started kissing. We didn't have much to say, and I wasn't feeling sexual, but it was nice to have someone in my bed, and we soon fell asleep.

In the morning, over breakfast in my sunny breakfast nook, he told me about his life. He was retired, and he and Ruth had grown children from previous marriages living nearby, so they spent time with them, helping them with their houses or kids. Concerts, spiritual retreats, and sensual parties rounded out their time. It sounded like my life, only without the job and with a marriage and kids. Because his life was familiar, I would not need to spend more nights exploring his "type." This one night had been enough. I counted it as date number 12.

For some reason, I didn't say, *Ray, this was a sweet night, but I'd rather not date more.*

"I adore you," said Ray. I was touched, but uncomfortable with the adoration.

But I still didn't tell him. I thought I could just fade away, since he was married. I had underestimated his interest. On a trip to Europe with his wife, Ray sent me postcards and emails saying he was looking forward to pursuing our relationship when he returned. I sent him emails back letting him know that I was trying to date a variety of men, so I was not sure how available I was for more dates. When he returned, I told him this in person on my front porch.

"I understand, but I'm sad," he said, with sad little-boy eyes, not understanding. I felt terrible that I had not been more honest with him before his trip, before he built up this longing.

I realized I could not just leap into bed with any sweet man who kissed me. Well, maybe I could, but I needed to let them know what I was doing—trying to date a lot of men and having more dates only if I thought they had partner potential. I was determined to have fifty first dates, and this meant I would be moving on after most of them. Since Ray was married, I had assumed that he would have no problem with my moving on. But even with married men in open relationships, I had to be careful with their hearts—as careful as I was with mine.

ECSTASY

~~~~~~~~~

Unrelenting ripples of pleasure were pulsing up from my feet through my calves and thighs, generating wetness between my legs, exploding in my heart, and exiting my mouth with a gasp of giggles. I could barely stay on the wooden chair's cushion. Luckily, Brad's firm grip on my feet steadied me as his alternating light and firm caresses on my skin caused successive waves of ecstasy and laughter. If he could make me feel this way just by touching my feet, what could he do to the rest of my body?

My giggles got him going, and his laughter fueled my own until we were both shrieking and chortling from deep in our bellies, gazing at each other fondly in the flickering firelight of Brad's living room in his house out in the country.

"Well, this is a side of you I've never seen!" Brad said, still chuckling.

"Which side—the ecstatic one or the stoned one?" I asked, my body still undulating in waves of bliss.

"This happy, letting-loose side. I've only seen you when you're in charge of things and kind of serious. You're delightful!"

"I feel like I'm back in Berkeley in the seventies!" Still giggling, I thought about that carefree era when smoking pot made me laugh and laugh just like I was doing now. Back then I was living in my seven-person vegetarian cooperative house with other twentysomethings, and pot enhanced our explorations of sex during that innocent pre-AIDS period. Thirty-five years later at Brad's house, away from my complex Bay Area life, I longed for that simpler time.

"I feel like I'm there with you!" He was looking at me appreciatively, perhaps for this experience of abandon he had never before had. He had spent those years as a young husband, father, and novice contractor in Healdsburg, a small town a few hours north of me. Now a divorced and successful builder, he'd been catching up socially by attending weekend HAI workshops on relationships and serving on the workshop support teams, where I was often the coordinator. Drawn to each other's fifty-eight-year-old sparkle, we had immediately liked each other when we met a year ago, and I had longed to spend time with him, but he lived too far away.

Now in April, I was driving north to visit a girlfriend in Mendocino during my spring break and had decided to stay with Brad on the way up and back. These two visits—our first real dates—were a chance to explore our attraction.

<hr/>

It was a relief to be visiting Brad after a few unsatisfying months of dating. Dates 13 and 14 had been Homer experiments. Date 13 was a threesome with Homer and a friend of his—more hilarious than erotic—and Date 14 was a blind date with a healer whom Homer thought I'd like. The most rigid healer ever, he insisted on choosing the restaurant and food despite my protestations and was not interested in the HAI workshops I was sure he needed. We detested each other. I'd gone back to choosing my own dates. In March, a HAI singles night had led to date 15, dinner with a polite businessman who soon lost his job and had to drop out of dating, or at least that is what he told me. Now with Brad, I could relax.

Our first date, my date number 16, was on my way north. Brad cooked me a gourmet pasta dinner and filled me with wine, cheese, crackers, and conversation as we stood around the huge island in his high-ceilinged kitchen and great room.

"Welcome," he said, holding up his glass of California merlot with a warm smile. "I'm honored that you're here. I've been wanting to get together with you ever since we met."

With his leisurely cadence, Brad was a mixture of Southern molasses and Californian new age sincerity. His unhurried manner of speaking sometimes tried my patience, but when I could slow down to meet him, his simple gratitude for ordinary moments always touched me. On this first day of my vacation trip, landing at his house after a two-hour drive through the glowing green hills of Marin and Sonoma counties, his pace was the perfect tempo for slowing my forward motion. With the wine seeping into my cells, I relaxed into his words and expanded into the uplifting space of this house he had designed and built.

"I've been wanting to spend time with you too," I said. I glanced up at the high white crossbeams and skylights. "You've created such a gorgeous home!" In a nearby alcove lined in cherry wood, amid scattered architectural drawings, a big orange cat slept on his desk.

"Thanks," he said. "I can feel how much you like it."

His smile warmed me as much as the wine. We stood across the island, grinning at each other. I had always found him adorable, with his boyishly handsome face and full head of wavy brown-gray hair. Although he was barely my height, he had made it through my filter against short men because he was so darned handsome. Plus, when I hugged him, he felt so substantial.

Due to our different tempos and locations, I didn't see him as a potential partner, but I was hoping we might be occasional lovers. That first night we slept together in his soft bed in the dark bedroom, kissing and holding each other tenderly. We'd had a safe sex discussion, but neither of us had moved to be more sexual.

The second date on my way back home, however, built up to that ecstatic moment. His foot-stroking talent was enhanced by the warm fire in his cold country house, the wine we drank during dinner, the pot we smoked afterward with the chocolate chip cookies, my relaxation after a week of spring vacation, and my comfort with Brad on our second date in a week.

With my body more aroused, we started out being more sexual in bed, fondling each other and moving toward intercourse. He reached for the condoms, and I got out my favorite lube. However, his cock, at first hard, seemed to shrink from the condom.

"It's hard to get this on," he said, smiling with amusement.

"Let me try," I offered. I sucked and stroked him. His cock swelled. But at the touch of the rolled-up condom, it shrank again.

"I don't think it likes condoms!" I said, now giggling.

"I know it doesn't!" he said, chuckling but looking a little chagrined.

I held his face up to mine. "You know, Brad," I said. "Despite your amazing foot-stroking ability, I really feel more affectionate than sexual with you. How about we just kiss and hold each other again?"

He laughed and looked relieved. "That is so fine with me."

In the morning we stroked each other's face and hair and gazed into each other's eyes.

"I adore you, Carolyn," Brad whispered tenderly in my ears, kissing me.

"I adore you too, Brad," I echoed as I kissed back. "It's amazing to feel so loved by you inside a friendship."

"I know," he said. "I've always been able to be friends with women, but to be able to be so erotic and not necessarily sexual is new. Thanks for your understanding last night."

"What was there to understand? Do you realize how blissed-out you made me feel? And our hearts are still connected. That's the most important thing to me."

"Me too."

Some things were still that simple. Sometimes dating was just a matter of enjoying the moment.

We showered in his skylit, Italian-tiled bathroom with the picture window view into his wooded backyard. His cat observed us from her perch on the top of the shower half wall. I felt loved, expanded, and grateful for this friendship. The cat blinked her eyes in approval.

HOPE ONE

~~~~~~

Another Marco party, this time a dancing one. It was May, and I'd spent the rest of April on several dates with a handsome architect (date number 17) but lost interest when we ran out of things to say. I would rather have no relationship than a boring one. I was glad to be back in Marco's never-boring scene.

When Marco first introduced me to David, I was put off by his gloomy frown. But when I ended up talking to him later that night, I was surprised by how much I liked him—the classic tall, dark, handsome stranger with curly black hair and neatly trimmed salt-and-pepper goatee, offset a bit too dramatically by a black fedora and black cape sweeping over his black clothes.

"Hello again," I said as I breezed by him in the hallway, feeling sexy in my black-and-gold sequined tank top and shimmery gold chiffon skirt. I could hear the dance music thumping and feel people bouncing in the next room.

"Hey," he said, like he had something to tell me. I stopped, and he leaned into me.

"Did you ever notice," he said, "how those of us who consider ourselves new age think we're so accepting of all people and situations, but we require very specific Starbucks lattes and organic cotton clothing to make it through the day?"

Responding to the bemusement in his eyes, I ignored the hat and cape and genuinely laughed.

"True," I said.

"You have a great sense of humor," he said. "Not everyone gets my jokes." He looked at me with curiosity. "Who are you? Tell me about yourself."

Warming to his attention, I paused to choose the aspects of myself I most wanted to present to this quick-witted man. "I'm a volunteer with the Human Awareness Institute. . . . I help with their relationship workshops. I do research at a community college, and I write songs." I said this in a stronger voice than I felt, proud of what I did but unsure whether any of it would interest him. I was still uncertain about my overall appeal to smart, attractive men.

"Most of my friends have done HAI workshops," he said. "People get a lot out of them."

I smiled with relief—he knew the value of the workshops. I would have liked to talk more about them, but I didn't know how long I could keep his attention.

"How about you? Who are you?"

"I'm a therapist, and I run workshops, mostly for men, on getting in touch with their joy and their power. I have a website if you'd like to see it." He handed me a business card with a dazzling but distressed looking sun on it and something about "joy" in the title.

"Oh, thanks!" I said, now thinking that I might be in over my head. Just by being at this sensual dance party, I knew we were swimming in the same pool—the Northern California personal growth culture of high-touch, high-feel experiences found in psychological and spiritual workshops, classes, ceremonies, and gatherings at retreat centers known for intense and earnest encounters, deep inner growth, and clothing-optional hot tubs. The HAI workshops were about love, intimacy, and sexuality. However, I only assisted at them; I did not lead them.

"I've been coming to Marco's parties for the last six months," I said. "How come I've never seen you here?"

"I don't come over to the East Bay much. I live in a big house on a hilltop in Marin, and until recently I was in a relationship. We just transitioned into being best friends, so I'm just starting to go out. I moved here from the East Coast a few years ago, and I haven't really explored the Bay Area."

"Really?" I wondered which thread to pick up. "My last relationship ended in October, and we're still best friends too. It's great when you can do that, isn't it?"

"Yeah, it's both wonderful and a heartbreak that we're still so close. How long were you together with your ex?"

"Seven years." He was right about the heartbreak. Being friends with Peter seemed to make me want him more.

"Wow."

"Yeah. He's been traveling in Europe and India for the last seven months since we broke up. He comes back next week."

"Really? To see you?"

"Sort of. He's stopping here on his way home to Hawaii." I was looking forward to seeing Peter to understand where we stood. Was it possible that after all this time and distance he would realize that we were meant to be together? His Skype call from India in January showed that he missed me, but we had only emailed since then.

Now David was looking at me, expectantly.

"Where in the East are you from?" I asked.

"New Jersey. I settled in Connecticut after I went to Yale. Do you know the East?"

"Some. I went to a boarding school in Upstate New York and college in western Massachusetts."

"What college?"

"Smith." Just naming one of the oldest women's colleges in the country placed us both in the Ivy League milieu of the early

'70s, given that we were both in our late fifties. Now I lived in Oakland in a little house on a little hill, one bridge and light years away from Marin, the county of wealth and new age repute.

"I can't believe we have so much in common! You're smart, you're beautiful, we speak the same language! I want to get to know you!" he said. His excitement reached into my heart and planted hope. Could he be a match? A potential partner?

We had started this conversation near the kitchen but had drifted into the dimly lit living room where couples sprawled out on soft cushions in front of the fire. The hope in my heart opened to him like a flower. We reached for each other, sank onto a cushion, and started embracing, looking into each other's eyes. In a party of people comfortable with sensual touch, eye gazing, and more, this felt like just enough closeness. I could see his smile spreading into his eyes, sending me a warm light.

"I'm so interested in you," he said, "that I don't want to touch more right now." I felt him protecting our potential for a deeper connection. My hope put down roots. I let myself sink into his embrace. As the party ended, we parted reluctantly, exchanging a few gentle kisses. We would see each other after Peter's visit. On his suggestion, we made two dates—a Friday night dinner at my house and a Saturday night dinner and show.

Although I was a little skeptical about David's intense interest in me, I was also thrilled. Seventeen first dates in the last seven months had not turned up anyone I liked better than Peter, and my heart had been turning back to him in my discouragement. This encounter with David could be evidence that my dating project was finally working and that I was ready to meet my match and move beyond Peter. I felt light and fluttery inside.

It was good timing to have met someone so compelling right before seeing Peter again. I knew that my hope for getting back together with him was unrealistic. With David in the wings, maybe I could look at Peter more objectively.

HOPE TWO

～～～～～

Peter arrived in the Bay Area the week after the party at Marco's, and he met me at my house Friday night. Objectivity disappeared as soon as I saw him on my front porch—his tall, tanned body and happy smile under his white-blond halo of hair jolted my heart with a familiar yearning.

"Peter!" I said as I opened the door. "Welcome back!" I was hoping the enthusiasm in my voice disguised the longing. Seeing him evoked a deep feeling of peace in me, and I realized why it had been so hard to find someone better—there was no one who made me feel as good. I wanted to bury myself in his arms right away. Instead I held back, waiting to see where he was.

"Carolyn!" he said, his voice starting high and ending low. His head tilted to the side and his smile held steady, but his voice sounded weary. For a second, we both stood there with our smiles frozen to our faces. A few dry leaves left over from the winter skittered across the porch.

Then he started moving, carrying his suitcase over the threshold. He walked across the living room to set down his suitcase, as he had done so many times before when he arrived from Hawaii. As he stood up, I moved toward him with my arms out for a hug, expecting to meet his eyes. But he wasn't looking at me when he hugged me back, and he gave me a just brief squeeze. *OK*, I reminded myself. *He was always a little standoffish when he first arrived.*

"How was your trip?" I said.

"It was quite smooth, actually," he said.

"Oh, I have some presents for you!" he added and turned back to his suitcase to get them.

I sat down on the big purple couch that he'd left me when he moved to Hawaii. As he brought a cylindrical object over to me, I tried to catch his eye, but he looked away and took two steps back. He always brought me presents, so this was a familiar ritual. It usually helped us ease back into connection.

Under the wrapping paper I found a purple silk scarf—my favorite color—rolled around an Indian Tantra poster of a sexy woman facing her lover in his lap, my favorite picture.

"They're beautiful," I said. "The poster's perfect for my bedroom!"

"I thought it would be," he said. I looked up at him. He was staring at the poster. That he had imagined it in my bedroom gave me hope.

He sat down next to me on the couch, and we hugged, longer and closer this time. I could feel his warmth through our clothes.

"Let's tell each other everything!" I said.

"OK," he said, sitting back. "Here, this will help." He pulled out a joint, lit it, took a drag, and offered it to me. I breathed in as much of the sweet smoke as I could and handed it back.

"So I've been on all these dates, but none of them are as good as you," I said as I exhaled.

"Oh, that's so sweet," he cooed. He always responded that way, and I never knew if he was taking it in or brushing it off.

"I met a girl," he said, looking at the joint.

As my peace shattered, I tried to hold on to the pieces. *This could be nothing*, I thought, but I knew it wasn't. Handsome as

Peter was, his shyness kept him from reaching out to women when he traveled. In an email he had mentioned someone from Paris that he'd met in India. If he was talking about the same woman, it was a big deal. I breathed and tried to sound neutral.

"The woman from Paris that you told me about? Do you think you'll see her again?"

"Yeah," he said. "I think so. She's going to visit me in Hawaii in August." I shifted out of my comfortable position, and my breathing sped up. Pieces of my shattered peace jabbed me inside—that was the only time this year I could have visited him. And now I couldn't.

"It's so good to see you, Carolyn." Peter was always good at getting back to the present moment. I didn't know if he was really feeling it or just saying it to soften the words before, but he was saying what I wanted to hear, so I went there with him.

"Oh, Peter. I've missed you so much!" I said. I wanted to crawl into his arms and cry.

"I know," he said. "Me too." He held out his arms. I crawled into them, and tears came in relief to hear him say that. Maybe the new girl didn't matter after all.

We went to bed, assuming we would make love. It may have been a delusion, but despite all my dates and his new girl, I still felt close, and he made love to me as sweetly as ever. As he entered me, I imagined that he still loved me best.

The next day, we spent an affectionate Sunday morning in bed, replaying similar mornings at my house or in his Hilo bedroom. In the afternoon, we drove out to Limantour Beach at Point Reyes, my go-to place for a larger perspective, where six months before I had gone alone to cry out my grief for Peter and feel the "waves comin' in"—but had ended up fantasizing about a handsome meditating guy and realizing I was *fine*. I was hoping that this wide expanse of sand and sea would help us clarify our relationship, which I had always likened to two souls frolicking together in the cosmos. The hour-and-a-half drive through the golden California coastal hills reminded me of our frequent drives from his house in Hilo to the beaches on the other side of the Big Island.

On days when it was raining, which it often did in Hilo, Peter would happily announce in the morning, "Let's go to the beach!" He meant the white sand beach on the always-sunny Kona side of the island, one and a half hours away. We would pack a picnic and drive along the emerald Hamakua Coast, soaking in the lush green fields rolling down to the blue sea or up to the jade mountain. "Isn't this beautiful?" he would say. "Yes!" I would say. My first few times there, he had stopped so I could capture the contrast of the dazzling green against the sapphire sea on my camera. I could still imagine him waiting by the car while I got the perfect picture.

Now we walked along the Point Reyes beach, enjoying the ocean in a peaceful silence. When we were settled side by side on my favorite sand dune, I asked, "So do you think we have to give up being boyfriend and girlfriend? You know, the special someone part?" I was hoping he would say no. Being with him had made me long for him again—maybe he was feeling the same way despite the new girl.

"Yeaaaaaaaah," he said, "I think we do. But we're still friends. Really good friends."

"And sweeties," I added. "Like sweet friends." Although being friends was a pretty good consolation prize, we had been sweeties when we were lovers, and I was holding on to that.

"Yeah, I like that," he said. "We're sweeties."

I turned my gaze from his face to the ocean, noticing how far the Point Reyes Seashore reached in either direction. I took a deep breath, filling my lungs and heart with that spaciousness. Waves were coming in like they always did. We were still lovers, and he still called me sweetie.

I breathed in again and noticed the rocks sitting in the wet sand that the waves had to flow around. Something like that was stuck in my heart. Peter was moving on to a new love.

A flock of pelicans flew by just beyond the waves, and a little seal poked his head above the water. David was out there, wanting to get to know me, looking like someone who could be my next partner. The hope that David had planted in my heart was growing, crowding out the sadness I felt about letting Peter go.

Peter and I spent the next three days doing the things we loved—talking, cooking, watching movies, taking walks, and making love. Thanks to Peter, I knew how to stay in the present and feel the moment deeply. Like savoring the last drop of good wine, we were relishing these last days of our relationship before letting it go. We reminisced about our favorite times and cried about moving on. We told each other we would always be close. By the time he left, I didn't need to cry. I was looking forward to seeing David for Friday night dinner at my house—date number 18.

HOPE THREE

~~~~~~~~~

I knew the date was not going well when he picked up a news-paper and started reading it while I was cooking dinner. That would be fine on maybe the fourth or fifth date—but the first? And he had forgotten the wine he promised and neglected to bring flowers. This was not what I expected after how delighted David had been to discover me at Marco's dance party.

Why was David reading the newspaper? How could he ignore not only me but my exuberantly colorful house, splashed with Mexican paint and Peruvian tapestries? My mantel and fridge were covered with pictures of my friends, family, and neighbors, and of Peter and me in places like Switzerland, Machu Picchu, and Puerto Vallarta. If David were interested in me, he could've been asking about any of these pictures or decorations. Or, to continue from the party, he could've been asking about my life in a passionately curious way. Or he could've been hug-ging me from behind as I finished dinner. But he was doing none of these things. He was standing across the kitchen from me, backed into the breakfast nook, sifting through my stack of newspapers.

I wanted to say something—to just name it—*This is odd for a first date!* But I didn't, falling into the trap of thinking I must seem really boring to him. *Is my house, or am I, disappointing him?* I tried to ignore his obvious disinterest.

I asked him questions. "So, what's it like leading those workshops? Do you see a lot of breakthroughs?"

"Yes, I see profound shifts and transformations," he answered in a controlled monotone.

Hmm, I thought, *for someone who teaches men how to be joyful and express themselves, this is the least joyful and expressive man I've ever met.* We sat through dinner—ratatouille and tofu—at the nook table with a view across the bay and politely exchanged more information.

Perhaps to salvage the date, he asked to hear some of the songs I'd written. Reluctantly, not trusting that this part of myself would be received any better than me or my house, I led him to the purple couch and got out my guitar. I sang my three best songs, all about love. I finished with the one about wanting to stop and hold on to good moments because I didn't trust them to last. It ends with the realization that "the blessings that surround me are constantly renewed." It was optimistic and applied to how we met, if not this date.

He sang the last words with me, "*coooonstantly reneewww-wweeeeed.*" I was taken aback. He was attempting to sing along, but he was off-key, and his loud voice drowned out mine. This annoyed me, but I smiled and finished the song. He offered a tepid response, showing no sign of being affected. We kissed, but more for lack of something else to do than to express connection, and then he left. I went to bed disappointed and puzzled, but hoping against odds for a better second date. I was still holding on to the good moments of our first meeting.

The next day, I got an email from him suggesting four options for Saturday night: a play, a comedy show about failed relationships (did he realize the irony?), a concert, or dinner and a movie. I could not see how any of these ideas would help us regain the closeness of our first meeting, and if the plans and his behavior the previous night indicated how he connected, I was fast losing interest. Before I could shape my feelings into words, he called.

"Hello, Carolyn?" He sounded strained.

"Hi, David! How are you?" I said as warmly as I could.

"Not good, I'm afraid. I've been thinking about last night and processing it with a friend this morning. I'm calling to say I want to call off our date. I don't think I can date you at all."

I took a deep breath. "Really, why?"

"Last night," he explained, "all my negative judgments came up, and I realized that this is how I always push women away. I judge them and make them the reason I can't be close to them. I didn't want to do that to you, so I just shut down last night."

"That explains a lot. I was wondering what was going on with you."

"That's what it was. I've been grappling with these feelings all night, and my friend helped me get to the truth this morning. I've concluded that I have a lot of work to do on myself before I date anyone."

He said some nice things about me that I couldn't really take in. I was working too hard trying not to fall off the cliff of rejection.

"Well, thanks for calling and letting me know. That took a lot of courage." I was trying to be appreciative of his honesty, but feeling more like I'd fallen off the cliff and landed on a hard dirt ledge.

When we hung up, I felt shaken from the fall, but not as bruised as I expected. Instead, I felt oddly relieved—he had spared me from his judgments. In the past, I had been hurt by the opinions of men I went out with, even if I barely knew them. David protected me by not letting me hear what he thought of me. Even though I would have intellectually known it was his "stuff," emotionally I would have felt those judgments deeply and used them as evidence that I was not lovable. I felt like he gave me a gift. I didn't need to know what he thought. I may have lost him, but I could still believe that my match was out there, wanting to appreciate me as I was.

The next day I wrote him an email thanking him for that gift, and he gave me one more: "Reading your email warmed my heart," he wrote, "and reminded me of how much I love your clarity and how articulate you are in expressing yourself." He explained more of what he was grappling with in himself. He ended with an appreciation of me as "a woman of depth and quality, fierceness and gentleness, brilliant intelligence and emotional spaciousness" and said, "It was a privilege to dance with you, touch hearts, and connect on so many levels."

This was the opposite of a judgment. It was an affirmation of myself in the dating world—someone whom my match would be glad to know. Reluctantly, I crossed David off my list of potential partners—a list of only him so far. In my eagerness to be lifted out of my sadness about Peter moving on, I had put David on that list much too early. Although I had been wary of his interest in me, my longing for a man who was my match had overridden those doubts even during a date that showed no evidence of connection.

Now I had neither Peter nor David. I had only this project, and I turned to it gratefully. I had thirty-two more men to go—surely my partner would be among them.

PART IV
LONGING

LONGING ONE

~~~~~~~~~~

"Give me another chance," Timothy said, when he heard I was still dating. This was the spiritual businessman who had shared tea in my living room as date number 4 back in November. I was taken aback, given that he'd ignored all my attempts at affection and hadn't contacted me afterward.

It was now June. I had lost both Peter and David in May, and my summer break had started. I'd plunged back into the dating project by attending HAI events—first a singles night in SF which led to date number 19, an intense attraction that flattened into a boring date.

Now at a HAI party in Sonoma, here was Timothy. He'd greeted me warmly and asked how dating was going. Surprised at his interest, I'd told him I was almost up to date number 20.

Later that evening, he came up to me and said, "Put me on the list."

"What list?" I said.

"I want to be on the dating list. Give me another chance." He was almost whispering.

"But you didn't even want to touch me!"

"Really? I don't remember that. Try me."

I remembered how attracted I'd been to him when we'd met at the singles night, and how flattered that such a clean-cut businessman would choose me, a new age California feminist. During our tea date, his remark that I didn't trust my intuition had felt like he could see right into me.

"OK," I said. "Would you like to go to the Fourth of July fireworks in Sonoma? It's right after the HAI swim party here that day." I loved small-town celebrations and hoped he did too.

"Sure," he said. "Let's meet at the party and drive over there."

<hr>

A month later we were lying on our backs on my Mexican blanket in a grassy field outside of town, waiting for the fireworks to begin. A rosy sunset was fading behind rows of tall trees. I snuggled up against him. He didn't reach for me, but he seemed to welcome my hand in his. As the evening grew cooler, he turned so I could cuddle up to his flannel-shirted chest. We kept our eyes looking skyward.

"This reminds me of watching fireworks in our neighborhood park in the L.A. suburbs," I said. "I'd be huddled on the ground with my family and neighbors, next to the boy I was attracted to, not touching, but there was all this erotic energy."

"Really," he said. "I'm enjoying this." He smiled.

It wasn't what he said but how he said it. He had a way of lowering his voice and directing his words right at me, like he was sharing the deepest revelation about himself and expected the same from me. My heart opened to that voice, thirsty for that depth. The fireworks exploded above us into big red, blue, and white spheres that glittered and dissolved, leaving my heart even more open. "Wow," I said. He just smiled.

Afterward, he walked me silently but companionably to my car, and we each drove home. Despite so little said, I wanted to see him again. My intuition couldn't tell whether this longing for him was because he had the emotional depth that I yearned for or because he had so little that I was left wanting more. It did not matter to my heart. She just wanted him.

◦————◦

We had three more dates that summer. The first two—a visit while I staked up my tomatoes, and a dinner date—were unsatisfying, but I still longed to be close to him. My heart was sure that we were about to explore a deep emotional connection. It was not like before I'd taken HAI workshops, when I was drawn to any good-looking man who seemed to like me, resulting in very short relationships. Now, I trusted my heart more. After all, she had led me to Peter. I continued to date other men, but no one captured my interest as much as Timothy.

Our third date that summer was spontaneous. Driving home from a weekend up north, I called him to see if I should take a one-hour detour to visit him at his home in Fairfax. I wanted to figure out whether we should keep dating or not. I was beginning to suspect that we were not compatible, but my heart was still yearning for him, and I had to find out why. He was surprised but glad to hear from me and offered to cook dinner if I came by.

He lived in a small second-story, one-bedroom apartment on a quiet street with trees. Sitting on his front balcony sipping wine before dinner, we looked across the street at a group of tall Eucalyptus trees in an empty lot. We had hugged briefly, and now we were sitting close together on a cushioned bench, our shoulders and legs lightly touching.

"Do you know the Enneagram?" he said.

"A little," I said. The system with nine categories of personality types had never impressed me—maybe because I didn't fit neatly into any of the slots.

"I'm pretty sure you're a type seven," he said, "which is pretty incompatible with my type. The differences would probably drive us crazy."

"I don't know about that," I said, "but your astrological chart is all Scorpio, Virgo, and Pisces—my least favorites. I do better with Geminis, Libras, and Sagittarians." I wasn't even into astrology, but at least it had more categories, and I had noticed which types I got along with.

"Well, that settles it," he said. "We should stop seeing each other right now." He laughed. "Besides, you're way out of my league."

"What do you mean?" I said.

"You've been going to all these workshops on love and intimacy. I've just been working to keep my business going. I'm still trying to learn what my feelings are, let alone love someone. How can you even tolerate me?"

"This is how much I like you—I just drove an hour out of my way to see you."

"Well," he said, "maybe I should give you more tests like that!"

My heart cringed—he had managed to push away the compliment and sound mean at the same time. I leaned my body away from him but continued, undaunted. I wasn't ready to give up, despite the mounting differences. I still wanted to know why I was so drawn to him.

"Do you want to know how you should have answered that?"

"Sure," he said, not so surely.

"Try, 'Wow, thanks!'" I said.

He said that and added, with an admiring smile, "Thanks for letting me do it over—good coaching." He hugged me.

I complimented myself that I'd been able to teach him something; however, his harsh first reaction reverberated in my bones, poking into my soft heart.

As I drove home that evening, I pondered, *Why am I still so drawn to him?*

A young woman psychic once told me, "We women complain that men don't tell us what they're feeling, but they do—it's just that we don't always listen to what they say."

Timothy had said very clearly that he didn't know what he felt, that he didn't know how to love, and that we were incompatible. If I had listened to him, I would have stopped seeing him right then. Instead, I continued to assume that my inexplicable longing for him meant that we had some sort of deep emotional connection. It turned out that we did, but not in the way I hoped.

PHONE DATING

By late August, I was back at the college after the summer break. Timothy and I started calling each other occasionally on our way to work and emailing at night.

"What does your workday look like today?" he would ask me on the phone during my morning commute.

Just having someone ask me that question felt intimate. I rarely talked about work with my nonwork friends. "I'm giving a presentation to the president's cabinet, and I'm nervous."

"Why are you nervous? You're so articulate."

"I thought I was, but my new boss finds something wrong with most things I say. I feel undermined by her a lot."

"Maybe your boss is just threatened by you. Tell me what you're planning to say."

And he would work through the presentation with me, until I was feeling clear and confident in my main points.

"Wow, thanks for the coaching," I said. "I feel like I'm getting your consulting for free!"

"Not exactly free," he said. "I'm enjoying talking with you. Anyway, you're saying good things—you shouldn't feel bad, even if she reacts badly."

I'd never had my work life taken so seriously. When I walked into my office, I felt taller.

———⋄———

"What are you facing today?" I asked him one morning on my way to work in September.

"I have to sit down with a guy who hired me and tell him that he's belittling his employees, and that's the reason for their lower productivity."

"Wow," I said. "Could that threaten his contract with you?"

"Yeah, but he hired me to be honest. I just have to say it in a way he can hear."

"You have so much courage to put your intuition on the line in your consulting," I said.

That night, he emailed, "Do I really have more courage than you?"

"We've both demonstrated a lot of courage," I wrote back, "but I assume you have more."

"I think you have more," he said. "You're putting yourself on the line emotionally with all these dates. I could never do that." It felt like some sort of balance between us—that we each admired what the other could do so easily. Was this the type of balance that partners have?

The next day, I told him, "I feel like I'm practicing my relationship skills with you. I have to show up and be honest." I didn't tell him that I'd been longing to do that with a partner.

"Thanks for practicing with me," he said. "That kind of honesty takes a lot of health."

That weekend, assisting at a HAI workshop on love and intimacy, I was reminded that intimacy comes from honesty, vulnerability, listening, and trust. I realized that Timothy and I had been doing all that—building intimacy. I was glad it was the intimacy part of relationship skills that I'd been practicing, since those were the ones I needed to learn. Still, I wished that Timothy wanted more of a relationship—especially touching and being sexual. I was getting plenty of touch from my lovers, Homer and Ben, and I'd kept up the dating project by going on dates number 20, 21, and 22—fun summer dates with HAI guys at Harbin Hot Springs, at an outdoor restaurant in Palo Alto, and at a folk concert in Berkeley—but my heart was still longing for Timothy. His caring attention on my work life was awakening a yearning for intimacy.

By mid-September we were talking on the phone almost every morning. Even though I was not touching or seeing him, our talks were becoming my main emotional sustenance. He understood my work life better than most of my friends and was an intelligent and insightful listener. It was a tumultuous time with my boss, and he helped me understand my hurt feelings and act assertively yet professionally. I could talk about ups and downs with my job, my friends, and my neighbors. I'd never had a friend I could talk to so often about so much. My heart felt heard.

One evening, I called him before his bedtime to follow up on something he had said that morning about leading groups.

"Why are you calling me now?" he answered.

"I thought you'd still be up. I ran into something interesting I wanted to run by you."

"I don't want to talk," he said sharply. "I suppose that doesn't matter to you, though."

"What?" I said. "Of course it matters. You don't have to talk. You don't have to use that tone of voice with me either."

"And you don't have to call me!" He hung up.

I was shaken. I wasn't used to being talked to like that. I didn't want to be close to someone who had such a hard edge and could not treat well-intentioned people gently.

The next morning, he apologized. "I'm sorry I spoke to you that way. You are much too nice for me. I'll be nicer."

After that incident, his allure started to diminish. He was right—I needed to be around a nicer person. Timothy was aware enough to apologize but not aware enough to change.

We stopped calling each other, but my heart still wasn't done. One weekend, Timothy happened to be in my neighborhood and stopped by. I sat down with him on my front porch.

"Timothy," I said. "My heart didn't get the memo that you aren't interested."

He laughed and laughed. "Get over it!" he said. "I don't have the skills to be with you."

Wincing at his harshness, I persisted. "But I'm still longing for you."

"Well, go out and have a lot of sex because you'll be waiting a long time for me!"

He had picked up that I was craving not only the intimacy we'd been building but the sexual touch he'd never offered.

That was a pretty clear rejection. I heard and felt it. Several mornings later, I woke up from a dream of feeling Timothy's and my souls together in India, and I cried that I could not have that. I released my heart's grip on him a little more.

⊶————⊰

The last weekend of September, my lovers and friends helped my heart unhook further. Friday night, I had dinner with Randy, my neighbor and first date; he was now a good friend. Peter called to say, "If Timothy isn't into you enough to touch you, just leave him!" That made me laugh. I had plans with Ben to see Bob Dylan on Sunday. Homer called to make a date for the following week.

Saturday I went to Farmer's Market with Kate, my therapist friend from women's group. She admired how I had let myself feel strongly about Timothy and how I was now wisely withdrawing.

"How could I have been so taken with someone who gave me so little?" I said, chagrined.

"You don't have to judge yourself for whom you're drawn to," she said, "and he didn't give you nothing. There was a reason you felt close to him—you got a taste of the emotional depth you want. It wasn't quite right and it wasn't enough, but you felt it. That's a gift."

It was true. I had tasted it, and I wanted more.

Sunday night found me happily cuddled up next to Ben under a blanket outdoors at the Greek Theatre in Berkeley. Dylan was singing, "I've got nothing but affection for all those who sailed with me,"[1] echoing how I felt about Ben and all my friends and lovers. Randy, Peter, Kate, Homer, and Ben were giving me the affection and love that Timothy could not.

That night, back in my living room, I turned from putting on my favorite music for lovemaking, Bill Douglas's *Eternity's Sunrise*, and ran right into an enveloping hug from Ben. He started kissing me passionately, and then, slowly, with lips locked, walked me into the bedroom. "You are so sexy," he said, peeling off our clothes as we fell onto my bed. His hands stroked me from the top of my head all the way down to my toes several times, and by the time his tongue found me, I was already wet. My wave rose with the crescendo of the music and then burst and rippled through me with him inside. I drifted off to sleep in the comfort of his arms. This was the kind of touch I needed.

<hr />

Timothy and I had one final conversation in October, at a restaurant where we met to say good-bye. I had two glasses of wine, one more than I usually have. I felt open and happy to see him.

"Given how much we shared on our first date," I said, "I was expecting more interaction."

"It's true," he admitted. "I don't need a lot of interaction."

I finally understood why those intense exchanges had not led to the close relationship I longed for. He had not even wanted, let alone been able to create, that closeness. It had been all in my head and heart—it was my own strong desire for an intimate partner that I felt. With just a few comments, a certain voice, and a month of supportive phone calls, he had awakened an image of the man I wanted. He was not that person; he was only an actor in that role, but I let him keep playing it. I could finally let him go. We wished each other well.

As I watched him walk away from the restaurant, I silently said in my heart, *Thanks for giving me a glimpse of the partner I want. Now I'm free to search for the real one.*

MR. RIGHT

~~~~~~~~

It was Halloween, and I was dancing with the perfect guy, a handsome Latino my age, who was at this moment twirling me around the dance floor in perfect swing dance form. At this fancy fundraiser dance for my college, I was looking both sexy and professional in a modest satin black skirt that fell just below my knee, a black shirred velvet strapless camisole around my torso, and my strappy black heels that tapped out my best salsa steps in response to my date's swing moves. My work colleagues, including a big contingent of Latinxs, were impressed that I not only had brought a date but could dance salsa so well. He was date number 23.

He had arrived at my door early, in time to hang out with me as I was getting ready. His white tuxedo showed off his white-gray curly hair and perpetually tanned, weathered face. "I brought this for you," he said, pulling out something from behind his back. "I thought you might like to wear it." He smiled shyly. It was a purple orchid, my favorite color, perfect for my outfit. Touched that he'd thought of bringing one, I hugged him.

"You look so beautiful!" he said, stepping back and smiling.

"And you look so handsome!" I said, giving him another hug. Then I returned to pulling on stockings, earrings, and shoes by walking between the living room, bedroom, and bathroom.

I was putting on my high heels in the living room when he said, "Oh, you look so sexy, I'm taking your picture," and he flashed away as I struggled with the clasps.

At the dance, he stayed by my side, chatting with my colleagues, agreeing with them when they said nice things about me, and adding his own. Everyone liked him, and for years, I was asked about how things were going with that handsome man I'd been dancing with that night. They had assumed we were partners. I felt loved, appreciated, and deliciously escorted to this dance. Jules was the perfect date and would have made a perfect partner.

The only problem—one I couldn't disclose to my colleagues—was that Jules was already married. This was the Jules whom I knew through HAI—he and his wife Tatiana were my good friends. He was on loan to me for the evening by Tatiana. I had invited him because none of the other men I was dating would have been presentable. Homer was too sexual and Ben was so young he looked like a student at our college. And Timothy was gone.

Jules was just right, and he had done me the favor of being my date because he loved me and wanted to support me in this dating project. After Jules dropped me off and drove home to Tatiana, I sat on the purple couch, savoring the evening.

In the midst of dating several not-quite-right men, the night had allowed me to experience what being with a Mr. Right could be like. Like Jules, Mr. Right would come to my door looking dashing, bearing flowers, and offering to serve me. He would help me get ready by giving me feedback about different outfits, and appreciating me in every one. He would take my picture in the final outfit before we went. He would drive me safely to the gala event and escort me proudly into the dance hall. He would smile and talk easily with my colleagues, and encourage them to say nice things about me. And finally, he would take me onto the dance floor and lead me through a smoothly flowing sequence of swing or salsa moves that showed how in sync we were. We would laugh and catch each other's eyes, and not let go, not even when we finished the dance. Yes, this is how my partner would be with me. Could I find someone like that?

COLT

~~~~

My next date was the result of attending a November Sunday gathering of an invitation-only spiritual/sensual/sexual group in a house high in the Oakland hills. It was my second time there. A young, smiling guy named Ross had welcomed me into the group my first time there a few months earlier, and I was eager to try to connect with Ross one-on-one. I chose him for a sexy exercise—marking each other's bodies with chalk to delineate erogenous zones. We lay down next to each other in our loosely sarong-wrapped bodies but then realized that the exercise called for three people, so Ross looked around the room for someone among the forty people there. Suddenly a tall, tanned colt of a man bearing a mane of brown curly hair around his long face with dark round circles under his eyes galloped over to us.

Leaning over me like an eager puppy, he said, "Could I be in your group?"

I recoiled—his energy seemed too much, and his circled eyes made him look ominous.

"Um, I don't think so. . . . I don't really know you," I said. I was hoping that Ross would support me if I didn't feel comfortable in this guy's presence.

The colt's eager eyes fell in disappointment and said, "Oh, OK." He turned to go.

"Wait!" Ross spoke up. "Carolyn, this is Phil. He is a gorgeous, sweet man. You want to know him. I guarantee you'll like him!"

I looked at Ross and remembered his warmth toward me. I decided to take a chance that he could tell who I would like. "Well, OK!" I said. "With that recommendation!"

Phil lay down beside us, and brushing aside our sarongs so our skin was bare, we each followed instructions to point out our favorite pleasure zones, while the other two marked the places with chalk, color-coded for intensity. When Phil and I focused on Ross, much giggling ensued as he directed us to draw maps that seemed to take up most of his body. Lightly touching those areas for erotic responses drew dramatic moans from Ross as well as chuckling from all of us. On ourselves, Phil and I pointed out a mix of silly and pleasurable places, except that I noticed that when Phil was drawing on me, and later stroking me, every place he touched felt electric. As he stroked my face and his eyes looked into mine, a flash of heat flared between us. As I hoped, he bent down and touched my lips with his in a gentle exploratory kiss that said, "Would you like more of this?" The heat flared again. Oh yes, I wanted more.

When we finished the exercise, we were all lying down embracing each other. I was thanking Ross for inviting Phil into our group when Phil said, "Do you want to continue our touching upstairs in the 'hot room'?" This was the private bedroom reserved for sexual trysts.

I told him I'd love to. It seemed like a not-to-miss experience in exuberant sexual energy. It may not be a date, but it sounded like a welcome sexual encounter.

I turned to Ross and said, "Do you mind?"

"Go for it," he said.

Phil and I raced upstairs to claim the room. It was carpeted and bare except for a double mattress on the floor, made up with sheets and a few pillows. I lay down and Phil lay down on top of me, looking into my eyes like a hopeful puppy.

"May I fuck you, Carolyn?" Phil said casually, as if he were offering to carry my groceries.

"Yes, please," I said, equally nonchalant. "Here, use my lube. Do you have condoms?"

Phil looked like a puppy who'd been given his favorite treat. Smiling goofily, he got out a condom, put it on, and smeared my lube all over it and me. His cock, bigger than I had seen on most men lately, looked like it might have trouble sliding in, but after a few tentative pushes, he plunged it inside me. I could feel intense pleasure as he forced open my vaginal walls, stopping just before the pain of too-big. He started a rhythmic beat—*in* out, *in* out.

"Oooh! Aaah! Mmm!" I said on the down beats. On the up beats I gasped for air. Between gasps I was smiling as Phil bounced us along on the bed. His whole body was fucking me, from his eyes with their joyful smile, to the cock that kept up a fast pace in my yoni, to the legs that were pumping us up and down and keeping us on the bed. Soon I was oblivious to anything but Phil and his body on top of and inside of mine. I felt happy in this joyful, playful rhythm. Afterward, we looked at each other and dissolved into laughter and smiling kisses.

"Let's do this again!" he said. I agreed. I wanted to feel that joy again.

⸺⸺⸺

I wondered whether Phil would be an occasional tryst or another lover in my dating project. He lived in Santa Cruz, an hour and a half south of Oakland, so we would have to go out of our way to get together. He was not a serious partner possibility, because he was at least twenty years younger than me and, like some of my other dates, was married but in an open relationship.

However, I hoped to see him at least a few times, so my first step was a phone conversation a few days later with his wife, Tracy, to make sure I had her permission. I had heard that she was very open to Phil having other lovers. I knew her as a warm mother goddess type who had welcomed me into the sensual spiritual gathering months before.

"Tracy, I want you to know that with married men, I keep my heart protected, so I don't go very emotionally deep with them." I was hoping my attitude would be reassuring to her. It was one thing to accept your husband making love to and sleeping with other women. It was another to worry about the women wanting to steal him away.

"Actually, you don't have to hold back from Phil," she was saying. "I don't want to deny him any experience he could have. Please go deep with him!" I could barely understand what she was saying. His wife wanted me to "go deep" with Phil? But what would be the consequence? I didn't think I wanted him as a partner, but what if I did? What if we fell for each other? What would happen to me if I felt deeply for him, but he was still married? I realized that protecting my heart wasn't just for his wife—it was for me.

⌖

Two weeks later, I got a call. "Hi, Carolyn. It's Phil."

Hearing his happy, high-toned voice made me smile.

"I'm interviewing in Berkeley for a consulting job tomorrow," he said. "And I was wondering. Um. Could I come stay with you tonight?"

The combination of puppy exuberance and shy hesitancy was endearing. I was glad I had no plans that night and told him of course he could stay—our first official date—date number 24.

He came by at eleven that night—early for us since we were both late-night people. I embraced him at the door and let him bounce into my house. Then I confessed that I still had some work to do in preparation for a presentation the next day.

"That's OK—I can work on my computer." He promptly opened his laptop and settled on the floor of my study, leaning against the filing cabinet while I sat at the desk. I had never felt so little judgment about not being ready for a date. My heart relaxed with relief. Phil's reaction felt so companionable. This is what I longed for from friends, lovers, and my future partner—an easy acceptance of my often-delayed schedule, a project of their own to work on, and an ability to focus on their own work during the minutes or hours I was delayed. I thought I just needed ten minutes, but one hour later, when I finally finished the presentation, he was still working.

"Time for bed!" I said.

"Yay!" he said.

He fucked me as enthusiastically as he had before, gazing directly into my eyes. His joy was contagious, and we were both laughing and squealing by the end. I fell asleep curled around his long lean body, my face close to his.

In the morning, he said goofy endearing things that made me laugh and rolled out clever word plays that tickled my mind. His playfulness evoked my own silly words and stories. Words did not need to make sense. I felt like a happy little girl who had found her favorite playmate.

⸎─────⸎

Phil got the part-time Berkeley consulting job, and we set up a regular late-night rendezvous for his weekly trip here. Like the first night, our time consisted of loving banter and enthusiastic lovemaking. Our mornings were sleepy and goofy. Once we went to the IMAX 3D theater to see *Avatar*—a science-fiction adventure that matched our high-flying imaginative relationship. He was becoming an ongoing lover.

"Do you know what I like about you?" he said one morning. Of course I wanted to know.

"I like how smart, easygoing, and sexual you are."

"Wow, those are the same things I like about you," I said. It was easy to be easygoing when I wasn't imagining Phil as a partner. He was just a very supportive lover.

Once when we were making love, I imagined that I was having sex with Timothy, the spiritual businessman I'd been longing for. But I wanted to be longing for Phil, so I told him where my mind had gone.

"That sounds like a nice fantasy," he said.

After he said that, I surrendered happily into sex with Phil. Telling Phil that I was thinking of another man allowed me to release the desire and be more present with Phil.

One evening, sitting at my kitchen table, I asked Phil to read the ad I'd written for an online dating site. I was running out of singles nights, parties, and HAI acquaintances and needed to generate dates from outside my own circles. Reed, my tenth date and ideal guy, whom I'd met with his partner Olivia at the New Year's Eve drumming party, had helped draft it. He'd convinced me to include my unconventional activities such as clothing-optional retreats, spiritual ceremonies, and personal growth workshops, in order to attract a man who liked the same things. I'd also included a vision of the relationship I wanted. I didn't want to waste time responding to men who did not want that. I wasn't sure how the ad sounded to a man, so I wanted feedback from someone I was dating.

Phil read my ad with interest, especially these parts about what I wanted:

I'm looking for a partner, lover, friend, and fellow adventurer who, like me, thrives on a variety of experiences, a loving relationship, friends, satisfying work, creative expression, music, exercise, outdoor and indoor adventures, being home, going away, and time alone. Like me, you are happy (and even busy!) with your life, and you know how to support and appreciate someone else's busy and independent life.

I'm looking for a man who, like me, enjoys growing closer emotionally, touching, sensuality, clothing-optional hot springs, personal growth workshops, and spiritual ceremonies, and who matches me emotionally, sensually, spiritually, intellectually, and energetically. After years of short relationships, I'm ready for a long-term monogamous partnership, and I'm looking for a partner who wants that too.

"This describes you and your life perfectly. I'd date you."
My shoulders relaxed in relief.
"Except for one thing," he said.
What had I left out?
"You're not monogamous."
"What?" I said, peering at the ad.
"It says here that you want a monogamous relationship. I don't see you as monogamous."
"Of course you don't. That's because I'm dating lots of guys. But once I find my partner, I'll just want to be with him." I knew that I wanted one man, and to be my man's one and only.
"Hmmm. It looks to me like you really enjoy having different lovers."
"I do, but once I meet my guy, I don't think I'll want that."
Phil looked doubtful.
"I'm leaving it in," I said, taking the ad from Phil. I was definitely monogamous.

HALFWAY

~~~~~~~~

Posting that ad yielded me date number 25 with a gentle graphic artist who hiked. We met on a Sierra Singles hike in Oakland, figuring that if we didn't get along, we would have lots of other singles to talk to. This was brilliant in theory, but in practice, we were swept along with the group on the hike and talked to others more than each other. We finally sat together at lunch, but by then it was apparent to each of us that there was not enough energy between us to justify another date.

Date number 26 was a Sunday lunch date with an artist whom I'd been wildly attracted to when I met him on the dance floor the previous Friday night at Dance Play, a free-form dance studio in Berkeley. Our dancing had been so in sync with each other, his long curls so sexy, and his smile so warm that I had wanted to take him home with me that night. However, my caution put the brakes on and suggested a daytime date first. That turned out to be a good instinct, because when he arrived at my house for lunch, I realized that he was too short—I must have overlooked it on the dark dance floor amid the strobe lights. I had never been able to muster an attraction for a man—or woman—who was shorter than me, no matter how sexy. It was a deep and unfair bias, I knew, but I didn't think I could change it.

The lunch proceeded like a job interview with an unqualified candidate—awkwardly. I learned that he had trained to be an artist but had never pursued it and was now in his forties without a means to support himself. I asked polite questions and made supportive comments about the time he spent with his nieces and volunteer work, but he was nowhere near the man I'd called for in my ad. Being in sync on the dance floor did not always translate to compatibility in life. After we finally finished lunch, I told him I needed to work. Neither of us followed up.

Only halfway through the project, I did not feel discouraged with these two dating duds. My project was working—I was finding men to date, and I was trying out lots of types. Onward!

SPIRIT ROCK

～～～～

It was late November, and I was sure that something would happen if I went to the Friday night singles sangha at Spirit Rock, the West Marin meditation center. Although many of my single women friends complained that they never met "anyone" at these events, I approached singles nights with a mixture of optimism, faith in the universe to provide some sort of meaningful experience, a refusal to generalize from past occasions, and no investment in actually finding a date. My last time at the singles sangha—a part meditation, part mixer event—I had been in a discussion group with a few nice but not particularly bright men, one of whom called me afterward. I had been turned off by his dull questions, and I'd finally thanked him for calling and said that I was not interested. But I refused to regard that encounter as the norm.

Now, a few years later, on the day after Thanksgiving, I was at a cozy West Marin party of several good friends, enjoying post-holiday visiting. The sangha was happening only a half hour away, about an hour closer than from my home in Oakland. Despite feeling particularly connected to my friends, something was nagging inside me, telling me to go. I had a dating project to pursue. I wrenched myself away from the party and arrived only a little late.

As I walked into the wide room full of chairs in a quarter circle around a corner altar, fifty people were listening to a dharma talk about gratitude. I crept around to the far side, where there were a lot of empty seats, so I could be closer to the speaker. Soon, he finished and asked us to form into groups of three to share about experiences of gratitude in our lives. I looked around and noticed that the nearest people to me were a scruffy, downward-looking man with a gray beard and shifting eyes, and a clean-cut, short-haired guy in a business shirt and slacks, who smiled widely as he made eye contact and came over to sit near me.

We decided that the clean-cut guy, Gregory, would start, and he told a story of feeling grateful for his life when he lived in Connecticut.

"Where did you live in Connecticut?" the scruffy guy asked.

"In Greenwich," said Gregory. "I commuted to New York."

"Did you like it there?" the guy continued.

"Excuse me," I said. "I suggest that we stay on the topic so we all get a turn."

"I'm just asking questions. You're trying to control me!" the guy said, his voice rising.

"I think it's a good idea for everyone to share before we start a discussion," Gregory said. I chimed in that that had been my intention. But the guy was too upset to hear us.

"Bitch!" he muttered under his breath, and suddenly stood up and strode out of the room.

While I was sure that the guy was unclear on the concept of small-group sharing, I was embarrassed that I had caused him to leave, especially if Gregory agreed that I was a bitch.

"Was I too hard on him?" I asked.

"No, you were very reasonable," Gregory assured me.

The event ended after some sharing in the larger group and a meditation. Although he looked too conservative for me, I stayed to talk with Gregory. I liked that he had supported me in our little group. He had volunteered for cleanup, and even though it was late and I had a long drive home, I found myself folding chair after chair to help him get the big room back in order. As we passed each other stacking chairs toward the end, he thanked me for the help. Afterward, he asked me if I wanted to have dinner the following weekend. I left the center with his business card and a big smile on my face. I had a date!

⊸———————⊰

We met for that first date, number 27, on a Sunday night in Berkeley. It was a cold December night in a hip but chilly Thai restaurant with a broken heater. We were both good-natured with the waiter about the low temperature and had an easy conversation, exchanging information about our lives. I emphasized parts of my life that might seem familiar to him—he was from New England, so I mentioned my East Coast college experiences; he had an MBA, so I told him about my graduate program in educational research; he had a successful mortgage brokerage career, so I described how my research career ups and downs had led me to the perfect job at the college. I did not tell him about my terrible mortgage in Phoenix.

"It sounds like you really like your job," he observed. He had listened to what I said. I liked his strong square face with neat brown hair along its edges. He looked familiar, like my brother.

"I loved my life in Connecticut," he said, referring to his marriage, daughter, and well-paying job. "It's been hard starting over," he continued, referring to his divorce and starting a brokerage firm in the Bay Area during a recession, "but I like what I do too." He smiled warmly.

There was not a big spark, but we left agreeing to "do it again." I was hopeful. A handsome spiritual businessman was one of the types of men I wanted to experience more of.

But before Gregory and I could get together again, someone came along who was even more to my liking.

WINTER SOLSTICE TWO (2009)

～～～～～～～～～～

"Would you like to come to my house for dinner?" said Dale. If he'd been a random Match.com guy, this invitation would have been much too forward. But we had several friends in common, and this adorable guy with a soft, open face and an early Beatles haircut had lit up the *Match!* lights in my head. In his late fifties like me, he was a therapist involved with Burning Man, men's groups, relationship workshops, meditation retreats, even community service projects—all part of the alternative culture I breathed. He was much more aligned with my life than Gregory had been. The invitation for a Monday night dinner in his home felt sincere and safe.

Earlier in the call, he'd told me he lived on a hill in the Napa wine country, in a cottage with a hot tub and balcony that overlooked the vineyards.

"I would make a fire," he said. "It would be quite cozy."

"That sounds wonderful," I said, attracted to the intimacy of the setting, and to him.

However, I had second thoughts as soon as we hung up. The drive would take over an hour from my house, and it was a work night. How would I drive home after the wine and hot tub we both said we liked? The obvious solution would be for me to sleep over. But my heart had second thoughts about that. "You don't even know him!" she said. "We could get really hurt!"

What was I thinking? I wondered. *What was he?*

Dale would be date number 28. By now in this dating project, I was ready to meet a man who matched me. It had been over a year since I started this quest. During that year, I'd gone out with a variety of guys who were not necessarily partner material, just to shake off my longing for a simple beach boy like Peter. Now I was more focused on finding a partner in the Bay Area and was alert to eligible men. And by now, I thought I knew how to protect my heart.

The next day I called him back and said that I'd be more comfortable if we met first so we could see if we wanted to spend a whole evening together. I suggested meeting at the Berkeley Marina on Saturday for a walk along the bay.

"OK, I understand," he said. "I hope I pass the test."

"I hope you do too!"

When Dale had first written to me, melodic chimes had gone off in the *Partner Alert!* area of my brain. I hadn't gotten many responses to my ad, and here was someone my age who had a profession, had probably done a lot of work on himself, and knew some of my favorite people. I was hopeful. It felt like we were meant to meet. The online matchmaker was actually working.

"So when was the last time you were in a relationship?" he said in that first phone call.

"I broke up with my last boyfriend a year ago," I said. "We were together seven years, and we're still good friends. I've been dating ever since, looking for my next partner."

"What are you looking for in a partner?" he said.

I liked that he was conversant and comfortable with relationship topics. I should have expected that from a therapist.

Phone conversations with online dates tended to be interviews, but they often circled around the important topics. He was getting right to the point of our ads—we had each declared we were looking for a partner.

"I want to be with someone who matches me on many levels," I said. "A balance of closeness and independence is really important. How about you?"

"I've been in several long-term relationships," he said. "I lived with my last partner for eight years. That was about five years ago, and we're still friends too. I love being in relationship, but I'm very careful about who I choose to be close to."

"So what are you looking for?" I said.

"Someone I can deeply share my life with," he said, "although I'm also very independent. So I'm looking for emotional, spiritual, and physical closeness without necessarily needing to live together or even spend all our extra time together."

I had said those exact words to other dates. In a dating ad a decade ago I had asked for "a committed but not daily relationship." My heart beat faster in a surge of hope and excitement—here was a man who wanted the same thing.

<hr />

Saturday was a warm, sunny December day, with clear skies above a sparkling bay. I got to the parking circle early and waited on a bench. Several tall men emerged from cars, and I studied each one hopefully. I wanted so much to be attracted to Dale, since I was drawn to everything else about him. Finally, a tall, somewhat rounded, young-looking guy appeared; he met my eyes and smiled. I realized that he looked young because his face was plump with a dimpled smile. The rest of Dale's body was large, not exactly fat, but substantial without any tone. It was not what I'd imagined from his picture, and I was not immediately attracted.

However, on the path, we quickly fell into an easy conversation. He shared his feelings—"I'm a little nervous about meeting you." He told funny stories—"So our whole Burning Man camp ran out of water, and we had to go begging from other camps!" He asked me deep questions—"What parts of you does your job satisfy?"—and really listened. I felt relaxed, interesting to him, and more and more interested *in* him. As we walked along, breathing in the fresh salty air, we touched each other's arms— not too much, but enough for me to feel a physical connection.

He suggested that we stop and gaze into each other's eyes— my favorite way to connect. We sat on a bench, facing sideways toward each other. His eyes were kind and exuded deep calmness and acceptance. Although I was not becoming more physically attracted, my heart was responding. "He makes me feel really good!" she was saying. I congratulated myself on proposing this "pre-date." Now I was willing to take the risk of ending up an hour away late on a work night.

<hr/>

The next evening, Sunday, I was holding my annual winter solstice gathering at home. Like the year before, I was offering this ceremony for my close friends to honor the darkness of the longest night of the year and celebrate the return of the light. It was the same format—a light dinner followed by a ceremony around the fire. We would declare to each other what we wanted to let go of into the darkness and then what we wanted to bring into the light.

In a gesture of inclusiveness and hope, I had invited Dale to the gathering, but he was busy. I was feeling excited about getting to know him. During the part of the ceremony when we declare what we want to "bring into the light," I would be declaring that I wanted to bring in a new partner, and thinking that it might be him.

About an hour before my guests arrived, Dale called.

"You must be busy getting ready for the solstice," he said. "But I wanted to tell you something. Do you have a minute?"

"Sure." He was right. I was in my usual last-minute rush of food and fire preparations.

"I'd like to cancel our date tomorrow. I've been thinking about it, and I just don't feel we're a match."

"Really? Are you sure?" I was thinking, *What???! That pre-date was for* me *not* you!

"Yeah," he said. "I'm sure. I wanted to let you know before your solstice gathering so you could get support from your friends."

Right, a therapist would think of my support needs, I thought, tumbling into hurt.

"Thanks," I managed to say. "But I'm disappointed. I was looking forward to getting to know you." I was thinking, *How could he know? I wasn't sure, but I was willing to risk another date.*

So I said it. "How could you know?" The rejection was sinking in.

"I just do," he said. "I trust myself a lot."

How could I argue with that? "OK. Thanks for letting me know."

"You're welcome. Best wishes on finding a partner."

"Thanks," I said. "You too. . . . Happy solstice."

Happy? Did I really say that? As I hung up, I wasn't happy at all. On this solstice eve, I would still be declaring that I wanted a partner, but it wouldn't be Dale. I let the waves wash over me—waves of tears, waves of lost hope—and went on arranging the celery, the hummus, the wine glasses, the kindling, trying to keep my tears off it all. It *was* the darkest night.

I knew that the light would return. My friends would be here soon.

But my heart was here now, hurting. "*How did this happen?*" my heart cried.

"I was trying to protect us by having a pre-date," I said. *"He wasn't supposed to reject us."*

My heart sighed. *"I felt something with him,"* she said.

"I did too," I said. *"I'm just glad we didn't have the dinner date and then get rejected."*

"Yeah, me too," said my heart.

"You're so brave," I said. *"Even though you get bruised along the way, you stay open. I love that about you."*

"I love you too," said my heart. *"Thanks for trying to take good care of me."*

And at that point, I knew that I had.

My heart and I could go on with the dating project.

◦———◦

And go on we did, to date number 29 on a bright sunny day in late December. In an unusual convergence of my dating and work life, a handsome colleague in my professional network had popped up on Match.com as a match for me, and after weeks of hemming and hawing on his part and fantasy on mine, we were finally hiking on the ridge of an Oakland park.

I hadn't known he was single and looking. Based on his ad and what I knew, I imagined that his mix of intellect, sensitivity, and hiking experience would be perfect for me. Before our date, I'd been dancing around the house to Bob Dylan's happiest song, "Spirit on the Water," excited and hopeful that my colleague would see me as just right for him.

We started up the rocky path, and I asked him a question about himself. From then on, he talked nonstop and never asked me anything for the whole hike. As we parted at the parking lot, he said, "I don't know about dating, Carolyn. My girlfriend wants to get back together with me, and I think I'll be doing that."

It was a short version of the Dale rejection. I had put my heart out one more time, and she was hurting again. But this time I knew that my heart and I could get through. I cried on the way home, then gave her a hug.

"*He wasn't good for us after all,*" I said. "*I love you. Let's find someone better.*"

She agreed.

PART V
VISIONS

BALANCE

~~~~~~~

On the last night of 2009, I was in a San Rafael two-story mansion filled with the high throbbing energy of more than a hundred colorful, sparkly, and exotically-dressed adults milling about celebrating New Year's Eve. Pulsating music and lights wafted down the stairs into the narrow, softly illuminated velvet entry hall, where a cozy, polite bottleneck of friends greeted each other and admired each other's attire. I spotted one of my favorite couples.

"Carolyn!" Grace called out, glowing in her blond locks above her silver shimmering gown, her arm held firmly by her beloved Galen, who was in a white topcoat and hat to match his soft white hair. They could have been Cinderella and her prince. "You look beautiful!"

"So do you!" I replied, glad to be enveloped in her glow as I was carried up the hallway stairs toward them by the surge of the crowd. Her generous gaze always made me feel beautiful.

As we got closer, her warm smile landed on the smiling young man who had his hand on my hip. "Who's this handsome guy?"

"This is Ross! We know each other from . . . around! Ross, Grace and Galen." I wasn't quite sure how to describe the various situations I'd been in with Ross, including the sexy party in which he had introduced me to tall, coltlike Phil, who had become my ongoing lover.

However, it didn't matter. As my friend, Grace knew that by date 30 of this project, I had needed to cast my net outside our usual circles, so she wasn't surprised she had never met him.

Ross beamed brightly as he greeted Grace. "Very nice to meet you," he said with a faux-cultured accent, bowing a bit and kissing the back of her hand as she grinned back.

Ross had a permanent smile on his GQ-handsome face. Although he was thinner and barely taller than me, the amount of joyful energy he exuded matched mine well. We had originally discovered each other at a HAI party in Sonoma six months before, and recognized high-energy kindred spirits in each other when we started talking happily, fast, and nonstop. Despite my enjoyment of Phil, I was still interested in exploring my connection to Ross, and he had asked to be one of my fifty dates. This New Year's Eve party was the perfect opportunity.

We made our way up a few stairs to the two main rooms—one with a long dining room table covered with finger foods, and the other an open space for dancing with couches and alcoves around the edges for watching the dancers. Both rooms opened out onto a wide covered back porch the length of the house, which overlooked a deep turquoise outdoor swimming pool on the lower floor. The porch was filled with well-worn couches and chairs in arrangements for conversations and smoking various substances. Men and women were perched on seats in each space, talking to each other as well as watching the guests walking by. I was feeling sexy in my short black leather skirt, high black strappy heels, gold-and-silver-sequined sleeveless top that hugged my torso from neck to waist with earrings to match, and a silver sequined hair band that echoed the glitter I had sprinkled on my hair, eyes, and skin. Ross was looking sexy in a slinky kind of way, in tight shimmery rainbow-colored bell-bottoms, a shiny moon-colored shirt, and a blue sequined hat. With his arm on my lower back, I felt we were a shining couple, waters parting for us in our magnificence, which was as much in our faces as our outfits. Indeed, when we first walked in, people at the dining table turned to look at us and nodded approvingly. I smiled back.

"Oh, there's Dennis!" I said to Ross. I had not seen Dennis, a good friend, for months. "I must hug him. . . ." I started guiding us that way.

"Oh," he said, looking in the other direction. "I just got a glimpse of Charlene, my ex. I think she needs rescuing from her date. How 'bout if we mingle for a while and meet up later?"

"Sounds great!" I said, happy to greet my friends on my own.

"First," he said, "a kiss!" We held each other's faces gently, looked into each other's bright shining eyes, and gave each other a deep smooch.

"You are the best date!" I said. "Time together and room to roam!"

"No, you're the best!" he said. And off he went.

As I made my way through the dining room to Dennis, two attractive men looked up at me from their chairs along the wall. One said, "You look so hot!" The other agreed.

I smiled, thrilled that my outfit was as alluring as I felt. I rarely got compliments from men I didn't know, and it made me feel brave and outgoing. Could they be potential dates?

"Thanks! I'm Carolyn. What are your names?"

"Delighted, Carolyn," the first one said. "I'm Bill, and this is Rocky."

We exchanged the usual info about where we lived and how we knew the hostess, but they didn't seem that interested in following up. Maybe they were already partnered . . . or stoned. In any case, I had already received the main message from their attention—that I was sexually desirable. Good to know at this stage in the project.

177

After visiting with Dennis and a few of my friends on the porch, I went downstairs to look for Ross. I found him bouncing in the middle of a pulsing crowd, dancing to loud music in a long room. At the end of the room opposite the music, they were serving drinks and offering marijuana for the taking in a big jar. The long side of the room opened onto the pool area, where torchlights were burning and a few men were setting up for fireworks. It was more crowded down here, and to get near Ross I had to squeeze by some of my favorite women and men, complimenting them on their creative and dapper outfits using hand signals over the loud music.

When Ross spotted me, he called out with bright eyes and a wide smile. "Carolyn! Come dance!" I could tell he was saying.

I went up to him and he circled my waist with his arms and then we were both dipping, bouncing, and swaying together to the lively tune, dancing close and then breaking apart to show off a salsa step (me) or a swing move (him). We anticipated each other's moves, moving in sync, feeling our mutual exuberance. Eventually I got tired, so I bowed out for drinks while he kept dancing. I went upstairs, where conversations were possible.

The evening proceeded that way—taking time apart, then coming back together. I was enjoying the comfort of having an affectionate, fun, upbeat date, as well as the freedom to come and go and connect with friends and potential dates as I wanted. *This would really be ideal*, I thought, *to have a partner I could do this with—share such positive energy, give each other space to have our own connections with others, and always return to each other.*

Right before midnight, I came downstairs and found Ross so we could watch Kate, my friend, the former pole-dance teacher, slink down the pole to the countdown. She did it very erotically, and we all cheered for her and 2010. Ross and I kissed deeply. Then we turned to others around us and kissed them too. I was feeling a lot of love coming my way, so I had a lot to give.

"You'd be welcome to come home with me," I said. We were in my car after the party had died down. "But I can't end up at your house in the morning. I have too much to do."

After a whole evening and half a night experiencing such an affectionate, generous, exuberant, spacious partnership, I wanted to continue that energy in an all-night embrace, and so did he. I could even imagine being sexual as part of the bonding, but knew we could decide that in the moment. He lived half an hour north of the party, and I lived about an hour south. If we were going to sleep together, one of us had to wake up very far from home on New Year's Day.

"I'm probably going to regret this," he said, "but I need to be home too. Rain check?"

"Definitely!" I said. I was a little relieved, feeling pressured by my to-do list.

I spent New Year's Day home alone, catching up on mail, cleaning the house, clipping back rose bushes, and researching local labor market statistics for a grant for the college. After all these dates, I craved this time alone in my house, where light poured into my colorful rooms and garden. I hoped that whatever partner I found, I'd still have this time alone at home.

The sleepover date with Ross happened just three nights later, on January 3. I anticipated another joyful evening and night of connection. However, in my house, his energy felt too high, and he was talking too much. He seemed to only operate on the high voltage level of the party.

"Ross!" I managed to break in. "This isn't working for me!"

"Yeah," he said. "Something doesn't feel right. What do you think it is?"

I thought of how to say it diplomatically. "Well, we really like each other's exuberant energy, and we were a perfect balance at the party. I loved going in and out of being together."

"Yeah, I loved that too!" He looked relieved that there was not something wrong so far.

"It's just that in this situation, one-on-one in a house, our energies seem very different."

"Yeah, I feel that." He looked pensive. "I have more energy than most women know what to do with."

"I don't know about most women," I said, "but it is a bit much for me. I'm sad, because I love your enthusiastic spirit and adore you. I just don't think I can be this close."

"I know, I adore you too. And I love how you can be so honest and it doesn't feel bad."

"Oh good," I said. "Then we can be good friends."

"Definitely," he said. We hugged, and he left soon after.

<hr />

The dating project had come through again. Although Ross and I turned out to be incompatible, he gave me another glimpse of the type of relationship I wanted.

I wanted a partner with Ross's high happy energy—but with equal parts exuberance and peacefulness. And I wanted the type of balance that Ross and I had created at the party between closeness and independence. We showered each other with affection, kept in touch, were always glad to see each other, danced together often, and shared special moments, like midnight of New Year's Eve. Yet we also encouraged each other to explore other guests and party activities. We were not threatened by mingling with others, because we knew we were returning to each other.

I could imagine going to a party like that with my future partner. We would return to our own nest of love and revel exuberantly as well as peacefully in each other, because of both the time apart and the time together. This should be possible. I could feel it.

MAGIC

~~~~~

After dinner, in the middle of a soaring piece of world music, George said, "Come outside. I want to show you something," and slipped out the back door.

By the time I got outside, he had climbed partway up a slope that rose steeply behind his house in the Hayward hills. I followed tentatively up the misty, mossy steps that I could barely see in the darkness. I knew he was proud of his garden, but I could only look down at each step I was taking. I had not worn shoes for outdoor tromping. I had my good sandals on, and I was afraid of slipping or stepping in mud on the unlit path. Even though we had met on a Sierra Club hike, I could not believe he was expecting me to trek out in the dirt on a cold drizzly February night, after such a warm and cozy dinner. But he was cheerfully insistent and was already high up the hill ahead of me, carrying only a candle for light, so I focused on taking one step after another. The steps went on and on, and while I had a nanosecond of fear that I was being taken somewhere unsafe, I basically trusted him. I started to enjoy the trance of the unending steps.

Then I heard the singing. Harmonious, ethereal voices were coming from somewhere. I carefully halted my precarious stepping and looked up through the mist. There, on the slope to the left, was the source of the music—a one-room hut, glowing with candlelight. I felt like I was in the high shimmering green canyon in *Lord of the Rings*, dotted with tiny houses. George was already traversing the slope toward the wooden hut, and I found the path and followed it. When I arrived at the little entrance deck, I saw that the room was simply furnished with a rug, a low table that held flickering candles, and pillows. I looked back over the deck railing and saw the house like a miniature cabin way below, glowing with its own light. It felt like we had flown.

"This is amazing!" I whispered, the view, the hut, and the music filling my heart.

"Welcome," he said softly as he arranged the pillows so we could sit facing each other.

Although this was our third date, we had not yet kissed, and I was still not sure I was attracted enough to him to kiss him. So when we were seated, I reached out and asked if I could stroke his face. He nodded, smiling.

"You've created such magic here," I said as my fingers tenderly explored his forehead, cheeks, and chin. His small face relaxed and took on an attractiveness that I had been trying to see. I could almost imagine loving him. My heart was softened by the peace and beauty of the hut, the otherworldly music, and the fact that this sweet man had imagined and built all this. We hugged, gazing happily at each other until we felt the cold air and walked back down the steps.

———

I wanted so much to like George more than I did. When I'd met him on the Sierra Club hike, I'd been impressed with his sharp mind, his caring attention toward me and others, and his kind comments on what we all said. He seemed gentle, smart, and funny. He worked as a social worker with foster kids, and he really cared about them. Although he was a white Midwestern guy, he was an accomplished African dancer. Yes, he was a few inches shorter than me, and I was not that attracted to his little face with his long thin hair pulled back in a ponytail, but he was so warm and interesting that I thought spending time with him would be enjoyable, whether or not it led anywhere. Besides, maybe I could get over my prejudices about short men and small faces.

On the hike, I'd told him I was enjoying talking and wondered if he'd like to have dinner sometime.

"Yes, I'd like that," he said immediately.

Our first date, date number 31, had been an uneventful dinner of information exchange, but our second date had endeared him to me. He'd waited for me to finish another late Friday work night, then took me to a Moroccan restaurant to pamper me after working so hard. We'd finished the evening at Dance Play, the free-form dance studio, and his dancing had been so graceful and intimate that I wanted to be closer to him. So I'd gladly accepted the invitation for a Friday night dinner at his house for our third date. Before he lured me outside, he had served an elaborate dinner of chicken in cream sauce with spices, condiments, and vegetable dishes in a cozy dining room filled with statues and masks from Africa. The meal and wine had felt sacred.

When we came back into his warm house after visiting the glowing meditation hut, the fire was still blazing, and the beautiful music was still playing. We sat down on the couch in front of the fireplace for a little more wine and tea. He sat close to me, and I snuggled up against him. A long week, the wine, and the magical evening held me there, and I sank into the cushions. As I was nodding off, I told him that I was dating several men and that some were lovers.

"That's OK," he said. We wriggled down the length of the couch until we were lying down and he was holding me. "Would you like to spend the night?" he whispered. Although I was pretty sure I did not want to start a relationship, I didn't want to leave, and sleeping with him seemed like the perfect end to the evening. By now I almost felt attracted to him.

"Yes," I said, "if we can sleep with our clothes on."

"Sure," he said. He got me a long T-shirt, and we found sleeping positions that allowed us to hold each other. With his strong arm around me, I sank into the comfort of being held close by a man and slept peacefully. In the morning, I watched him as he tenderly prepared my tea. He was so kind, and this date had been full of magic—why wasn't I more attracted to him? Was it only that he was short? Pondering this, I packed up my things and left to go start my Saturday.

⟡————⟡

I really thought I could change my attitude about his shortness, so I accepted his invitation to come over and sleep with him the following week. We had another romantic dinner and ended up in bed, knowing we would make love this time. His fingers and tongue skillfully explored me and I almost came. His plunges were gentle, and he came soon. We fell asleep curled up. In the morning, feeling open and tender toward him, I decided to enlist his help to get over my short prejudice. I chose a moment when we were sitting on his bed, so we were about the same height.

I looked into his eyes and said, in my most sincere relationship-speak, "George, I really want to be close to you, and something's getting in my way."

"What is it?" He squinted at me, looking like an animal that was used to getting beaten.

"I'm taller than you. Usually I'm attracted to men who are taller than me," I said softly.

"Why are you bringing this up when I can't do anything about it?" He was now glaring.

I was taken aback by his reaction. I was used to having lovers try and understand my feelings before talking back. I soldiered on. "I thought that bringing it up would help me get over it. There are so many things I like about you."

"Well, it's making me feel terrible," he said. "I don't see why you're talking about it."

Most people I knew understood that my feelings said more about me than about them and that feelings often changed once one expressed them. Clearly George didn't have experience with this type of communication. However, maybe he was right—maybe I was being insensitive to tell him how I felt. Perhaps my bias against short men could not be overcome as easily as I thought. But I so wanted to like him. I decided to have a fifth date with him on Saturday.

⟶———⟵

And that was the site of the awkward conversation at the cozy Ethiopian restaurant, heard clearly by the other diners.

"You're still sleeping with other guys?" he'd asked in a shrill voice.

"But I told you that on our third date," I whispered, "before we slept together."

"How could you do that to me?" he asked with sorrowful brown eyes.

We never recovered from that night. He had expected monogamous dating, and I had not known he expected that. He could not hear my apologies or my intent to not hurt him. In one long painful phone call, I apologized and listened to his anger, but he didn't understand my style of dating or communicating. I was starting to think that I should limit my dating to men who did. And men who were taller. I sent George a long email detailing the many things I appreciated about him, and wished him the best in finding someone who matched him better than I could, adding that that person would be a very lucky woman.

LONGING TWO

～～～～～

Soon after I started dating George, Gregory, the handsome mortgage broker I'd met at the Spirit Rock singles meditation night, called to see if I wanted to get together for a second date. I did—maybe his combination of spiritual and mainstream would work.

We decided on a Sunday afternoon hike to Inspiration Point in the Berkeley Hills, with dinner afterward in Berkeley. It was a warm sunny February day. The hills glowed neon green, the orange poppies waved gaudily along the trail, and the sun hinted at the warmth of spring and summer. This annual spring-in-winter awakening of the California hills always makes me feel affectionate and lusty, as if my juices are rising with those of the grass and the flowers. I usually want to be touching someone. However, given Gregory's conservative background in the heart of New England, I didn't think he would welcome a lot of touch. He was certainly not initiating any. As we hiked along the paved path through the hills, he opened up a little.

"I'm not in a good financial position to date." He looked down and frowned at the dirt beside the path. "My business is barely making it." He glanced over at me with a strained smile.

"I can see how you'd feel more like dating if your business were going better," I said, bending my neck sideways to catch his eye and send him a sympathetic smile.

"Yeah, I would." He smiled back at me, his face more relaxed.

"I can't speak for all women," I said, "but some, like me, don't expect men to pay for everything or spend a lot on dates. There are lots of things to do that don't cost much—like this!"

I was trying to reassure him. I liked him, and I didn't want his finances to stop us from getting to know each other. I wasn't in the best financial shape myself, with the Phoenix debt hanging over me, but I was still dating. I wasn't looking for a man to support me. While I preferred a man to earn as much as I did so we could do a few extra things like weekends at hot springs or dinners out, I knew that my tastes were not extravagant. Besides, I assumed that his mortgage business would pick up.

He had returned to frowning at the dirt. "I just don't feel I have a lot to offer right now. It's really affecting me emotionally."

"Well, I think you're really sweet," I said, meaning it. "That's what's most important to me." I reached out my hand and asked, "Could I take your arm?"

"Sure," he said, offering his elbow. I slipped my arm through it and felt more connected, squeezing his arm and pulling him closer as we walked. He did not pull away. I worked my way down to his hand, which he did not pull away either. It felt warm and light resting in mine.

When we returned to the car, he said, "You did that very gently and skillfully, just taking my arm like that and then holding my hand. It was nice." We both smiled.

But back in Berkeley in a sushi restaurant, he seemed dazed, and conversation lagged. He said he was tired and needed to go home. It was true that we had covered a big subject on a long hike, but I was not tired. He had also asked very little about me. His tiredness and not asking were red flags, but I disregarded them—there was something about him I wanted to explore.

He suggested another date—a Friday night movie. Afterward, I served him tea on the big purple couch. He had declined to hold hands in the movie, so I figured he was just not into touching. Given my need for physical contact, I didn't want to date him, so I was going through the motions of completing the evening when he suddenly asked, "Would you cuddle me?"

I must have been wrong about the touching. How did he know I was a cuddling expert? He lay back on the couch pillows, and I eased my body down alongside of him, putting my arm gently around his waist and holding him close. He responded by wrapping his arms around me and pressing his body against mine. Warm, erotic energy started rising in my pelvis. His hands wandered down my back under my loose blouse and suddenly darted under my jeans, grabbing the back of my thong panties and giving them a firm yank. This commanding jolt against my vulva made me want to surrender to him right there. His hands caressed the sides of my breasts from outside my blouse, and I melted more. I squeezed his body under me.

"You have strong legs," he murmured in my ear. "I find that really sexy."

"Mmmmmmmm," I said, wondering how sexual he wanted to be. I decided to find out. "Shall we talk about whether we want to be sexual?" Later he thanked me for asking that. He was not ready, which was a relief to me—I was savoring this erotic but clothed kissing and cuddling stage. He said that if we were sexual, he wouldn't want to use condoms, and he would want to be monogamous. My mind couldn't compute the contradictions: he wanted monogamous dating, which to me meant being committed partners, but he was too shaky financially to even date, yet here he was on a date. So I ignored them. It's astonishing how much one can ignore in the beginning.

Two nights later, he texted, *I found it hard to concentrate on my meditation class because my mind kept returning to the sensuous sensations of my hand on your firm, smooth butt.* I was still thinking about the thong incident too and was thrilled that the turn-on was mutual. I wanted more.

He called me the next night, and we talked for an hour.

"We've talked a lot about me," he said. "Tell me more about you and your life." One by one he was turning off the dating alarms.

I decided to tell him what I was afraid to say, given what had happened with George.

"I told you I'm dating other men," I said.

"Yes," he said.

"Well, I'm trying to date fifty men," I said. "I call it the Fifty First Dates Project, and the purpose is to find a partner. I'm dating two other men now."

"Yeah . . . ," he said. He must have known there was more.

"I've been dating for about a year," I said, "and some of the men I've dated have become my ongoing lovers, even if they aren't going to be my partner." I conjured up Ben, Homer, and Phil. "They're a big support to me while I'm dating. I want you to know about them and see how you feel about that." I breathed. I felt vulnerable now, but also closer to him.

"Thanks for telling me," he said. "I don't think it matters how I feel at this point, since I don't feel I can be a partner. It would matter if we started being sexual, but I want to be friends before we do that. As long as we can keep kissing!"

"I agree," I said, "I want to be friends first too. Yes to kissing!" I was relieved that he had not rejected me outright. Kissing, I thought, could lead to being sexual, and by then I hoped we would be dating on the way to becoming partners. He had such potential as a partner—smart and open enough to communicate his thoughts and his feelings. His strong sexual energy made me long to be taken by him. Plus he liked to hike. I could wait for him and his business to catch up. I was still seeing Ben, Homer, and Phil.

After that, he must have felt closer. Texts started coming from him more frequently, during work hours, many times a day—*How are you? How is your day going? I'm on BART, thinking about you.* They felt intimate, these little missives arriving on my personal cell phone at work, wanting to know how I was, like we were connected on some deeper level. I was being drawn in, as I had been by Timothy, with a type of intimacy and connection that I was craving. It made me feel like I was in a relationship, even if we were just exploring one.

I brought it up with Gregory over dinner in a Napa tavern. By now it was March. We had spent the afternoon at a friend's art show, and we were stopping for dinner before driving home.

"Our texts and emails have made me feel closer to you," I said. "It seems like you're drawn to me too."

"I *am* very attracted to you," he said. "I just don't think I can be the partner you want."

"Really?" I said, trying to take that in. "You're the first person I've dated whom I've seriously considered as a partner. You don't have to be ready to be one. I just want to get to know you with the possibility of being partners in mind. You're the main scene for me."

"I don't even have a scene," he said. "I'm really liking getting to know you as a friend, but I'm just not there as a romantic partner."

One part of me knew I should accept that he was not ready to be partners, but another part refused to hear this, as I had not heard Timothy before. That part kept hoping that he would change his mind once he saw what a great partner I'd be.

When we arrived back at his house, he asked me if I wanted to stay over. I considered it. I was so tempted. I wanted to be close to him. But I was starting to hear the part that knew he didn't want to be close in the way I wanted. After a long debate with myself, I landed in my own sense of self-preservation and said, "No, I don't want to stay unless we want the same things."

When I got home, I cried. I'd *wanted* him! I wanted a partner so much, and he was the closest I'd come. When I stopped crying, I felt my Higher Self/Spirit holding me, whispering that Gregory was not the one. I would find a better partner.

◦———◦

He called the next morning.

"I feel like we broke up last night, and I didn't want to," he said.

His plaintive voice tugged at my heart and awakened a hope that was still in me. Was he changing his mind? "You said you didn't want to be my partner," I said.

"True," he said, "but I still want to keep seeing you. I'd consider seeing you as a partner sometime in the future, but not now. Right now, I have no money to show up as a partner."

Ignoring his financial struggles, I selectively heard that he wanted me and would consider me as a partner. My longing for him flooded back. He was offering that partner quality I craved—intimate connection with a smart man—and had not yet found with anyone. I was falling into the trap that my dating project was supposed to guard against—thinking that there was no one better out there.

Erotic phone calls and texts continued to sizzle between us. One night at my house, we slipped deliciously into sex, with a condom that I'd convinced him to use. A week later, he invited me to spend the night at his house. We got into bed between sumptuous Egyptian cotton sheets and kissed. He reached over, pulled me to him, and entered me with a condom, and I opened. We slept entwined. When his alarm woke us, I moved to get up. "Where are you going?" he mumbled, still asleep. His strong thigh reached over mine and pinned me down. He was not letting me go. I felt held and desired, and I wanted more of that. I stayed.

But when he called the next night, I knew something was wrong.

"I can't be lovers with you," he said.

"No," I cried. "Why?" I'd slipped into the entrancement of being sexual with him.

"I'm not comfortable with you having other lovers—it increases my chances of getting an STD. I need a relationship to be exclusive. And I can't be in a relationship right now."

Feeling him pull away, my throat dropped into my stomach, and my stomach tightened in the knot of his contradictory needs.

I stammered, "You knew about my lovers, and you were still sexual with me! And I'm the one who insisted on safe sex. You know I'm healthy. Now you're changing your mind?"

"I'm surprised you're so upset," he said. "You have those other lovers."

"Gregory, the other lovers aren't important. You have my heart!"

"I don't see how that works," he said. "I'm sorry." And he hung up.

My heart, still longing for him, was broken. I had become hooked on his texts, his touch, and his attention. Peter, Jules, and my women's group helped me absorb my pain, wailing with me at Gregory, hinting that he was not right for me, was not who I wanted.

My women's group understood the deeper truth when we met that week. "There's a reason you felt so open to Gregory," said Kate, "even though you were not a match."

"What was it?" I said, sniffling.

"He was available in a way that fed you," she said. "Men like that aren't easy to find, and when we find them, we tend to overlook many things about them that wouldn't work."

She was right. I was inside a dating project that was meant to keep me searching for the best possible partner, but I was still susceptible to clouding the truth with my longing.

———

Our last meeting was in a bayside park on a crowded and dusty path. As we walked along, I asked him why he kept going back and forth between closeness and distance and why he would not consider being partners. He looked down at the path and said he was sorry—he had wanted closeness but could not do it.

"What do you want?" he said, turning to face me. How could he not know by now?

I looked into his eyes. "I want to be lovers and partners with you."

He looked back and said, "I can't do either of those things."

I was shaken, but grateful for his clarity. Why had I not been able to see this myself? I'd been so focused on his touch, sex, and attention and so hopeful that Gregory would grow into the partner I longed for that I was blinded, not only to how far he was from that partner but to what he was saying. I finally heard it, or was finally ready to hear it. I drove home crying.

Friends and lovers comforted me again with the same words as before. I heard those too. Date number 27 had taken a long time to figure out.

RELATIONSHIP CLASS

B y late April 2010, after more than a year and a half, I'd been on thirty-four first dates and did not feel close to finding a partner. The last several dates had tested my ability to identify the type of man I wanted. Date number 32 was a therapist my age who said he was available to date and met me for a walk at the Berkeley Marina, but revealed that he had a girlfriend and they wanted me to join them in a threesome. Even though they later broke up, I never trusted him after that.

Date number 33, the husband of a friend, was a kind caretaker type and an expert with his fingers. His wife let me experience him over several sweet dates, and I soaked up his caring and lovemaking, but I could tell that his type of simple niceness would not be enough to hold my attention—I needed a more complex man. Date number 34, a referral from Reed's partner Olivia, was a supposedly enlightened man who did bodywork, but we found each other uninteresting.

In the weeks after these dates, I would swing between optimistic hope about my prospects for finding someone, and lonely sadness. One day I would be missing Peter because he'd been so perfect for me, and another day I'd be missing Gregory because he had touched my heart. While I still basically trusted the unfolding of the project and believed that it would lead me to a partner, I was beginning to get discouraged and wonder if I would ever find him.

So during May and June I signed up for a teleseminar for singles who wanted to be in a relationship, called *LoveWorks: Singles Breakthrough to Love, Breakthrough to Relationship.*[1] It was time to clarify the type of relationship I wanted. I needed to explore whether I had some ambivalence about commitment and monogamy that might be preventing me from finding a full-on relationship. And I wanted to more completely let go of Peter and Gregory.

This class promised to do all that, but as soon as I signed up, I felt resistance to everything about it. We were asked to create visions of what we wanted, and I suddenly had doubts about whether visioning really worked. Although I had manifested many big visions, like my job and my house, others had not come true, such as my real estate investing and a partner, and I focused on those. I was afraid to articulate my vision—what if I said what I wanted and didn't get it? I started feeling worse about myself because of my inadequate visioning skills. I was also very touchy about the title of the course. I did not want to call it a "singles" class. I thought the title would condemn me to remaining single, so I insisted on calling it a "relationship" class. I refrained from talking about my dating project during class sessions, slightly embarrassed that I had embarked on something with such a grand goal that I was not sure I could pull off.

But slowly, I warmed up to the class. The lectures gave us positive ways to love ourselves, appreciate our lives, and see dating as an information-gathering adventure, all beliefs I already had but had somehow lost sight of. Group phone calls allowed me to talk out my doubts and fears. Homework exercises made me list what I loved about myself—my full potential self, they called it—and then helped identify what I wanted in a partner and what I was willing to give to another. Writing exercises allowed me to pour out my stories of how great Peter and Gregory had been, see their shortcomings, and slowly let them go. The lectures and phone calls were recorded so I could listen to them over and over, and the messages slowly sank in.

I felt lucky to have a circle of friends who supported and admired me and egged me on, both in my dating project and in this class. When I reported my discouragement about finding a partner to my women's group, another member, Rachel, said, "You'll never have to worry about being alone—you'll be eighty-five in the nursing home and dating all the men there!"

At a party of my favorite women and men who had been hearing my dating stories, one of the men said, "I want to be date number 50!"

"How about number 35?" I said, thinking that by 50 I would have found my partner.

"Yes!" he said, pumping his arm. I felt not only supported but wanted.

The class slowly worked—there were signs I was changing. I noticed I was loving myself even when I felt sad or rejected. I was letting go of Peter and Gregory by turning to the vision I wanted. I was appreciating myself and starting to believe that my full potential self was possible. After going on date number 34 in late April, I didn't have another first date until the end of June. I was alternately healing from Gregory, letting go of Peter, and enjoying my ongoing lovers (Ben, Homer, Phil). I was feeling optimistic about the summer. Where was my heart? She was slowly healing. I had conversations between my heart and mind on topics like *What was I thinking to want Gregory?*

On my most optimistic days I felt this: I know I can do this! I can find that partner! All that I'm doing is leading me there! I'm in a singles class that is really a relationship class! I'm letting go of Peter and Gregory! I'm visualizing my partner—and it's the best of each of them! I'm picturing myself in my highest potential, and I'm great! I'm on my way to being a wonderful person and partner, and to finding that love and partner who matches me—all of me, not just part of me—all of me! I'm meditating every morning about my good intentions for myself and others and about what I'm grateful for.

And on bad days, well, there were fewer and fewer bad days. Thanks to the class, I was enjoying being single, acknowledging what I loved about myself, and imagining a relationship that would combine the best aspects of being single with my best relationship vision, including some combination of freedom, commitment, and monogamy. I was letting go of Peter as well as the men like Timothy and Gregory who had captured my heart during the project.

My vision filled up a single-spaced page and described in detail my future relationship with a man whom I adore and who adores me, who reflects and supports all the best parts of me, and who is committed to me and to our personal growth. I distilled the essence of the vision into these words, which I posted next to my bathroom mirror where I would see them often:

I am in a relationship
in which we adore and accept each other
and joyfully and creatively celebrate
our deep connections
of heart, spirit, body, and mind!

With that relationship vision in mind, I vowed that beginning with date number 35, I would only go out with men who I seriously thought could be my partner. However, I started out a bit wobbly. Date number 35 was a picnic with the friend who had asked to be one of my dates. We'd shared a crush ten years before, so I thought we might rekindle the flame. However, after ten years of friendship, we could not find a romantic level to connect on, even on green grass by a shimmering blue lake. Date number 36 was a man recommended by a woman friend who'd found him online. He seemed perfect on paper and the phone, but our first date at his house fell flat, his smaller physique and lower energy failing to match mine.

I was glad I had explored these men who had been offered to me—you never know. But finding men who fit my vision of a partner was harder than I thought. Soon I started longing inexplicably for a man named Rob, an older white-haired dancer who was probably not that partner.

DANCE

~~~~~

My first encounter with Rob at the Friday night dance, Dance Play, had caught us both by surprise. I had started going to Dance Play by myself every week for contact and touch while I was taking the relationship class. I had noticed Rob's lean body and youthful surfer haircut in the small dance studio called the "warm room," where they played the slow music. Thirty of us were moving leisurely to the spacey music, all individually dancing in free form, touching occasionally in a casual stylized way. I was feeling slinky in my black leggings and loose sleeveless tunic of gray-and-black swirls. Rob was swaying, facing the wall, lost in his own dance. His sea-green T-shirt and multicolored dance pants hung soft and loose on his frame. With his eyes closed, he turned around and slowly slid down along the wall until he was lying on the floor, gracefully undulating and stretching out into the room.

His face had that weathered but noble look that older men with high cheekbones are blessed with, and his handsomeness and grace drew me toward him. I got down on the floor and stretched toward him, lightly brushing his fingers with my hand. He responded by curling his fingers around mine and pulling me to him across the polished wood floor, still keeping his eyes closed. I felt a surge of being claimed and wanted. I answered by pulling him to me as well, and then we mutually pushed each other away in a way that was just as erotic, knowing we would return. At the next pull, I rolled toward him, brushed his side with the side of my arm, and stretched out in another direction. He followed by stretching out his arm and brushing the back of his arm along my side, as I grazed my arm down along his shoulder and neck. We were both following the loose, unwritten rules of contact dance, which allowed touching only in nonsexual, nonromantic ways, staying clear of the usual dance positions like holding hands or embracing each other face-to-face or using our hands at all. It was usual to avoid eye contact as one exchanged light touch between various safe but sensual body parts. So with only occasional glances at each other, Rob and I rolled, bent, and curled around each other, sliding and stroking, eventually working up to sitting and then standing, leaning against each other from the back, looping in and out of each other's arms and legs. I loved it—a man's touch without the complications of a sleepover date.

Later he would say that he thought our meeting was by chance and meant to be. He was disappointed when I told him I had purposely reached out to him. Still, we were both caught in the wonder of discovering touch with another that was so balanced and mutually satisfying.

The music ended at twelve thirty, and we were on the floor, still pushing and pulling each other to and fro. We continued our slow dance without music until the spell was broken by the lights coming on and our friends scurrying around cleaning up.

As we got up to leave, he said, "My friend Jake rents a studio in this building, and has asked a few of us over for some food and more dance. Would you like to join me?"

His formal, well-to-do East Coast accent was surprising

from a guy with such a casual look, but it went with his age and the serious expression that he had held for most of the evening.

Wanting to keep touching him in some way, I said, "Sure, will others be there?"

"I don't really know, but Jake usually attracts an interesting group."

It turned out to be just Jake, me, Rob, and a younger guy named Fred, whom I knew and trusted from HAI workshops. As the only woman, I watched for any threats to my safety but didn't detect any. To energetic new age music, Jake, Rob, Fred, and I started dancing around the large, high-ceilinged, empty room, stretching our legs and arms exuberantly, filling up the space with our bodies, and touching only occasionally in passing. Jake and Fred kept dancing up to me, and I gave them some attention, but their movements felt jerky and hard to get in sync with. I just wanted to be dancing and touching Rob, so I kept returning to him.

Later, as the music and our energy wound down, we lay breathless on a few futons near the wall where Jake had laid out some fruit and cookies. He dimmed the lights, set out candles, and put on peaceful music. As the others talked, Rob and I lay down beside each other, and using the excuse that the studio was cold, I snuggled up to him. He wrapped his longer body around me, and to our astonishment, we fit perfectly, like two puzzle pieces.

"Wow," I said, "you feel good."

"I was just thinking the same thing," he said.

I didn't want to move, and apparently neither did he, so we dozed and snuggled for hours, occasionally glancing at each other in pleased surprise, not saying much. Sometime after three o'clock, I looked up at the skylights high above us in the flickering candlelight and smiled. This was definitely one of the benefits of being single and dating—staying out as late as I wanted and ending up in an enchanted studio in the arms of a handsome and touchable stranger.

———

A week later I looked forward to seeing Rob at Dance Play, anticipating more entwined dancing and sensual touch. As I walked into the cavernous studio entrance hall, I spotted his tall white-blond head across the room and smiled in greeting. To the left was the "hot room," where the fast music was just ending. To the right was the "warm room," where we had danced before.

"You're late," he said with a stern frown when I got near enough to hear him. He turned and flounced toward the warm room studio.

It was eleven o'clock, two hours later than I'd optimistically told him I might arrive. Being late was normal for me. I knew I could never be with someone who was a stickler about time. Sighing, I told myself I'd made a prediction, not a commitment, and followed him into the room.

"Look," I said, "that wasn't a very nice greeting. How 'bout 'hello' and 'glad to see you'?"

Still frowning, his face seemed to soften a bit into just a mild pout. "Well, OK," he said, "it *is* good to see you. I just wanted to dance fast with you in the hot room."

"I'm sorry I'm later than I predicted," I said. "This is when I usually get here. I don't like fast dancing; I like slow dancing. We still have an hour and a half of that, so let's enjoy it."

After that snippy exchange, we were not as in sync as before—we danced mostly vertically, with some touching, with little of the back and forth flow we had experienced before. We did share a very friendly dance with Conrad, a big cuddly man who had been one my dates. After Rob's earlier outburst, I thought that he would be possessive of me, but he was quite inclusive and affectionate with Conrad, and all three of us gracefully wove in and out of touching each other. I felt more open to dancing with Rob after that. However, I had no interest in talking or staying afterward with such a critical man, so I pled tiredness and left.

The next day, he left me a phone message: "Carolyn, I just want you to know how good you make me feel, and how much I appreciate that."

His appreciations seeped through my emotional armor, and I called him that night after work. I wondered how I could make him feel so good when he had been so critical.

"Rob, that was a very sweet message you left."

"Well, it's true," he said. "Being around you makes me feel happier."

I felt a surge of warmth in my chest, but it didn't make sense. "I'm surprised," I said, "because the first thing you did when you saw me was criticize me."

"I know, and I regret that."

Feeling tender toward his mistake, I forged ahead, nonetheless. "Well, it hurt."

"I was wound up," he said, "from wondering if you would show up. And they were playing particularly danceable music in the hot room."

"I understand, but could you listen to what it was like for me?"

"Of course. I'll shut up."

"Thanks. I got there with all these warm feelings about you, but your criticism shut me down. That's why I didn't stay afterward." I hoped he heard the part about the warm feelings.

Silence.

"Rob?"

"Yes, I'm listening."

"I'm done."

"Oh. I can see that was a terrible way to greet you. Will you give me another chance?"

"Maybe," I said, smiling to myself. He was socially awkward, but I was impressed by his non-defensiveness and his desire to change—admirable qualities in a partner. My heart had softened to him when he said how happy I made him feel. There was something in the way he took my presence so seriously—positively or critically—that made me feel deeply seen.

Two weeks later, I arrived for our third Friday night at Dance Play. In those two weeks, I had celebrated my fifty-ninth birthday with my favorite women and men at Harbin Hot Springs, and was feeling loved and appreciated by those friends and lovers. However, my heart was turning toward Rob. We'd started talking by phone, and he'd drawn me in with his focused presence and sincere interest. He wanted to know all about me, and everything he heard he lauded.

"You are so educated," he would gush, referring to my graduate degrees. "I admire a person who values that. And you are so loving."

Even though my friends had just filled me with appreciations of my favorite qualities, I was surprisingly susceptible to this type of admiration, flattered that a man I was becoming interested in would also value these achievements I was proud of. I'd soaked up every word and was glad every time he called. By this Friday, I was longing to touch him.

I surprised Rob in the hot room and joined him in an expressive fast dance, staying connected with our hands and arms. There were others on the dance floor I could have danced with— friends, former dates—but I only wanted to dance with Rob. I was feeling bonded with him, as if we were a couple already.

In the warm room, Rob and I fell into a luscious love dance to the slow music, bringing together the enchanted first night of touch with the longing I was feeling from our recent talks. When the music ended, I wanted to keep touching him and suggested that we cuddle on the pillows in the corner. We sank into each other's warm bodies like coming home. However, the cleanup crew soon ousted us, and we were out on the street in the cool Berkeley summer night.

"What's the inside of your van like?" I asked. I knew that he lived in Santa Cruz and his van looked camper-like.

"It's kind of messy, but I have a bed in back so I don't have to drive all the way home. I usually stay here on Friday nights." This was just what I was hoping.

"Could we cuddle there for a bit?"

Usually when I was feeling this much longing for a man I knew, I would invite him home to sleep with me. But I had no community context for Rob. No one I knew appeared to know him, so I didn't feel safe bringing him into my home. Somehow, cuddling with him in a van on the streets of Berkeley was deemed safe by my protective yet easily swayed mind. She viewed it as a perfect compromise between security and lust.

Rob neatened up the sleeping area, and we took off our shoes and crawled under his blankets with our clothes on. Warming up almost immediately, we held each other closely but tentatively, our most private embrace so far. I was enjoying the buzz of attraction between our warm bodies that I could feel through our clothes. He didn't try to kiss me, and when I started to, he gave me his cheek instead. It was fine with me to go slowly; this understated turn-on was exhilarating. We snuggled into each other's arms and dozed for the next four hours, awakening occasionally to smile and hold each other closer. At one point, his hand snuck up under my blouse and lightly stroked my breasts. Second base is irresistible and appropriate third date material to me, so I welcomed it. My body purred and melted. His hand continued roaming downward along the outside of my leggings, which I also welcomed in my melted state. But when he headed toward the spot between my legs, I pulled his hand back up to my shoulder. I wanted more but was not ready to go further.

At five o'clock, the morning light woke us, and I realized that I'd spent the night in a van with a man I didn't know, whom I was becoming fond of and sexual with. Kissing him firmly on the cheek, I pulled myself together and drove home, where I went to bed and brought myself to orgasm with my vibrator and a fantasy of making love to him.

A REGULAR DATE

The following Friday, on a hot day in July, I was driving north to a workshop over a high Napa hill, thinking about the four men I had dated that week and another I would see that day.

Suddenly, this message appeared on my phone:

"Hi, beautiful," he sighed in a deep voice. Rob started every phone call that way, and it always made my heart smile. The rest of the words were said gently and wistfully. "I just want you to know that I'm feeling very connected to you. I'm enjoying it, but I don't quite know what to do with it. I feel that I could love you. You don't have to respond. I don't want to do anything about it. You're just affecting me in a way that no one has for a long time."

But I do want to do something about it, I thought as I called him back. I was longing to sleep with him, to draw him closer. *He could love me? I could be loved?*

Of course, it was much too soon for either of us to say that, but oh, how his words reached inside me. I needed to protect my heart, who wanted exactly what he was offering. I needed to use different words, downplay it. I still had no context for him. I had asked around at Dance Play, and everyone knew him from dancing there but had never spent any time with him.

"Rob, that was quite a message," I said when he answered the phone.

"It was? I was just saying what I was feeling." He was downplaying it too.

"No, really, I was touched. And I feel the same way. I'm very drawn to you. I just don't know you. How about if we have a regular date next week and get to know each other?"

"A regular date?" He didn't seem to know what that was.

"Like going out to dinner," I said. "We've only danced and held each other. I'd like to spend time talking. How about a nice dinner next Friday before the dance? Would you like that?"

"Oh, well, yes," he said. "I know a few good restaurants in Berkeley. May I arrange it?"

"That'd be great! Let me know. I look forward to it."

I hung up and drove on, hoping that the dinner would make it clear whether I should keep seeing this handsome but strange man to whom I was so attracted. He would be date number 37. As my car wound its way down the hill to the workshop, I let my heart feel his offering.

⚬———⚬

When I saw Rob waiting for me in the Sicilian restaurant, my heart gasped. Handsome with his slender build, sculpted WASP face, and white-blond hair in that boyish cut, he appeared thirty years younger than his seventy years. My skin tingled, my face grew warm, and I felt unreasonably happy. I took in his stylish black shirt and slacks. *Dashing*, I thought. After three Fridays of dancing over five weeks, I was finally seeing him out of his casual dance clothes on this first "real" date.

He got up from his seat against the wall, smiling like he was pleased with himself and with me in my dressy black tunic. He reached his hand across the table to welcome me.

"Find the place OK?" he said, his eyes crinkling in amusement.

208

"Yes. It's perfect," I said, smiling back like I was pretty delighted with him too. "It feels so European!" I gazed admiringly around the room, decorated like an Italian villa, and then back at him. He was holding two wine bottles with Italian labels, one red and one white.

"I thought you might like some wine," he said in his formal low-key voice that for some reason resonated deep in my bones. "Would you like one of these?"

"I'd love the red," I said, looking into his eyes. We were talking about wine, but we were really gazing at each other with lust and longing. My desire had been building for five weeks.

<hr />

But the dinner hadn't resolved anything—certainly not the question of whether to keep seeing him. I learned that he led a peaceful retired life—tending his house and garden in a town south of Santa Cruz, swimming every day, visiting his married daughter in San Jose, and dancing two nights a week in Berkeley. A few years earlier, he'd lost his job in the stock market crash and had retreated to this quiet life on the coast. Between his simple life and my full one—how could we possibly relate in an equal partnership?

I cuddled with him in his van two more times after Dance Play that summer, but I didn't trust or understand my attraction to him. I told Rob I needed to keep my dating project going and turned my attention to finding other dates.

<hr />

Date number 38 was a single man in my spiritual/sensual community who had the same values and lifestyle as I did—so he seemed like a good prospect. We'd been very attracted to each other when we'd started talking in a hot tub at a Sonoma swim party that summer, and I had high hopes for a close connection.

However, the hot tub must have mellowed us both out, because on our subsequent dinner and hiking dates, his frenetic energy made me so nervous that I could not imagine him as a partner. When I gently told him my feelings, he became defensive— something I had not expected from such an aware man.

⊸————⊷

So when I drove to rural Oregon to attend a new age summer retreat in early August, it was Rob I talked to until I lost cell reception in the woods.

SUMMER RETREAT:
POLY EXPERIMENT

~~~~~~~~~~~~~~~~~~~~~~~

"Honey, would you like to sit together at the morning gathering?" asked my handsome, dark-haired boyfriend of two days.

"I'd love that, sweetie," I said, gazing affectionately at Daryl. "I'll save us seats."

I sank into the comfort of not only having someone special to sit with at the daily morning meeting of this summer retreat but actually having a boyfriend, albeit ephemerally.

⊳————⊲

Soon after arriving at the rustic retreat center where I'd be spending ten days with a hundred other growth-seeking, sex-positive adults, I'd gone from assuming I would sleep alone and just attend as many personal growth and spiritual workshops as I could, to wanting to explore sensuality with a variety of people, to realizing that I really wanted to be sleeping with one person. I'd been longing to do that with Rob, but this crowd was a much better choice—they were my people. However, at the introductory meeting, I noticed that there were very few men who were single—most were either there with their partner or had one at home. I'd had enough of dating men with partners. I wanted a man all to myself, and I wanted one here.

Daryl was exactly what I wanted in a temporary summer boyfriend. He was taller than me, with a lean body, shaggy black hair, and a wickedly sexy smile that melted me. He was an expert at sex—both intercourse and finding other ways to pleasure me—and wanted to do it as much as I did. Although he'd been attending the retreat for years and knew everyone, he was single and wanted, like me, to have a "primary" or main sexual partner while he was there. His vision of a primary partner matched mine: to go through the days coordinating our time so we spent some of our free time together and some agreed-upon time apart. Besides hanging out with friends, the time apart included dates or even overnights with "secondaries," romantic partners who were not as central, as long as we returned to each other. It was a long-term relationship model I wanted to try out in this short-term community—a type of polyamory.

I hadn't seen his potential at first. When I arrived at the retreat, Daryl drove me to the meadow where I pitched my tent. As I set up my gear, he told me that he was looking for a primary relationship and that he would love to sleep with me. Amused, I told him I'd think about it—he was at least fifteen years younger than me, and I figured that he said that to all the new women. But I'd noticed his strong muscles oozing sexuality above and under his short blue tie-dyed sarong. Two days later, after brief dates with the few single men, including an erotic kissing and cuddling date with Daryl in my tent, I decided he was the best option—I liked his smile, his voice, his body, his outgoing warmth, his wanting me, and his enthusiastic youthful energy. Also, he lived in Portland, so an ongoing relationship was out of the question. I approached him during a lunch break.

"Daryl, I'd love to sleep with you and try out being primaries. Would you like that?"

"Are you kidding?" he said. "I'd love to be your primary here!" He looked into my eyes and kissed me deeply. "Especially if it includes a lot of sex."

"It will!" I said, and kissed him back. "Let's go to my tent now!"

———

A few mornings later, as I threw my purple sarong over three backrests in the front row of the meeting room to reserve them for Daryl and a few friends, my secondary walked over.

"May I sit with you?" Galen asked.

"Of course," I said, beaming up at him and patting the seat next to me. His smile radiated out from under his long blond hair. The day before, I'd chosen Galen to be my secondary boyfriend after a satisfying cuddle date, and we'd spent the evening feeding each other sensual finger foods at an erotic feast. We had not been sexual, and I had returned to Daryl for the night.

As Galen folded his large, sturdy body into the backrest, Hannah, a willowy yoga teacher, rushed over. She was one of my favorite women there because she reached out to women as much as to men.

"I want to be with you too!" She usually sat with her husband, Sean, but today she was gravitating to our little group.

"Would you like to sit behind us?" I said. "We could all hold hands!" In the round dome where we had the morning gatherings, backrests were arranged in a semicircle three to five deep, three quarters of the way around the big room.

"I'll sit in the second row with you!" Galen said, circling Hannah with his arms.

In the end, Sean appeared and sat with Hannah. I sat in Daryl's lap, between my friend William and Galen, holding each of their hands, with Hannah and Sean stroking our hair. I felt held by these friends and lovers, and I took it in deeply, right down to my soul, like a flower soaking up warmth from the sun. This is how I wanted to live.

Check-In was about to start, and we turned our attention to the woman moving in the center of the room.

"I'm having sex! I'm having sex!!" Sharon, a woman my age, gleefully shouted to all of us gathered in the circle that morning. She skipped around the space within the circle of back-rests, declaring this over and over. Everyone's eyes were on her, reflecting her delight. She was plump with a soft face and short brown hair, wearing a loose nondescript T-shirt and short jean shorts. I admired her bravery and confidence—I would have been self-conscious sharing something so personal and wearing something so plain, but in her exuberance, she was not. She added that she hadn't had sex in years, had come here alone, and had met a man who was the perfect sexual partner, at least for now. What impressed me most was her ability to make this happy declaration of what was true in the moment, even before she knew where it was going.

That was the purpose of Check-In, as the morning gather-ing was called: for a few people to get up in front of everyone and tell their truth—the good, the bad, and the confusing—and to be supported for being honest. This open transparency was meant to help us become closer and more trusting of each other. The shares were also supposed to help people push through any stuck places with the support of the group, and for that reason, staying in motion was important. Facilitators were available to walk around the circle with the speakers, encouraging them to say more, keep moving, express their anger or fears.

No one needed to help Sharon speak or move—she was skipping, commemorating this happy moment for herself, and asking only that we witness it. I was glad for Sharon, but I won-dered if I'd missed my chance to share my immediate delight at finding Daryl and Galen for my experiment of primary and secondary relationships. Anything I said after this morning would be very premeditated and planned out. I had never been one to share in front of a group without knowing what I'd say, and now I was chastising myself for not pushing myself to be more real and in the present in this daunting but supportive Check-In.

Why can't I do that? I thought as Sharon pranced gleefully around the room. Those old critical voices in my head were showing up again, judging me for whatever I did.

That afternoon, I wanted Daryl and told him so. His face lit up, and he suggested we go to his tent, which was on the shaded edge of the forest. He took my hand and led me over. Inside was a mattress covered with brown sheets, a blue sleeping bag, and several tie-dyed sarongs of blue and purple. He cleared off a space, and I slipped off the purple sarong I was wearing, draped it over his sheets, and lay down on it. He wanted to pleasure me, so I showed him the best ways to touch me with his fingers and tongue. Eventually, with the combination of his touch, his cock in my mouth, and me stroking myself, I surrendered into a delicious orgasm. The release expanded my heart, and when he entered me, my wetness welcomed him. I was definitely having sex and loving it.

The next day, Galen and I did a workshop together focused on finding compassion for the people who were driving us crazy—for him a coworker, and for me my mother. We ended up in tears, finding both compassion and love for them and an opening in our hearts for each other.

"Would you like to spend the night with me?" Galen asked. "We can see the stars through my netting—it doesn't look like rain tonight." I had learned that rain in the summertime in Oregon was the norm, so a clear night was a rare gift.

I was tempted. We had already shared a cuddle date and the sensual feast. This would be the fourth night of my experiment in primary and secondary relationships—the first three nights had been spent in sexual explorations with Daryl. Galen was in an open relationship with Valerie, a woman he lived with in Seattle who had not come to the retreat. He could sleep with me as part of their agreement. Since I already had Daryl as my primary partner, I would not feel bad being "secondary" in relation to Valerie. If I were single, being someone's secondary partner would only rub salt in the wound of not having a primary partner and imply that I was not good enough to be a primary. Now, with a primary partner, even a temporary one, I could emotionally afford to spend the night with Galen. But would it fit into Daryl's and my arrangement?

I found Daryl in the dinner line. "Daryl, sweetie, how would you feel if I slept with Galen tonight?"

"Great!" Daryl said, and added, like a Yelp review, "Galen's a good man. I've known him for years, and I know he'll treat you well. Besides, I could use a break tonight to get some sleep!" We grinned at each other. Our sexual romps had gone late the last three nights, as Daryl rekindled my erotic energy.

I was relieved and delighted that Daryl supported my being with Galen. This was the type of primary relationship I had envisioned, but having an actual person respond in this way was a visceral lesson in how it could work. Daryl and I agreed to meet at breakfast the next day.

That night, Galen waited for me after the evening activities, and we walked up the hill to his tent under a sky full of stars. I felt the excitement and shyness of a first date, and he held my hand and said he felt happy to be with me. He welcomed me into the soft warm bed he'd created out of an air mattress, flannel sheets and blankets, and a big down comforter on top. Twinkling stars smiled down, and Galen was sweet and playful, nuzzling me with his cheeks, sweeping his long hair over my face. I nuzzled him back, giggling in the happy starry moment.

"You are very adorable," he said.

"You are too," I said.

Celeste, his longtime friend and my new friend, came by to visit, and we invited her into the bed, where we all cuddled, rotating who was in the middle. We told each other what we loved about each other, creating what felt like a love bubble under the stars. Then she left, and Galen and I cuddled affectionately and fell asleep. He got up for Tai Chi at dawn, and I slept in. Waking, I left him some colored beads on his pillow and walked down the hill to breakfast.

When I saw Daryl, we hugged warmly. I was glad to see him, and he was happy to hear I'd had such a sweet night. He was sitting with Hannah, and I hugged her too.

I was a little envious of Daryl and Hannah, because they were both able to "run tantric energy"—send heart and sexual energy up through their bodies and out to others. Since I had never experienced it, I was not sure what they actually did. They described it as letting love and sexual energy flow through the vertical channel of their chakras—the seven energy centers in the body recognized by spiritual and healing traditions that are stacked up along the spinal column from its base to the top of the head. Each chakra—root, sacral, solar plexus, heart, throat, third eye, and crown—is connected to certain physical, emotional, and spiritual feelings. Daryl explained that to run tantric energy, he drew energy up from the earth into his root chakra, which holds survival energy, through his sacral chakra, which holds sexual energy, and then breathed that energy up through all his chakras, picking up love in the heart chakra and sending this combined energy out through his heart and crown chakras to lovers or friends. It sounded like a combination of a strong imagination and actual physical sensations, and they'd been trying to teach me, but I could not feel anything. Two nights earlier, before we made love, I had cried in frustration to Daryl that I felt like such a failure.

"Hey," he said. "You don't have to feel that for me to love you. You're a great lover just as you are."

I believed him, but still felt disappointed in my body.

Later, when I walked into Check-In with Daryl, I saw Galen nearby and felt a heart pull.

"Would you mind if I invited Galen to sit with us?" I asked Daryl.

"Not at all, honey," he said. "Please do. You should keep up your connection." As a primary, Daryl was really all I hoped he would be in his generosity toward my other "lover."

So I was sitting there in the front row, between Daryl and Galen, holding their hands. Suddenly I felt my heart open and connect to both of them, and felt energy running through me from my heart, through each of my seven chakras. I felt Daryl's and Galen's hands and legs touching me but felt the energy coming from me. It was filling up my own heart and flowing back and forth between us, responding to who they each were. As I sat between them and felt this moving energy, it expanded, and I could feel that I was creating or sourcing it, as Hannah and Daryl had done. This was the tantric energy—a deep flowing heart connection—that I had wanted to feel. It came from asking for my heart's desire and opening my heart to these men who had each touched me. I sat there for many minutes, feeling this energy flowing between us, relishing that I could feel it. Maybe I wasn't so blocked in my heart and sexual energy after all.

Two nights later I slept with Galen again, still more affectionate than sexual, and felt close to Daryl afterward. I liked this! If this is what it meant to be in a polyamorous relationship, with a primary and a secondary, I loved it! I had a growing closeness with Daryl, who I felt would always welcome me back after I had "roamed," whether or not I had been sexual. This assurance fulfilled my need for security with one person. His ability to so easily send me off to sleep with another man supported my freedom, so precious to me. Actually, it blew my mind—could I be that generous to a lover? Daryl was showing me the best of both worlds—security and freedom. Of course I wanted this. Maybe having more than one partner would work for me.

The following day at Check-In, I was sitting with Daryl in the front row by the side. Pressure had been building in me since Sharon skipped around the room, sharing her delight at having sex after such a long dry spell. I wanted to be visible in this community, and I had to stop criticizing myself for not speaking up earlier. Maybe now was the perfect time for me to share. I forced my hand up, and before I could change my mind, they chose me. I rose, ignoring the heavy weight in my chest—my terror of being judged, by myself or others. At least I liked what I was wearing—my long purple broomstick skirt and the little purple-blue cami that complemented it. The outfit gave me a little confidence. True to myself, I had rehearsed my words over and over, so they came pouring out as I walked around the circle:

"So I'm trying an experiment here at the retreat. I'm single, looking for my next partner, and I have this project of going out with fifty different men to find him. It's been almost two years, and I've been on over thirty-five first dates, and I haven't found him yet. So for these ten days I've stopped trying to find the right guy. I just want to experience the kind of relationship I might like. I want to know—is a poly relationship for me? Of course, being single, during dating, I *am* poly in that I have different lovers. But that's just dating!"

A few chuckles from the audience confirmed that at least a few could empathize.

"Dating is different from having a primary lover and sharing him with others," I said. "I thought I wanted a monogamous relationship, but even a good one feels so confining. So I'm having a practice primary relationship with Daryl, and a practice secondary relationship with Galen. So far, it's working! I just wanted all of you to know what I'm doing with these guys you know and love."

I stopped to take a breath. A few people had laughed; many people were looking at me with kind smiles; some looked confused; and others were frowning. William was looking at me affectionately, Daryl was beaming, and Galen and Celeste sent warm smiles. I focused on the smiles. By the time I sat down, I felt relieved and relaxed—I had shared. I had been honest. I had been transparent about what I was doing with two men in the community. I felt lighter. In the weeks after the retreat, it would be my share at Check-In that I most remembered. I had stood up to my critical voices and told my truth when I was ready. Although it was said in front of everyone, the person I had spoken to had been myself.

<hr />

As I drove away a few days later, through the bright open hillsides of chaparral and occasional pine forests of rural Oregon, I was filled with the shimmering afterglow of the connections I'd created, as well as a longing for Daryl. However, by the time I reached the Bay Area eight hours later, reality seeped in. As perfect as Daryl and Galen had been for me in this ten-day fantasy community, they would not fit into my real life. Besides the fact that Daryl lived in Portland and Galen lived in Seattle, Daryl had a very different lifestyle from me—he was a handyman who had not gone to college and lived on the edge financially. I would not feel met by a partner who was such a mismatch in education and resources. We also moved at different speeds; although I had slowed down during the ten days, I was usually in constant motion and talked fast, whereas Daryl tended to move and talk slowly—another mismatch. At the retreat, our sexual connection had captured my imagination and met my yearning for a primary partner, and I had allowed him to touch my body and my heart deeply. I would long for him for a while but eventually let go.

The imprint of this polyamorous relationship would remain. I counted my entire time with Daryl and Galen as date number 39, as if to fuse the dates into my own vision of polyamory. Could it work for me back in real life?

PART VI
DISCOURAGEMENT

SANTA CRUZ BEACH

Some of my favorite people were in polyamorous relationships, so I had a front-row view of how they worked. Reed, my tenth date and ideal guy, was still with Olivia and thriving two years and many lovers later. A Southern California couple I knew, Rosemary and Blair, had raised three children while being poly. My coltish young lover and twenty-fourth date, Phil, and his wife, Tracy, joyfully supported each other having other lovers and still stayed close.

A woman acquaintance of mine was in an open marriage, and I had met her husband, Jay, at a party earlier that summer. He looked as boyish as a Kennedy and was just as charming, asking me questions about my experiences in HAI.

"Helping with the HAI workshops must be amazing," he said, looking into my eyes. "What do you like about it?"

His eyes were bright and peaceful at the same time.

"I love that I get to open my heart to everyone in the workshop," I said, realizing that his attentive gaze was opening my heart right then.

"I can see that you have an open heart," he said.

Afterward, he had emailed me. "Would you like to get together sometime?"

It was bad timing. I liked him, but I was coming up on the fortieth date in the project and was only interested in actual partner prospects. I had done enough dating of unavailable men just to experience their types, so I didn't think I would want to date him.

Nevertheless, when I saw his wife at a party, I asked her how she'd feel about my going out with him. She told me that Jay had had other girlfriends for years and that she was in love with her current boyfriend. She encouraged me to date Jay.

Even though this didn't sound like much of a marriage, it sounded too complicated for me—I didn't want to be just another girlfriend.

"No thanks," I told Jay in response to his email. "You're married and poly, and I'm looking for my own partner."

⊶————⊷

The August weekend after I returned from the summer retreat, I drove down to Santa Cruz for the day. Phil, my coltish young lover, was having his Aikido black belt exam, and he and his wife, Tracy, had invited a handful of lovers and friends, including Jay, to watch. As we stood in a big gym along the mat and applauded Phil after each move, I chatted with Jay. He introduced me to his friend Barry, an attractive dark-haired guy with dreamy eyes and a swimmer's body.

"What do you do?" I asked Barry.

"I'm a physicist. Jay and I were helping start an airline company in Florida, and it was just about to be profitable when the economy crashed," Barry said as Jay nodded.

"What did you do in the company?" I said, wanting this dreamy guy to keep talking.

But Jay answered. "We were the mathematicians who figured out the algorithm to create an on-demand airline service for executives. We were living there part-time."

So they were not only cute but smart. "What happened to the company?" I asked.

"It folded, just one loan short of succeeding," said Barry.

"We had to leave Florida and return here to work," said Jay. "I was building a house with a girlfriend there." I hadn't realized that he and his wife had been leading such separate lives.

"But I'm glad I came back," Barry said, "since I met my girlfriend here."

I sighed and turned back to Phil's performance. Were all the cute, smart guys taken?

<hr />

A few hours later, I was on the Santa Cruz beach at the annual HAI bonfire, put on by the local HAI support group. About forty people were milling around the barbecues between the sand dunes and the ocean, and I knew about half of them. After talking with various friends, I spotted Ben, my young lover, sitting in a low beach chair on the edge of the crowd, and he held out his arms.

"Carolyn," he said. "Come sit with me." I snuggled into his lap, relieved to feel his familiar arms around me. He hugged me and whispered in my ear, "How's the dating going?"

"Not so good," I said. "I had a great experience being poly at a summer retreat, but I don't think I could pull that off here. I feel very far from finding my partner."

"Oh, you'll find him, and he's going to be one lucky guy," he said. I believed him, kind of.

"Thanks, Ben," I said. "I'm glad I have you."

"Hey, we should go to Burning Man together," he said.

"I'd love that," I said, "but I can't get off work that week. Enjoy it for me."

Just then Phil bounded into the crowd, straight from his Aikido exam. "I passed!" he said. He was wrapped in a new rainbow tie-dyed T-shirt gift from Tracy.

I went to hug him, and he pulled me down into another seat. We kissed and held each other tight for a minute, nuzzling each other's necks.

"Thanks for coming," he said as he finally let go. "I always feel happy around you."

"Yeah, me too," I said. "I miss you."

"Me too," he said. "I wish my Berkeley job had continued."

The sun was starting to set, and I had a long drive home. I'd spoken to everyone I knew, so I headed up the bluff to my car. In the dark, a figure emerged. I froze, wary of strangers.

"I just wanted to say good-bye." I relaxed. It was someone I knew.

"Who's that?"

"Jay. Hey, it was good to see you." His voice was gentle, and he sounded sincere.

"Yeah, it was nice," I said. Inside, I was sighing. Although he wasn't in much of a marriage, I didn't need another even slightly married man.

AN EVENING IN OAKLAND

~~~~~~~~~~~~~~~~~~~~~~~

In September, I walked into Reed's house in the Oakland hills for a sexy sensual party to celebrate our friend Katrina's fiftieth birthday. Reed greeted me with a big kiss. "So good to see you, Carolyn." As the host, he was welcoming everyone. I gave him a big kiss back. Since meeting Reed and Olivia two years ago on New Year's Eve and having one date with him, Reed and I had morphed into friends. He was still my ideal type, with his focused presence, his creative way with words, his connection to Olivia while seeing others, his passion about his work, and his interest in mine.

I wondered if I would get to enjoy any lovers or lovers-to-be at this party. Then I saw Ben.

"Would you like to join me in a bedroom?" he said. We made love as joyfully as usual.

It was a rare warm evening in Oakland, and people who weren't having sex were sitting or lounging in groups on the outdoor deck or nearby in the kitchen and dining room. Jay was at the party with Sandy, one of his girlfriends, a plain but curvy redhead.

I wandered outside and sat near the end of a long folding table, in a chair next to Jay with Sandy on his other side. A few heavy casserole pots had been placed in front of us, but no one was eating. A group at the other end of the table started talking about the falling prices of Bay Area real estate.

"It's not just here," said Jane, a realtor. "Prices have crashed all over the US, thanks to those sub-prime mortgages." I thought glumly about my Phoenix property. Now I'd never be able to sell it. Would I ever get out from under that mortgage?

"It's happening in Europe too," said Todd, a world traveler. "The Greek economy just crashed from the weight of too much European Union debt."

Just then our end of the table started to make an ominous creaking sound, like the table's legs were buckling. Yikes!

Jay, Sandy, and I grabbed the tabletop to stabilize it as Jay called out to the people discussing the economy, "Hey, our side of the table is about to collapse from too much debt, I mean weight! I know you're not the European Union, but could you please bail us out? Like take some of these heavy pots? With everything going sub-prime, we don't want a sub-table crash."

We all laughed, and they took the casseroles. As we propped up the table, I looked closer at Jay. How had he managed to connect the world economy with the creaking table so fast? This was the kind of mind I liked to play with. Plus he was cute and sexy. A full mop of brown-red hair framed his boyish face, a bright light beamed out through shining eyes, and a warm smile enveloped everyone near him. When he had walked into the party, I remembered how he had held his tall body both loosely and strongly, emanating health and a delicious sexuality.

This is the type of man I should be with! I suddenly realized. Leaning into him, our hands gently touched, and electric shivers confirmed a mutual attraction.

I turned to Sandy. "Are you willing to share tonight?" After all, it was a sex party.

"Um, no," she said. Jay looked disappointed but didn't object.

Oh well, I thought. *He's marginally married and has multiple girlfriends. At least he's loyal to the one he's with.*

OASIS

~~~~~~

In late October, I started longing for Rob, my dancer, van-sleeping friend. I had just been turned down by an online date, and my lover Homer was now seriously attached to my friend Clara and not available. My other lovers, Ben and Phil, were now seeing others too.

Date number 40 had been another married man in an open relationship. I made an exception for him because we had a long-standing flirtation. Despite the risks to my heart, I was hoping to explore being sexual. Luckily, he just wanted to eye gaze, so I evaded heartbreak. I was finally done with married men. I only had ten dates to go, and I turned my attention to available men.

Date number 41 was a Friday dinner date in Berkeley with a single man I was very attracted to. However, he started the date by being annoyed at my working late, even though I had made it to the restaurant on time. Our conversation never recovered from that, and the date ended after a long discussion in my car, where he was still accusing me of disrespecting him by calling to tell him I *might* be late. When he finally said, "I don't think I can date you," I readily agreed and let him out of my car before he could change his mind.

Shaken, I went to find Rob, who by now seemed like a safe and familiar friend.

"Rob, would you like a visitor?" It was one in the morning, and I was talking to him on my cell phone from my car, parked right next to his van in the Dance Play parking lot.

"Not really. I'm sleeping," he said in a muffled voice.

"Even if I'm right here already?"

He opened the van with an incredulous look on his face. "What are you doing here?"

"The worst dinner date ever. I need a hug." This got me into the van out of the cold air.

"What happened?" He looked concerned, hugging me gingerly. He hadn't seen me in over two months.

"Date number 41! This guy and I totally offended each other. We tried to talk it out, but we couldn't. I'd been planning to come to Dance Play and dance with you after the date, but he talked until Dance Play was over. I finally cut it off so I could come see you now."

"Well," he said, finally smiling, "my gain!"

"Would you come home with me and sleep with me? *Please?* We could just cuddle." "OK, I will," he said with a bemused expression. "I'll follow you there."

"Oh, thank you!" I cried, hugging him close and kissing his cheek.

⊱————⊰

We walked into my house together, and I went into the next room to turn off the alarm. When I came back into the living room, I found him examining the pictures and objects on the mantel.

"Who's this?" he asked, peering at a picture of a man with a pipe leaning casually against the railing of a ferry with a camera in his hand.

"That's my father—my favorite picture of him. I took it when we were whale-watching."

"And these people?"

"That's my mom, sister, brother, and their families in Cabo for my mom's eightieth birthday."

"And where are these tapestries from?" he asked, pointing to the long runners on two walls.

"Those are from my trips to Peru."

I couldn't believe it. He was the first man on this dating project, and maybe ever, who had expressed an interest in the decorations in my house. Inquiring about each picture and object, it took him a while to get through the living room. When we got to the kitchen, he asked about all the pictures on the fridge. I had to cut off the questions so we could get some sleep.

I took him into the shower and then to bed, cuddling him with my nightgown on. With fewer clothes, our fit was not as perfect as it had been in the dance studio or his van—our bones collided more. And he didn't want to kiss, saying it felt too intimate. This bothered me, since I felt I was being fairly intimate by sleeping with him. However, I let it go—his finger resting on my belly turned me on and comforted me at the same time. We slept off and on until noon.

I spent the afternoon on Saturday errands—nails, food shopping—while he read. Later he cooked us a simple stir-fry of onions, garlic, broccoli, and tofu. We gazed lovingly at each other over dinner. I reveled in the simple companionship.

<hr />

I was feeling so connected to Rob that I invited him to a party I was attending at Marco's that night. The party included high-energy dancing, another magical warm pool ceremony, and food and friends spread out over about five rooms. Once there, Rob danced some with me and some on his own, which gave me the freedom to visit with my friends. He wore a blissful grin no matter what he was doing. When we passed one of my friends in the halls, I would introduce him.

"This is Rob, from Dance Play," I would say and smile meaningfully. My good friends knew I had been lusting after someone there. They looked approvingly at this handsome guy.

"Nice to meet you," he would say, with a conspiratorial smile. "Carolyn knows how to throw a good party, doesn't she?" They laughed and found him charming.

When the pool ceremony started, we all paired up and stood around in the warm pool. Rob followed the directions to gaze into my eyes in the dim light, while laser lights pierced the misty air. I could feel his heart gazing at mine. The ceremony ended with all the couples kissing, and he almost kissed me but pulled back. I was disappointed, but then he lifted me onto his back and carried me around the pool. The magical mist and lights permeated my cells, and I felt more alive and happy than I ever had in that pool, despite all the kissing sessions I'd had there.

Back home, I tried for another cuddly night with no sex. With a shirt to cover my breasts and shoulders, he could reach more of my skin. I loved his touch, and he finally kissed me.

In the morning, there was no time to talk. I was meeting date number 42 in San Jose. Even though I was the one leaving, my heart ached, as I loved having Rob's presence in the house, and I didn't know when he would be back.

Date numbers 42 and 43 were both OKCupid.com dates that came to naught. Guy, date number 42, was a happy-go-lucky telephone repairman who said he had been to HAI workshops, but he'd only been to HAI introductory nights, so I'd overestimated his communication skills. We met for our date in San Jose at a friend's guitar sing, where he was loud and insensitive to others. At dinner, I suggested that we weren't a match, and he agreed. However, walking to our cars, I took his arm, longed for more touch, and proceeded to kiss and have sex with him in his van.

Chagrined at my behavior, I called my friend Sarah on the way home. "Is it OK I did that?"

"Of course," she said. "Totally understandable. I would have done it too if I was in that longing place." I had to allow myself some detours.

Two weeks later, Terry, date number 43, was a much better match for me on paper—a progressive lawyer and white Spanish-speaking adventurer who lived in Marin. On a Sunday afternoon, we strolled around Oakland's downtown Lake Merritt and stopped in on a Spanish-speaking mass at the majestic Cathedral of the Light. However, despite the alignment of our lifestyles, I could not warm up to him. He felt like my first college boyfriend—his words came more from his head than his heart—and Rob had been touching my heart.

◦————◦

A week later, I tugged Rob into my bedroom. The dark clouds of a rainy afternoon softly illuminated the room. I opened the curtains on the corner windows above the bed to reveal as much sky as possible. It was cool in the room, and I thought of turning the heat on but then had a better idea. I drew back the purple flannel sheets.

"Let's cuddle in bed," I said. I never got in bed during the day, but his invitation to take a nap during the rainstorm had penetrated through my usual Saturday errand rush.

His presence calmed me, the way Peter's serenity had. Peter had been my vacation oasis, first in his San Francisco Twin Peaks apartment with the panoramic city view, and then in his cozy Hilo home far above the ocean. Now Rob brought a feeling of serenity to my own home, and I responded with a feeling of peace. His desire to stay with me for the weekend rather than leave on Saturday morning after our Friday night dancing made me feel wanted and supported.

However, this man had very little going on in his life, while my life was a whirl of projects—social, work, volunteer, home, and creative. I could feel his stillness as I went about my Saturday errands. He would do his exercises or read in my living room, or lie in bed looking out the window. I knew that he was waiting for me to be free, and this imbalance made me uneasy. I wanted a partner who was busy with his own activities, as my ad said.

But right now, his presence soothed me. We cuddled naked between the sheets. We had attempted to make love a few times in the last few weeks, but there wasn't enough passion from either of us to entice the other into sex, and my strong attraction had dwindled to a companionable affection. In this moment, we just delighted in each other's skin.

Crackle! Boom! A flash of light in the dark sky and the subsequent thunder thrilled me as much as an orgasm. The light patter of the rain became heavy thumps on the roof and the backyard garden. Rob's angular face was lit up, and his contented smile reflected my own. We were in the right place for this rare Northern California thunderstorm—in a warm bed with someone we were fond of, under corner windows that outlined the show. As the light pierced the dark sky and illuminated my bedroom in bursts of light and the thunder exploded from not so far away, I *oohed* and *aahed* my delight and held him tighter. Although Rob was not the right partner, I was glimpsing the type of relationship I wanted—an oasis of calm, warmth, and affection in the middle of an exciting life.

WINTER SOLSTICE THREE (2010)

It was two in the afternoon of my winter solstice ceremony. I still had shopping to do. But I had asked my guests to take time to ponder what they wanted to let go of and bring in this year, and I needed to take that advice myself. So I sat back against the cushions on my bed, where I did all my major pondering, picked up my journal, took some breaths to slow down, and started writing. I already knew the two major things I needed to let go of:

1) My Phoenix property. It was draining my savings. My realtor had proposed a daring end-of-year short sale offer to the bank: forgive my loan and take the property, even though it was worth much less. It was in escrow, but what if it didn't go through?

2) Waiting for Peter. Even though it was wishful thinking, I had to admit that I still thought of him as my backup plan. It was time to really let him go. Could I do that?

Taking a breath, I closed my eyes to envision what I wanted to bring in. It was not as specific, but one image was clear. I wanted a loving partnership—a love that fills and excites my heart, spirit, and body in a relationship that enhances each of our lives. A partnership that supports me to develop my highest emotional, spiritual, creative, and professional self.

Besides that partnership, I envisioned more—spaciousness in time, finances, relationships, creativity, and work; being in loving communities; generosity and being of service in my work, friendships, and HAI communities; doing more than I think I can in all areas of my life; and contributing to my communities from my larger, deepest, and most creative self.

After writing all this down, I felt I had already released what I didn't want and had sent my visions into the universe. *That should do it*, I thought.

Just as I was about to get up, my cell phone rang. It was my realtor in Phoenix. *The sale closed!!!* I was released! I immediately felt a letting go of that heavy financial weight—the debt that had made me feel undesirable as a partner, the stranglehold on my financial security, the drain on my monthly income, and the drag on my psychic energy—just in time for my ceremony. I thanked the universe for answering my prayer, at the perfect time.

It would be harder to let go of Peter, but I trusted the universe to work on that too.

"Your house is like a shrine to Peter," I suddenly remembered a friend saying when she visited my home for the first time and saw all the pictures I had of him. That was back when Peter and I were together, but now I realized that most of those pictures were still on my fridge. Why had I not taken them off?

I shot off the bed and charged into the kitchen. There was the picture of him in Machu Picchu, the one of us on the cruise ship in Cabo, and the ones with our faces glowing in the Hawaiian sun against the dark lava rocks. There was his handsome face and white hair shining in the sun on my deck the day he left for Europe, and me looking at him a moment later. My heart remembered each of those times. I had kept these images of Peter with me for this whole dating journey—to support me, but also, I had to admit, to keep alive the hope that we could return to those precious days. His long-distance support of my dating ups and downs had given me the illusion that we were still close, even though I had worked hard to let him go during the relationship class earlier that year. It was only now that I realized I wanted to go forward more than I wanted to stay in that past, as beautiful as it was. I was ready to let go.

I started taking the pictures down. Some came off as soon as I took the magnets off; some had stuck permanently to the fridge, and I had to peel them off. It felt like they were all permanently stuck to my heart and that I was ripping out a core part of me, but I did, gently. I rearranged the remaining pictures of friends and family and thought of new photos I could add. I took the Peter pictures to my study and put them in my "Peter" file with all our cards and letters. I walked back to the kitchen, took a deep breath, and felt the space I had made.

I drove off to the store, thinking about who was coming to the ceremony. It would be some of my favorite friends—Chandler and Carrie, as usual; Kate and Sarah from my women's group; Olivia and Reed, my original ideal couple; Luke, my wispy-haired, self-taught counselor; and three others. All of them knew how hard I had tried to let go of both Phoenix and Peter these past few years, so I was looking forward to making my declarations in front of them.

I'd decided to include Rob in the evening, despite a growing awareness that I had to stop seeing him. I knew it wasn't fair to him to keep acting like we were partners—I was stringing him along, and I needed to focus on the search for my real partner. However, I wasn't ready to stop yet—we'd just spent another loving weekend together, and I was still appreciating his presence. When I got home, he was waiting in his car, and he helped me unpack. I started the mulled cider, and he stacked the wood in the fireplace. As the scent of cinnamon and oranges from the cider filled the house, we arranged chairs in the living room around the altar and worked in the kitchen, setting out plates and utensils and arranging the appetizers.

People started arriving, and soon the kitchen and living room were filled with my friends munching on spanakopita, sipping cider or wine, and filling each other in on their lives. I stayed in the kitchen, replenishing celery and cider, talking to anyone who was near me. When I suggested that we move into the living room for the ceremony, they flowed into the room, finding their favorite chairs or places on the couch. Rob had made a fire that blazed confidently.

"Welcome to winter solstice," I said, gazing around and feeling embraced by my friends.

"This is the longest night of the year, the time to state what we want to let go of into the darkness and what we want to bring forth into the light. I invite you to bring your deepest selves to your declarations and those of others." I was saying this to myself as much as to them.

"Who would like to call in the directions?" Chandler, Kate, Olivia, and Reed each took east, west, north, and south and led us in calling out their qualities and lighting each candle. I called in the center candle for our deepest selves. "Now, write down what you most want to release into the darkness of this night, and we'll burn them in the fire, to be released by the universe." I put on some peaceful music by Hilary Stagg, and we wrote our declarations on purple paper. My writing didn't take long, so I waited until everyone had finished.

When everyone had raised their eyes from writing, I stood up. I wanted to be the first to declare. "I am letting go of my property in Phoenix—it just closed today!" There were murmurs of hooray. "And I'm letting go of Peter and the hope of being with him in the future. I know I've been letting go of him for the past two years, but I'm more ready this time than before. His pictures are finally off my fridge, and I'm no longer hoping to be with him."

"Yes!" Chandler said.

"Hooray!" said Kate.

"And so it is true," said Reed.

"I agree," said Olivia.

They were with me, my friends. They knew how big it was for me to let go of Phoenix and Peter, and because of their support, I could deeply feel my letting go.

As they rose one by one to make their own declarations of release and, later, their intentions, I realized that they had brought their deepest selves to this ceremony. I had created the space, and in it they had profoundly witnessed themselves and each other. I felt peacefully successful to have done that for them and for me. And Rob was the perfect fill-in for the partner I believed would come—he washed dishes, held my hand, and kissed me a lot.

The next night, alone in my hot tub under a full and fuzzy moon, I had an exquisite orgasm, feeling expanded into the universe, not even thinking about Phoenix, Peter, or Rob.

TEST

~

Finally, we were meeting. After two months of almost-meetings and phone calls about meeting, I was waiting near the Berkeley Marina on a chilly but sunny January day for a walking date with Steve, a man who had great potential to be my partner. A broad-shouldered man with an attractively craggy face and thick tousled salt-and-pepper hair, he had a busy life and was immersed in personal growth activities familiar to me. That he was also truly single, intelligent, my age, and interested in me made me hopeful. Although I was still lingering with Rob, I was looking for someone like Steve who might match me on more levels than Rob's peaceful one.

Rob knew I was dating others. "I know I'm not your partner," he would say, sighing and looking down like Eeyore. "I'm not enough for you. Of course you must continue with the project."

He assuaged my guilt by saying this, but I could feel his sadness. I had to admit that I saw him as a comforting bridge to my real partner. Like my lovers, he was sustaining me on this journey, not with sex but with companionship, something I now knew I needed. But he hadn't signed up to be a temporary partner, and I knew I had to release him to find someone who could love him better. The problem was that neither he nor I seemed inclined to let go.

I'd met Steve in November, at the type of event I rarely attended—an art exhibit opening. My old friend Carson, a photographer, was displaying his stunning shots of shorebirds and egrets at Lake Merritt, a tidal lake and nature preserve in downtown Oakland where I often went running. I wanted to support Carson and see "my" birds, but I hadn't cultivated any birder friends since the bird-watching days of my lesbian years, so I was there alone. Carson had invited his men's group to the celebration, a group I had heard about from Carson and his wife—it sounded like they supported each other to be strong, sensitive, spiritually conscious, service-oriented men, and Carson exemplified that. This was the type of man I wanted to date.

During the reception, I had noticed Steve—he was a bit taller than me and the most interesting-looking man there. I had even gone up to Carson when he was surrounded by Steve and his other friends, hoping for an introduction, but the focus had been on Carson.

Then it happened without my doing much about it. We were all standing around one of the biggest pictures while Carson explained how he had gotten the close-up of the egrets doing their mating dance on a nest high above the island.

Suddenly, Steve was right next to me, asking, "Don't I know you from somewhere?"

The warm flash that he had noticed me quickly turned into a smile, and I said, "You look familiar to me too. Have you done any HAI workshops? I assist there a lot."

"I took the first one," he said. "Maybe I saw you there, or maybe contra dancing?"

"I've only done that once in Santa Cruz," I said. Contra dancing, a European folk dance performed in long lines of couples, was not my favorite. "Do you do that often?"

Now in our own mating dance, we launched into a conversation about our lives and where we might have met. He told me about weekends spent dancing, the lucrative medical supplies business he'd started with a friend, and the volunteer work he did with the men's group. I told him about my college job and my Friday nights dancing in Berkeley. In the end, we realized with a laugh that we'd seen each other's ads on OKCupid.

"Would you like to go out sometime?" he said.

Oh, the words I'd longed for but had rarely heard on this dating project. A man I was attracted to, who had just met me, saying that he wanted to see me again. So many of my dates had been initiated by me or had happened by mutual agreement after sexual encounters or longtime friendships that I was starting to wonder if I was attractive to men out in the world. Just having Steve ask this question made me feel desirable.

"I'd love to," I said, trying to subdue my wild enthusiasm but not the sincere interest.

We exchanged phone numbers and began two months of trying to make a date, but we were never free at the same time. It was not until January, when I'd started a six-month sabbatical from my job, that I had time to make this bayside walking date.

◦———◦

"So what are those dance weekends like?" I asked as we walked along the Berkeley shore. I turned toward him and kept my eyes on his face, which was looking down.

We were strolling along the path that circled the park on the edge of the bay. To the left, the spindly Bay Bridge arched twice across the water to reach the city—first from the nearby shore to a landing on Treasure Island, and then from the island to the edge of downtown San Francisco, with its hodgepodge of skyscrapers, the silver pyramid rising above them all. Straight out across the shimmering bay, the graceful silhouette of the

Golden Gate Bridge spanned the far opening to the ocean. To the right of that bridge, several tree-spotted islands floated in front of the taller green hills of Marin County. The sun sparkled on the water in all directions, and the chilly sea breeze made us wrap our jackets tighter, but we did not touch. Every once in a while, we remarked on the spectacular view, but mostly we asked polite questions and munched on some cheese and dried fruit I had brought.

"It's a dance festival out in the country," he said, brightening up from the serious look he had had up to now. "There are dance floors spread around the property with different types of music, and you can go from one to the other, trying out everything from African dance to contra dancing to waltzing. We just keep dancing all weekend for hours and hours."

"I love dancing," I said. "I danced salsa every Sunday night for years, and I remember how energized I felt. You must really build up your stamina on one of those weekends."

"It was tiring at first, but now I leave with more energy than I came with." He was smiling to himself about this, still looking down.

I wondered where I would find the time to squeeze that amount of dancing into my life if I started dating him. Between work I had to do for my sabbatical and consulting jobs, social groups I was in, and volunteering at workshops, I didn't have many free evenings or weekends.

"What do you like about helping with the HAI workshops?" he asked, looking at me briefly but mainly gazing straight ahead.

"At first I liked paying back what I got out of the workshops," I said. "I learned how to really love myself and appreciate people, so I wanted to help others experience that. Then I realized that being on the team helps *me* be more loving. I have to stay in my heart as I do my logistical jobs, and that's a challenge for me, so I keep going back to learn."

I was having a hard time feeling a warm emotional connection with him. Despite exchanging information about activities we cared about, his questions and answers were not reaching me at the deeper level I'd hoped for. I sensed that what I was asking and saying was not bringing out his deepest self either. Like this walk, we were enjoying parallel lives in highly compatible but separate communities. And we had not found the connecting bridge between.

Back in his car, out of the cold wind, he brought up what really seemed to matter to him.

"Have you read any David Deida?" he asked, turning toward me.

"A few of his early books," I said, "and I saw one video. I've given the books as gifts to men friends." Deida wrote about the sexual and spiritual growth of men and women and conducted workshops to promote his ideas. I was trying to show that I was familiar with—even supportive of—Deida, without immediately revealing that I did not agree with all of Deida's views. One of his points was that women wanted their men to claim power over them.

"I've been studying him for a while," he said, "and I'm interested in how he says that a man's power can be drawn out and supported by how a woman relates to him."

"Like in what way?" I asked, hoping it was different than what I thought.

He was looking forward, glancing only briefly at me. "Like being a true reflection for him of how he is being in the world, and supporting him to live out his life purpose."

"Wouldn't you want to do that for each other anyway?"

"Yeah," he said, "but there's a particular type of mirror that men need from women to help them reach their full potential, and I need that at this point in my life." He was looking straight ahead with a worried frown, like he was afraid he wouldn't get it.

I wondered what he meant specifically. "That sounds like a really valuable role a partner could play. I'd be glad to find out more about it. I haven't read his recent books."

"That would be good," he mumbled. However, I had a feeling I'd lost him by not being able to answer his question with the understanding he wanted to hear. He was still looking straight ahead, a little dazed, but he finally turned toward me to say good-bye.

"Well, this has been nice," he said. "Thanks for bringing the snacks. Let's be in touch."

I was hoping that the date had not ended as badly as I suspected. Despite our differences about Deida's theories, I believed that if we kept honestly sharing our needs as Steve had done, we might find that deeper way of relating. I emailed him a short appreciation for the walk, but when I didn't hear from him for several weeks, I was afraid my suspicions were true. Although I had other dates to keep me busy, I wondered how I could have "answered" better.

⊷————⊰

One day, while I was cycling along the shoreline of the suburban island of Alameda, enjoying the sun on the water, my cell phone rang, and I could see it was Steve. I braked, stopped in the middle of the path, and answered.

"Hi, Carolyn," he said. "It's Steve. I'm just getting back to you after our walk last month."

"Steve!" I said, stalling as I got my earphones on and settled my bike against a nearby bench. "Good to hear from you! How appropriate you'd call me now—I'm biking in Alameda." We had talked about going biking on this island. "How are you doing?" I sat down on the bench.

"I'm doing fine," he said. "That's nice about the biking. Hey, I've been thinking about why I haven't called you since our walk."

"Oh, yeah," I said, trying to pretend I hadn't noticed the long silence. I took a deep breath, wondering if this would be good news or bad. It sounded bad.

"I like you," he was saying, "and usually I would've called you sooner so we could go out. But I haven't felt strongly compelled to do that."

Likes me but not compelled to call me. Not looking good for dating.

"In the past," he continued, "I've ended up spending time with and even getting into relationships with people who aren't quite right for me. So now I'm trying to only go out with women I'm feeling really drawn to. And I'm just not drawn enough. I'm sorry. You're really nice, but I think I need to trust my feelings on this."

"Um, of course you do," I said, feeling disappointed and hurt. *Why is he not drawn to me? Damn his feelings, but at least he's being honest and clear. I can give him credit for that.* "I can see how that'd be a good strategy for you. I really appreciate you telling me. If you change your mind, let me know."

"I will," he said, sounding relieved that I had understood. "Have a good bike ride, and I hope to see you around."

I was left to continue my solitary ride, knowing that I had lost him as I'd thought. Maybe it was during the Deida conversation, or when we didn't connect deeply on the walk. Whenever it was, I felt sad and let down that he was not giving me another chance to find that connection. Dressed in my multicolored biking pants, purple shirt, and matching headband, I felt like a colorful butterfly, but Steve had picked me up and put me down as if I were a dull gray moth.

Steve was the forty-fourth date. Because we had matched on many levels, I had considered him to be my best partner prospect so far. The fiftieth date was fast approaching, and none of the foreseeable dating prospects looked remotely like my match.

I'd been so sure that dating all these men would lead me to the partner I had envisioned. But now, as I biked through the empty streets of Alameda on a weekday afternoon, I wondered, *What am I going to do when I get to the fiftieth date?*

PART VII
REVELATIONS

SEX PARTY

"Carolyn, give Blair some loving," said Rosemary with a toss of her curls and a wink in her dewy blue eyes. She was referring to her husband as she slipped out of the party with her boyfriend. I had just stepped into Clara's living room of soft couches spilling over with women and men in silky clothing and sensuous lingerie. Rosemary and Clara, my friends, and Homer, my cowboy lover and date number 9, now Clara's lover, had greeted me at the door with warm hugs. They had all been admiring my short slinky black dress with the fishnet stockings and my high strappy black heels.

It was the kind of party where wearing a sexy outfit and loving up someone else's husband was normal—the kind of party I was in the mood for after Steve, the Deida-loving man who'd been my best partner prospect so far, had rejected me. I knew that several of my recent lovers and a few potential ones might be in this group, which ranged in age from early forties to my late fifties. Although I was hoping to meet someone to date, I was also anticipating at least one sexual encounter if the atmosphere felt safe and comfortable. So far, I was feeling enveloped in love by these friends, and honored by Rosemary to trust me with her husband. She was very particular about the women she allowed him to be with, despite the fact that their marriage had been open for years and they both maintained other partners. Offering Blair to me was a big step up for our friendship. I had talked with Blair before, but this would be my first one-on-one time with him.

I had arrived just in time for Homer's welcoming speech. As Clara's lover and cohost, Homer took his responsibility seriously to set the tone of the sensual sex party so that everyone, especially women, felt safe. His handsome, rugged face and large, commanding presence made him a compelling speaker. As the thirty friends, lovers, partners, and acquaintances draped themselves onto couches or into laps around the long room, arms and legs entwined, Homer's lilting Iowa farm boy drawl permeated the room. Blair and I squeezed into a nearby couch.

"Everyone is at choice, here," he said slowly. "Everyone's 'no' is to be absolutely respected. All the women here are to be honored, worshipped, and cherished as goddesses at all times, whatever their choices are at any moment. Does everyone agree to that?"

The room was filled with affirmative murmurs and nods. In a crowd that had been carefully trained in workshops on love, intimacy, and sexuality to always respect each other's choices, he had a receptive audience. By also honoring the women as goddesses, he was ensuring that women would feel treasured as well as empowered. He wisely knew that if we felt that way, we would be much more open to the men. I was touched by his combination of passion and reverence for women. It was what had endeared him to me when we were lovers. Here, he had definitely created that safe and comfortable atmosphere I was looking for.

Blair and I spent the first part of the evening mingling in the living room with our friends, nuzzling them on the couch, or swaying with them to the music on the dance floor. Jay, the marginally married poly guy I had decided not to date, appeared, and he and Blair, longtime friends, hugged me from either side and rocked me. I felt proud to be with Blair, as we were a well-matched couple—about the same height, his uncombed wispy brown-and-gray hair to my tousled blond, and we both smiled a lot as we peered out from behind wire-rimmed glasses. Plus the kilt he wore made me feel that he was as quirky as I was.

As Blair and I roamed around the room, he stayed close, his arm around my waist or over my bare shoulders, including me when he talked to his friends, showing interest when I talked with mine. His light touch on my skin, the pressure of his body against mine, and his steady presence generated a warmth that trickled through the layers of skin into my heart. Although I knew I couldn't have him as my own partner, I knew he was the kind of man I was seeking. Just by being with him for the evening, I was giving my heart and body the imprint of the type of man I wanted. I sent a psychic thank-you to Rosemary for the loan.

Eventually, Blair and I made our way to the master bedroom, where Homer, Clara, and others were alternately talking and making love on Clara's king-sized bed. In the center, Homer was on top of Clara's long curvy body, moving in and out of her in a gentle rhythm. Clara was giggling; Homer was gazing down at her fondly. Stretched out naked on Clara's right side was Sue, another friend, discussing meditation techniques with a man who stood beside the bed, caressing her lightly along her waist and hips. Without the sex and the naked stroking, it could have been any normal party scene.

As if he didn't see or hear the others, Blair tilted his head to one side and smiled at me, exuding both confidence and amusement. "May I pleasure you, Carolyn?" he asked.

Coming from anyone else, this might have sounded corny or clinical, but with Blair's twinkling eyes shining into mine, it felt like a precious offering. Although Rosemary's suggestion was to love him up, I sensed that he was used to being the giver and was offering to "do" me without any expectation that I would return the favor. Accepting it *was* loving him up.

"I'd love that," I said.

I slipped out of my dress and stockings; Blair's shirt and kilt fell to the floor. After we washed our hands and faces, he enfolded me in a standing naked hug, pressing his mustached lips lightly against mine. I felt cherished in his arms, and his warm skin against mine made me long for his touch. He guided me to lie down on the open section of the bed, on the other side of Homer and Clara.

Sitting by my side, Blair gently spread open my legs, drenched a few fingers with silky lube, and started slowly stroking the outer lips of my anticipating yoni. He smiled through his mustache, gazing at me with half-closed eyes. I dissolved into the bed.

Gradually his fingers strayed into my inner lips, and my yoni opened like a wet mouth, wanting a kiss. Circling around my clitoris, his caresses darted over and around it, evoking sharp internal jolts of pre-orgasmic delight. Delicious shivers of sensations spread from my pelvis to the rest of my body.

Slowly his fingers slid into my yoni, opening me further. Deep inside, his fingers found my G-spot and caressed it lovingly but firmly. He was an expert at finding and lingering in just the right place. I surrendered into the pressure, past the point of feeling I needed to pee, into a widening, a letting go. A flash flood of warmth pulsed through me. I melted into a yummy openness, oblivious to anything else for many moments until I became aware again of the tender talking and lovemaking on the bed.

On my left, Blair's body was nestled closely with his arm around my waist. On my right, Clara's soft skin pressed against my hips, and Homer's arm around Clara brushed my arm. When I'd first started attending these types of parties, it had seemed too personal to have sex in front of my friends or see them making love, let alone be close enough to touch. Gradually, I started seeing the beauty of it. The presence and touch of those I loved at such intimate moments created a connection between all of us—another way of being close.

Now, surrounded by my new lover Blair, my friend Clara, and my ex-lover Homer, I felt that closeness. For a while I just lay there, entwined with the bodies of my friends and lovers, in blissful appreciation of the trust, safety, and sexual openness we had created.

DEEP

~~~

I drove home from the party feeling loved and touched. Rosemary
and Blair lived in Southern California and were staying with
other friends that night. Blair and I had made a sleepover date
for the following night, when Rosemary would be staying at her
boyfriend's house. The date with Blair would be my forty-fifth.
Blair was married, but after being rejected by Steve, date number
44, I needed some nurturing. I was giving myself the gift of a man
who not only was a match for me but liked me, even if he could
not be my partner.

◦━━━━━◦

The next morning I woke up feeling peaceful but wondering
again how I would find a partner if I kept being lovers with
polyamorous men who already had primary partners or wives.
Where was my primary partner? A better option might be to
date only monogamous men. However, monogamy felt so confining. I'd already brought grief to the men who had expected me
to give up my other lovers after sleeping with them only once or
twice. I wished I could find someone like Reed, who supported
Olivia to seek other lovers when she wanted, or Daryl, the generous primary partner I'd had at the summer retreat.

That night, sitting in my kitchen over tea, I told Blair about my dating project and how I wanted to go deeper with a partner than I'd gone with Peter. Blair's eyes smiled at me through his wire-rim glasses. His elflike face, messy salt-and-pepper hair, and scruffy goatee looked disheveled, but his presence felt sincere and comforting.

"Do you still miss Peter?" Blair asked.

Tears came to my eyes. "Yes, I do. I felt so loved by him." I wondered if I'd ever find someone who loved me that much.

Blair held my gaze, which allowed me to say more. "I'm afraid that I'm not that attractive as a partner to most men, and I'm not sure why," I said. That was the truth, and I felt safe admitting that to this kind and present man.

"You're very attractive," he said. "I can see why you'd be sad about not finding someone."

He hugged me while I cried a bit. "What does going deeper mean to you?" he asked.

"I'm not really sure," I said. "I think it has to do with sharing our deepest feelings. Peter and I only shared happy things, and that didn't seem very deep, but I don't want it to be just about the hard, struggling stuff. What do you think?"

"I think it's being vulnerable with our feelings, no matter what they are. It can be very vulnerable to share deep happiness as well as deep grief and fear."

"Hmm. That sounds right," I said. I couldn't take in what he said. Going deeper sounded both obvious and abstract. I was suddenly very tired. "Let's go to bed."

As we crawled into my purple flannel sheets, in my room filled with peaceful music, I assumed we were going to have another blissful sexual encounter. Instead, we both fell asleep and cuddled closely all night, which was just what I needed.

We woke at the same time.

"Good morning!" Blair said. His eyes were bright and happy to see me. "Happy Valentine's Day!" I had forgotten—it was that day. That night, we would be at a Valentine's Day dance—he with his wife, and me with Rob—but right then, I was glad I was waking up with him after my tearful confessions the night before.

I smiled back. "Happy Valentine's Day!" We kissed.

"Hey, how come you never got married?" he asked. I took a deep breath, trying to come up with a short version of why I never did.

"I didn't in my twenties 'cause I thought I'd become a dependent housewife. I didn't in my thirties 'cause I was afraid it would get me off my career and grad school track. I also tried being a lesbian from my midtwenties to midforties, but I never found the right woman. I decided I preferred men, so I've been looking for the right male partner ever since."

"Oh, I did kind of get lesbian energy from you," he said.

"Really, what kind?" I was surprised that he could feel that. It had been almost twenty years since my lesbian days.

"Well, mostly it's the independent, taking-care-of-yourself energy."

Tears came to my eyes again. Blair had named the exact strength I had purposely developed as a lesbian in order to counteract my fear of becoming a housewife. For the first time, I could see a conflict between what I was so proud of—the financial, practical, and emotional independence from men that I had learned in my years as a lesbian—and what I wanted now: a close, interdependent relationship with a man. Maybe I'd been repelling the men I now wanted to attract—those who wanted to be vulnerable and close.

We lay there in bed, breathing together. Blair's presence never wavered, staying with me in mind and gaze. He held me as I cried. He was seeing the real me.

"I'm so sad," I said through my tears, "that I haven't been putting out energy that would be attractive to the kind of partner I want. And I'm not sure what it means to go deep."

"You're doing it now," he said. "Being vulnerable and sharing your feelings."

"Really?"

"Yeah."

I breathed into that.

After a few breaths, I felt reassured, less sad, and more hopeful. Maybe I could find someone like Blair, who could be with me just as I was.

⸻

That night, at the Valentine's Day dance, fifty women and men floated around the room to romantic new age music. Separating myself from Rob and dancing on my own, I spotted Blair and Rosemary and Jay. I felt a pull toward Jay but reminded myself that he was not available. As they danced by, I reached out my arms and gathered up Blair, Rosemary, and Jay.

"You know, the main reason for dating someone like Blair or even Jay," I said to the three of them, "is to give myself the experience of being with someone who's my match, so I reinforce in my bones that I deserve a man like this."

Blair and Jay glowed with the compliment, and I smiled at them. They were both men of emotional availability, sexual sensitivity, warm intelligence, kindness, and presence. They liked me just as I was. I wanted a man like them. But one of my own, not one to share.

"You do deserve someone like them," Rosemary said, smiling at all of us.

I needed to rethink what partnership meant to me. Men like Blair became my lovers and friends, and by doing so they became my partners in a way. Since I'd shaped myself as so

independent, maybe I needed an independent type of relationship that also allowed me to be close and vulnerable. Blair felt
like my partner for the night. Several of my lovers during this
dating project had become part-time partners. Peter had been a
long-distance partner.

*Maybe this is just how I do relationships—more independent
than most,* I thought. *I wonder what a good relationship for me
would look like.*

OPENING

~~~~~~~~~

On a cold rainy evening later in February, I sat in my study at my computer, clicking through men's OKCupid profiles. No new ones. It had been over two years since I started the dating project, and I'd gone on forty-eight dates. The last three had been coffee dates with Match.com prospects, but none were anywhere near partner potential—too boring, too arrogant, or so inexperienced in relationships that I recommended a HAI workshop. I seemed to be scraping the bottom of the dating barrel. I still believed that I would find my partner eventually, but I was starting to suspect that I might not find him soon.

I broke away from the computer and wandered into the living room. *I might have to go on another fifty dates*, I thought. I flopped onto the purple couch as I imagined the energy I'd need. I didn't have it. I needed a break. What would refresh me enough to start this project again?

Suddenly I sat up. Greece! I'd always wanted to go to the Greek islands during May, and I'd been saving United miles for years for such a trip. Now that I was on sabbatical from my job, I could go in May. Why had I not realized this before? My sabbatical work would be done before May, and I was turning sixty in June. What better milestone birthday present to myself than a trip to Greece? I rushed back into my study and opened up the United web page to see how many miles I would need to fly to Europe. I had more than enough. In fact, I had enough for a round-trip first-class ticket. My heart beat faster. What a birthday gift! But were there seats? Miraculously, there were, in the first row of the first-class cabin.

I booked seats for the whole month of May and sat back, relief and excitement flowing through my body. I'd rescued myself from the dating doldrums. The trip had come together effortlessly, as if the universe had responded to my solstice wishes. I hadn't even asked for travel. Maybe the universe didn't have a partner lined up for me, so it had given me my dream trip instead. Or maybe I was destined to find my partner in Greece. In any case, I was grateful.

I had to talk to myself about going alone, though. *Carolyn, I know you'd rather go with a partner, but you don't have one yet. Some of your best trips have been traveling on your own. You're outgoing and friendly—you can finish the project there!*

It was just what I needed to hear. Suddenly, I had energy for dating in Greece. Imagine! I could enjoy sexy adventurous male travelers or Greek men for the last several dates!

It was even possible that someone I knew could meet me there. In the days after I booked the flight, I said to whoever would listen, "I'm going to the Greek islands in May, and anyone who wants can visit me!" Well, not anyone. I had to like them and want to spend time with them. I thought Peter might be able to go, since he now had two girlfriends in Europe and was going to visit them that spring. I didn't know anyone else with the time, money, or miles for the trip.

⊶————⊷

The day after I made my reservations, I was driving on the freeway, talking on the phone to Jay about whether I should consider dating him. I mentioned my Greece trip.

"I could go," said Jay. "I have the time and the miles."

My heart almost jumped out of my car, and my car almost swerved into the next lane. "Really?" I said, getting the car under control. I suddenly longed for him to join me in Greece. How did I know I wanted to travel with him when I was not even sure I wanted to date him? At that moment, with my heart still pounding, I realized I wanted to do both. My vow to not date married men had flown out the car window like yesterday's to-do list. Besides, Jay was only sort of married, and he was the type of man I wanted. He might be the perfect companion for this trip to Greece. I could have a date with him to see if he was.

Peter was about to visit me for a week, so I told Jay we'd set a date for some time after Peter left. During Peter's time at my house, we went to a friend's birthday party, and there was Jay, also a friend of the birthday boy. I introduced Peter to Jay, so he could meet someone I might be dating. Peter and I were normalizing our friendship by sharing about our dating lives.

After greeting Peter, Jay turned to me. "What number date are you up to?" he asked.

"Somewhere in the high forties," I said.

A look of panic went across Jay's usually cheerful face. He said to Peter, "Oh no—I don't want to miss the bus! I want to get on the bus!"

Peter looked amused, and I took note. Jay and I made a date for the following Sunday. He would be the forty-ninth date.

———

Peter had just left for the airport and I was still teary from the good-bye when Jay showed up at ten o'clock. Despite letting go of Peter at solstice and normalizing our friendship, being with him always reminded me how much I loved him. I brushed off my tears and welcomed Jay.

We had a full day planned—a bike ride, a memorial service for a mutual friend, and an Oscar party. This was unusual for a first date. However, each of the activities touched on something we loved—exercising outdoors, supporting our friends in sorrow, and socializing with our friends in joy. We were both very high energy, so doing three things in one day seemed normal. We figured it would be a good opportunity to get to know each other.

"Let's see how the date goes before deciding about Greece," I said when we planned the day. It felt like a big leap to travel with this almost stranger.

"Good idea," Jay said, "I'm on board if you want me." I trembled inside, wanting to leap.

We drove over to Alameda for the bike ride. As Jay helped me get my bike and gear out of his van, I noticed how gentle and kind he was in making sure I was all set up.

As we rode near the Oakland airport, planes flew low right above us, and we both looked up, our eyes shining. My father had been a Navy pilot and then worked for Lockheed. I remembered that Jay had also been in the airplane business, so I suspected he liked planes as much as I did.

One flew very close, and I stopped to watch it. Jay came to a halt next to me.

Gazing at it, I said, "Airplanes remind me of my father. He loved planes. He died sixteen years ago, and I still miss him."

"He must have been very special."

"He was," I said, touched that Jay had heard the feelings under my words. "Once in the 1970s, I went to the Oakland airport and took the perfect birthday picture for him—a plane flying past the American and Californian flags—and he kept it on his desk from then on."

"I feel like your father, you, and I are here together, enjoying the majesty of planes," Jay said. "And I'm seeing your father's bright eyes in yours."

Tears filled my eyes, feeling the comforting presence of Dad and Jay at the same time.

The memorial service was held in a large, cavernous hall, once a sanctuary, in downtown Oakland. As I drove us there in my Corolla, Jay rested one hand on my thigh. "May I?" he said.

"Yes," I said. It felt natural and comforting, like he'd been doing that for a long time.

Inside the hall, about a hundred folding chairs had been set up facing an altar in the middle of the room. Tables in the back held the potluck dishes that people had brought.

Jay and I had both known Ruth, the woman who had died. She was the wife of Ray, who had been date number 12 two years earlier when I met him at Marco's Valentine's Day party and took him home with me. Ruth had been there with her boyfriend and had given me permission to take Ray home. I hadn't kept in touch with them enough to know what led to her death, but whatever it was, she was our age—too young to die.

We were there to share our grief with friends who knew and loved Ruth. However, Jay knew many more people than me, and we hadn't discussed how we were going to be together at this event—would he want to stay together or mingle with his friends? I was used to being independent, so I assumed we would mingle with different friends and meet up now and then.

Jay had introduced me to an old friend of his, and they were now talking behind the food tables. I stood around for a bit and noticed that people were finding chairs and sitting down. About to go off on my own, I called out over the table, "Do you want to sit together?"

"Of course!" Jay looked pleased I had asked, and moved toward me.

I was pleasantly surprised and glad he wanted to. My independent self relaxed a bit.

We sat next to each other and started holding hands, without thinking about it and without stopping. On the other side of me was Ray, now Ruth's widower. While still holding Jay's hand, I reached over and held Ray's too. The slideshow of Ruth's life started. Her life looked so familiar—like mine, it was a combination of professional work and a wild hippy-like life of friends and lovers, including women and pagan rituals. I ached knowing her life was over, and I squeezed Ray's hand. As we mourned Ruth together, I was comforted by the aliveness of Jay's hand in mine.

⊳————⊲

Back home getting dressed for the Oscar party, I suggested to Jay we lie on my bed and just hold each other. Feelings from the day were filling up my chest and about to spill over.

As Jay held me gently, I started crying. Jay just gazed at me tenderly.

"I still love Peter," I said through my tears. "This week I let go of our relationship a little bit more, but now I really miss him." Jay nodded.

"I can see why you'd miss him," he said gently.

"And Ruth and I were so alike," I said, sniffling, "and she died—it could have been me."

"I know," said Jay.

"And I'm feeling drawn to you, but I don't know where it will lead. It feels complicated!"

"I know," said Jay.

I was crying for still loving Peter after all these dates, for letting go of him, for Ruth's and all our wild and precious lives, for the new and scary space I was opening for Jay to come in. Jay held me in such a respectful and caring way my tears all flowed out. After a while, they stopped. I felt more space. I smiled at him. We didn't kiss. The moment felt too tender.

———

At the Oscar party in my friend Sarah's roomy apartment, the wide-screened show had already begun. The forty or so guests were strewn around the living room on couches, chairs, and the floor, mesmerized by the spectacle. Jay and I crept in and sat in the front row of backrests on the floor. We watched the show, but we mainly just kept holding hands and staying close. I noticed that I was feeling more peaceful holding his hand than doing anything else with the forty-eight men who had come before.

———

Jay left that evening for his house in Los Gatos, a suburb of San Jose. I was leaving the next day to drive to Los Angeles on a sabbatical trip to study other colleges and visit my mother. When we realized I'd be driving relatively near him on the way down, he offered to meet me at the crossroads in San Jose.

"Would you let me practice narrating how to stroke each other's faces?" I asked. I was in training to lead face-stroking exercises in HAI events and was going to be tested after my trip.

"Do I want to stroke your face and have you stroke my face?" he said. "Um, of course!"

He showed up with the back of his van all decorated like a HAI workshop—beautiful sarongs were laid neatly over a carpet and two backrests sat at opposite corners. I felt so supported and met. As I tried out a guiding and appreciative patter, we stroked each other's faces, looking into each other's blue eyes, trying to see who this other blue-eyed person was that we were suddenly getting to know. In his eyes I saw the tenderness and kindness of the day before, plus a twinkling hint of adventure and fun.

As I drove down to L.A., we talked on the phone; when I got there, we texted. On the road between my mother's house and the colleges, we kept up an ongoing phone conversation. It didn't matter what we covered—the sights driving through the Central Valley, my interactions with my mother, his memories of L.A. freeway driving, my L.A. parking challenges, stories of our pasts—it was all engaging, and I didn't want it to end. As we spoke, traffic jams miraculously opened up lanes for me, college visits went smoothly, and my mother became less critical.

⊸————⊷

On the drive back up north, I stopped in San Luis Obispo at the home of Rosemary and Blair, the poly couple who had loaned me Blair for the sex party. Blair, who had helped me accept my independent, post-lesbian nature during date number 45, invited me to cuddle with him on a sunny bed. In the safety of his arms, I started crying.

"I think I'm falling in love with Jay," I said. It was literally a falling feeling, something inevitable that felt delicious but scary. I was hoping Blair would cushion the fall.

"I don't blame you," he said. "I love Jay too." Like our date before, Blair's soft gaze and arms around me were reassuring. "Just feel it," he whispered, holding me close.

On the rest of the drive home, I talked with my close friend Anne, who lives in Arizona.

"I'm really falling for this guy, Jay," I said. "And I'm not sure I should—he's still married."

"I wondered the same thing when I was thinking about getting involved with my Jay," she said, referring to a man with the same name. "He was in a relationship with his wife and another woman. How could I get what I needed? Would it distract me from finding my partner? So I asked Jesus." Anne was a retired pastor and could just ask Jesus to help her with her problems.

"And Jesus came to me one night and said, 'Love Jay.' And I did. And I'm so glad I did. Later we both moved on, but it was perfect at the time. We don't have to predict the future. We just need to respond to the offer of love when it shows up."

I knew I wanted to respond to my Jay's offer. Love Jay. I wanted to do that.

＊＊＊

A week after I got home, on a Friday, Jay and I had our first sleepover date. We met around noon at my house, so we had the whole afternoon, evening, night, and morning.

"I want to honor this time we have together," Jay said. He had just come into my house and was looking into my eyes earnestly, with a touch of eagerness.

"I have an idea," I said. Given our shared background in spiritual and sexual communities, I was hoping Jay would be open to what I had in mind. "We could have a ceremony and create 'sacred space' like they do in Tantra gatherings."

"I love the sound of that—what would it look like?" Jay said.

"We'd set up a little island here in the living room with sarongs and backrests. Then we'd clear out any qualities we don't want for our time together, and bring in qualities we do."

"Oh, I've done something like that before," he said. "Go on!"

"We'd say what we appreciate about each other and give each other a gift—something that symbolizes how we feel about being together. Then we'd state our intentions for this time. After that, we would sit closely and breathe together, in and out, matching each other's rhythms, getting in sync. Whatever we did after that would be a sacred connection."

"I love it!" he said. I was relieved that he was not only open to having a ceremony but enthusiastic about it. I hoped it would have the result I wanted.

We sat down facing each other on the sarong-covered island on my living room carpet. We waved our arms in an arc around the space, creating an imaginary bubble around us.

"I take out fear and worry," I said, gesturing as if throwing something out of our bubble.

"I take out expectations and time pressure," Jay said, mimicking my throw. His words dissolved two major sources of fear and worry for me.

"I bring in joy and open hearts," I said, pulling them in with my arms as I smiled at him.

"I bring in love and fun," Jay said, grinning at me. "And what I appreciate about you is that you know how to connect so well, and you live your life in such grace and heartfulness."

"Ooh," I said, touched by what he said. "I appreciate your warm smile, your kind intelligence, and your enthusiasm." He beamed.

"The gift I have for you," I said, "are these purple stones on a string, a string for each of us, to symbolize the connection with our spirits that we are creating." The necklaces had called to me from a crafts booth that week—a sign of my budding intuition. I put one around his neck and the other on mine. He held his to his heart, his eyes softening as he looked at me.

"And I give you my open heart," he said. My heart thumped open as I felt his.

Our intentions were similar—to experience each other with our hearts, minds, and bodies. As we breathed in and out together, absorbing the words of our ceremony, I felt us creating a union of heart, mind, and spirit, and I felt him giving me the freedom to be just who I was. This was what I had imagined. I wondered if this guy was for real.

Afterward, we floated through the rest of the day, opening our lives to each other. We wandered around my neighborhood, telling our stories in bits and pieces. We held each other on my bed, where I told him my relationship history and he told me about his marriage.

Jay's marriage was not only marginal—it was almost over. Although he and his wife were still living in the home where they had raised their three children—all college graduates with successful careers—they were living as if they were already separated, with separate bedrooms, activities, and relationships. His wife wanted a place of her own so she could start a new life with her boyfriend. When she moved out, they would be officially separated, and they intended to dissolve the marriage as soon as they could unravel their finances. Jay's relationship in Florida had ended when his airplane business had collapsed, and now, though he had several lovers, he was not committed to anyone. He seemed more available for a partnership than I'd thought. I felt a surge of hope and a bold impulse to take a chance on him.

It didn't matter to me when his marriage would be officially over, because I wasn't interested in being married. I just wanted to know that Jay was free to make a long-term emotional commitment to me, and it sounded like he was. I didn't yet know if I wanted to start a relationship—that's what dating was for. Until then, I would protect my heart—I told myself that I was still getting to know him, and I could leave at any time. But I knew that my heart had started longing for him.

⊷————⊶

Months earlier, I'd stood in front of a HAI workshop and declared that I was ready for a partner.

"I want to share my life with someone," I'd said, and described that life.

The facilitator had said gently, "It sounds like you want a husband."

I'd sucked in my breath. I had never thought I wanted to be married, but when he said that, I realized that marriage might be the label for what I wanted. "Yes, I want a husband," I'd said, blushing with the strangeness of that idea.

⊷————⊶

Now I saw that I had found *a* husband, just not necessarily *my* husband. Next time I'd be more specific with the declarations. But maybe I had not misspoken. I was glad that Jay had a life in Los Gatos—it gave me time to focus on my own life in Oakland. Marriage still looked too confining. Maybe a relationship with an experienced husband whom I did not live with was the exact amount of independence I needed.

We took another walk and talked about safe sex, so we could be sexual later. For dinner we went to Ikaros, a new Greek restaurant in Oakland, run by a couple from the island of Ikaria. There, we smiled and laughed a lot. The staff there said we were so *cute*! In this restaurant island, I could feel the Greek island trip getting closer, and I imagined going with Jay.

Back home, after more talking, I sang my song, "Stop and Hold the Moment," for him. He got it—when things feel so good, I want to hold on to them, but I need to trust that "... the blessings that surround me are constantly renewed." He didn't try to sing along but smiled warmly and nodded as I sang.

Finally, we went to bed, wanting only to hold each other. I put on the same song that had comforted me so long ago: "Waves are comin' in, waves are comin' in." We wrapped our arms around each other and drew each other close, kissing. Falling asleep, waking a thousand times, each time finding ourselves still kissing each other, holding, and gazing into each other's eyes, feeling the waves of closeness. It felt so complete. Neither of us moved to make love.

⊶————⊷

In the morning, we lingered in bed with tea and then got up and started packing for our separate Saturdays. We each had other plans—I was going to a retreat with friends up the coast in Bolinas and he was heading home. On Sunday, we were both planning to be at the spiritual/sensual gathering of our friends in a big cliff-hugging house on the San Francisco Bay in the town of Sausalito; we would see each other then. Jay, however, would be there with his occasional lover Lavender, a woman who was descending into Alzheimer's and who needed a lot of attention. So I could not expect to spend much time with him, let alone private time.

I suddenly realized that I would yearn for him at that gathering.

"We should make love now," I said. "I don't want to be longing for you tomorrow."

"OK!" he said, smiling. "I love your logic!"

I wanted him inside me, to be as close as possible, and he was glad to oblige. He licked my yoni to moisten me, then covered himself with a condom and lube. As he entered me, I felt the fullness of him I longed for, like my yoni was Cinderella's slipper, and his cock fit it perfectly. His arms around me felt like being held by the gentlest prince. His thrusts were caressing my clitoris more than intercourse usually did, and it made me long for more. With a vibrator on my yoni, I came as he stroked me from breasts to feet. He said he didn't need to come, so he entered and moved inside me slowly while we gazed into each other's eyes. It was the exact closeness I'd wanted. After a lingering kiss, we jumped up, packed, and left.

Later that day, texts trickled in:

Helloooo, Bolinas . . . hello, dear Carolyn . . . In awe from our date. . . . Hope you made it safely and on time! Have a beautiful retreat. Love and more love, j

I'm here and feeling so happy and supported by you. . . . Much love & awe & excitement & appreciations. Carolyn

We were both falling.

The next day, at the daylong gathering, while Jay was with Lavender, I cuddled with my other men friends, among them

Marco and Chandler. But I was aching for Jay. Finally, in the early evening, Jay, Chandler, and I snuck away to the heated swimming pool down the cliff from the house, where we found ourselves gazing out at the San Francisco city lights.

"Let's imagine that those lights across the bay are the island of Crete," I said to Jay and Chandler, "and we are there together." We were standing naked in the warm water of the enclosed pool, looking out through the windows. Chandler and Jay stood on either side of me with their arms around my shoulders and waist.

"I can see it," said Jay, gazing across the water and hugging me tighter.

"Even if we can't all go," I said, "we have this precious moment right now."

We breathed in the steamy air in silence, holding each other, softening our gaze, seeing the shimmer of an ancient Greek island in the distance, and imagining ourselves there.

I really am going to Greece, I thought. *Will this moment transport us all there?*

"I know it's going to happen," said Chandler, pulling us both closer so we all had our arms around each other, our slippery warm bodies meeting affectionately under the water. Our faces met in the middle, and we started kissing each other with many kisses, sealing in the vision.

In fact, Chandler and his partner Carrie had booked flights to Crete soon after they heard about my trip. We were planning to meet up somewhere on that island but hadn't worked it out yet. So it was mainly Jay who was the question—and I hadn't decided yet.

But then I surprised myself. "I hope you join us, Jay," I said through my kisses.

"So do I," said Jay as he kissed me.

We three held each other close for a moment. Soon, friends from the gathering came into the pool area, looking for Jay and Chandler. I had to let go of them for now.

Still, a connection had been made. The Greek island fantasy with these two men had evoked something deep in me. I knew I was meant to be with them in Crete. I was still single, but my three dates with Jay had been profound, and I could feel us becoming closer. I was moving toward him, and my fears were receding.

GREECE

~~~~~

Greece would be in May, but in March, I was going to Mexico. I was spending a week there with my friend Jules, who'd been my model for Mr. Right as date number 23. He and his wife, Tatiana, had bought a house in a town near Lake Chapala, and I wanted to see it, practice my Spanish, and keep Jules company since he was alone there that week.

Jay and I had been seeing each other for the past three weekends. We were feeling unabashedly happy together. I couldn't imagine being with anyone else, and neither could he. Rob and I had said our good-byes, and I'd wished him well with a gift of a HAI workshop.

What about the fiftieth date? I thought about the men who were waiting in the wings to go out with me—a blind date offer from my plumber, an online ad guy who had looked promising a month ago. But I couldn't summon any of my usual interest in new men. It felt misleading to date them since I was so sure I wanted to be with Jay. *The fiftieth date would have to remain undone.*

My researcher mind protested. *No! We have to go on all fifty dates to complete the project!* But my heart answered quietly, *The purpose of the project was to find a partner, and we may have found him. I can't go on another date when I'm so in love with Jay.*

Siding with my heart, I let go of the need to have a fiftieth date. My researcher mind grumbled, but she accepted my decision.

⌾—————⌾

We had been discussing Greece. Should he come? Did I really want him to? Did he really want to? The night before I left for Mexico, he called.

"I did it," he said.

"Did what?"

"I'm on your flight to Greece," he said. "In the first-class seat next to you. Hope that's OK."

"Oh, my god!" I said. "That's more than OK—it's wonderful, and incredible!"

I flew down to Mexico feeling loved, wanted, desired, and lucky. I had a date for the first week of Greece! Now that someone was coming with me, I had to find us places to stay. Just me, I could drift around, but for Jay and me together, I wanted to line up spaces we would enjoy.

Jules was the perfect friend to share all this with. "Sounds like you found someone really special," he said. "I knew it would happen—you deserve this."

While Jules worked on the new brick wall for his upstairs patio, I planned the Greek trip. As I started to research lodging, I checked with Jay about whether he agreed with my preference for places with views. "I didn't know I preferred that," he said, "but now I do." I felt unexpectedly supported, like he had signed up to be on my team and was going to stay on it.

I was working out the schedule for that first week when Jay called and said, "Um, I just can't pull the trigger on coming home after a week. Do you mind if I stay for two weeks?"

"Oh, my god, of course not!" I said. I was thrilled to have him on half of my trip—I hadn't let myself feel how much I wanted him there, and now I could not imagine it without him.

Rooms with spectacular views appeared on my computer—on Crete and on Santorini. It helped that we were sharing the costs, but I checked with Jay when the price seemed like a splurge. He always said, "Let's go for it." We both had the sense that it was a once-in-a-lifetime trip.

<hr />

Two months later, Jay sat in the first-class seat next to mine, and we were off to Greece. The first-class crew said we had that just-married glow, and indulged our sleeping together on one reclining seat. From then on, we called the trip the honeymoon before the relationship. Even this early, it felt that we were embarked on a grand adventure of the heart.

We landed in Heraklion, on Crete, where our room had a view across the harbor. The first night, Jay surprised me with an amethyst ring that he had bought on a whim from a second-hand store months before he met me. "I want you to have this as a symbol of our deepening relationship," he said. My heart burst open, and I wept when I realized how much I had wanted a ring to feel like Jay was committing to me in this grand adventure. He really was. Amethyst was my favorite gem, and it fit perfectly on my left ring finger. It was as close to a commitment as a marginally married man and a marriage-phobic woman could get.

We spent the next day gazing at each other, the view, and wandering sleepily around the harbor. At the Heraklion Archeological Museum, we learned about the artistic, goddess-worshiping Minoan civilization, which had flourished on Crete between 3,000 BC and 1,450 BC.

On the second day we visited Knossos, the ruins of the largest Minoan palace, arriving only an hour before it closed. We sped through the palace, and just as we were rounding the corner to go up the last set of stairs, I took Jay's arm, slowed us down, and said, "Here we are in ancient Minoan time, and we are going up to the temple." I could imagine the king and queen holding a ceremony in the central court.

Immediately, with no hesitation, Jay slowed, squeezed my arm, and joined in the fantasy. "Yes," he said, "we hope to be blessed by the king and queen in a ceremony."

"I'm so happy with you, Prince Jay," I said. "I'm sure they will bless us."

"Oh, Princess Caroline," he said, "I don't think they bless everyone."

"I think they can see how happy we are," I said. "After all, they put us together."

"True, Princess Caroline," he said. "Oh, we are almost to the platform!"

"Here we go, Prince Jay," I said calmly. "I'm proud to be presenting myself with you to the king and queen."

We reached the courtyard, and the air shimmered.

"We are walking up to the king and queen," I said as I guided us to the raised platform in the center of the yard. When we reached it, Jay got on one knee and bowed his head, and I followed. "They are putting their hands on our heads!" I said.

Jay spoke. "The king is saying, 'We bless you, Princess Caroline and Prince Jay, as a royal couple in our community. We grant you a dwelling on our palace grounds.'"

I looked up, astonished to hear such a blessing. I added, "And the queen is saying, 'May your love grow and prosper, my children. May you feel the love of all of our kin with you.'"

"Thank you, thank you, Your Highnesses," we both murmured, bowing again. I looked up and imagined their kind and shining eyes, gazing lovingly at us. They were giant spirits, this king and queen. We had been blessed by the gods.

We were silent as we walked across the plaza and down the stairs to leave. Through my hands and arms, I could feel Jay's excitement and relief echoing mine as we squeezed each other hard and gazed ecstatically straight ahead, stealing sideways looks to affirm what we each felt.

When we had gone down the stairs and around the corner, we turned to each other and embraced. "They blessed us! They blessed us!" Jay exclaimed.

"I knew they would!" I said. "We are truly blessed."

As we gazed at each other, I sank into a peaceful place in my heart—a deep knowing that our union was ordained by the universe and that this whole trip had been to affirm that. We'd traveled back to Minoan days to see it. And we had the rest of the trip to feel it even deeper.

⊱————⊰

Every place we stayed supported our honeymoon feeling. In Chania, we spent three nights overlooking the harbor in a spacious Venetian room with high ceilings and a four-poster bed. I confessed to Jay that I liked to be tied down, and he said he'd love to do that to me. As we wandered around the harbor among colorful clothing booths, I picked out four iridescent scarves of purple, silver, blue, and black swirls, pulsing inside as I imagined how he might use them.

That night, he bound my arms and legs firmly, a different color holding me to each bedpost, and my naked body trembled with anticipation.

"You just have to accept whatever I do—or say," he said. I nodded, starting to get wet.

"Yes," I said, expecting the standard domination dialogue.

"You are so good," he said, looking into my eyes. "Will you accept that?"

"OK," I said, searching his eyes, not knowing where he was going.

"*Really* accept it?"

"I'll try—"

"You are beautiful, lovable, brilliant, and exciting to be with, and I want to be with you. Can you let that in?"

He was stroking my whole body softly and looked both loving and serious.

"Yes," I said, though I squirmed trying to absorb it. These were not the usual words of domination. But they were the words I'd been longing to hear for so long, and he was saying them, over and over. My heart resisted, afraid of believing, but he kept saying, "You are so good, you're perfect just as you are," again and again. I could feel my heart letting go of a tightness I hadn't known was there. "Now you say it, over and over," he said.

I squirmed but said it. "I'm beautiful, lovable, brilliant, and fun to be with." When I had said it enough for him to see that I believed it, he began pleasuring me with his fingers, tongue, and cock. My body melted, our bodies joined, and I surrendered to him completely, coming like never before. My heart had never felt so loved, safe, or open, and my body had responded deeply.

In Myrthios, high on the southern coast, we spent three nights gazing at each other, making love until noon, and passed afternoons on a nude beach, frolicking in the water and reading a child's version of *The Odyssey* out loud. Pictures show us ecstatically happy, splashing in the calm sea.

On the ninth night, to celebrate my sixtieth birthday, Chandler and Carrie met us for dinner at the Blue Palace, a fancy hotel on the northeast coast. I wore a long white Aphrodite dress with black trim that made me feel like a Greek goddess. As we gazed out from our restaurant table across the bay to the twinkly lights of a nearby island, our fantasy from that warm pool many months before came true. We were all here together. And Jay was with me.

We stayed near Chandler and Carrie's place on the north coast so we could go hiking together. Carrie led us up a mountain to Karfi, the last stronghold of the Minoans. In that high valley, with fog swirling around us, we again felt surrounded and blessed by ancient spirits.

Jay and I left Crete for Santorini, where we spent four romantic days making love, enjoying the spectacular view from our patio, and hiking on nearby cliffs. Then Jay flew home.

"You know, I'm in for the whole thing," he said at the airport, "not just the honeymoon."

I kissed him good-bye but couldn't take in what he was saying. I'd loved our honeymoon and hoped it would continue; now he was giving me more hope than I was allowing myself to feel. What did he mean by "the whole thing?" A whole relationship? Was I ready for the whole thing?

GREEK ISLAND FANTASY

After Jay left, I missed him so much it hurt, but my heart was smiling. I ferried over to an island known for hiking and beaches, rented a studio on a clothing-optional beach, and Skyped with Jay every night.

Each day, I went walking naked for miles along the sandy shore. The warm sun caressed my skin and danced across the turquoise Aegean Sea to the next island. I passed a smattering of people, some clothed, some not, spread out along the dunes pursuing their own Greek island fantasy.

Along the way, I swam, sunbathed, did yoga, ate, read, and looked for the naked Dionysian Greek guy who had beckoned me from the dunes on my first day. He'd been darkly tanned, with an upturned nose and a twinkle in his smile that broadcast "Fun here!"

"Come sit down," he'd said, patting his beach towel.

"No, thanks," I'd said with a reflexive no, and kept walking. I'd been feeling close to Jay and protecting my three precious days at the beach.

Later, I realized that this Greek stranger would've made the perfect fiftieth date—unlike the men at home, he would not expect a relationship. Playing on the beach with this guy would have been a harmless and fun way to finish the project. I told Jay about him, and Jay rooted for me to find him. We called him Adonis, and I looked for him for the next few days. Jay even urged me to take advantage of any "not to miss" experiences, so I knew he'd be comfortable with whatever I did.

Finally, on my last day, there he was, right where I had passed him before, about a mile and a half from my own beach. We were both delighted to see each other, politely ignoring the fact that we were both naked. His name was Dmitri, and we talked enough for me to know that I felt both drawn enough and safe enough to spend more time with him. Born on this island, he'd been married to an American woman, which explained his ease with English and me.

I was carrying only my sarong. I had left everything else— towel, bathing suit, food, sun block—on the beach with my next-door neighbor Dan, a cynical L.A. world traveler in the business of selling teddy bears internationally. Dan sat on the beach for hours, tanning and catching up on business news. I'd told Dan that I would be right back . . . unless I found the cute Greek guy.

"I need to get my things," I said to Dmitri. "I'll be back."

"Come back," he said.

I walked the one and a half miles and debriefed with Dan.

"You don't have to worry about Greek guys on this island, in my opinion," he said.

Reassured, I went back to my room and emailed to Jay that I found Adonis. I could almost hear him shouting "Hooray!" and "You go, girl!" in my laptop. I walked back the one and a half miles.

It had been almost two hours, and Dmitri was glad to see me. "I thought you not return," he said. We smiled. We laughed. We lay down on our stomachs on our beach towels and inched closer together as we talked.

And suddenly I was in my own Greek island fantasy—frolicking naked with a cute, tanned guy on a beach, splashing each other in the water and massaging each other in the dunes.

"Just touch, no sex," I said.

"You're driving me crazy!" he said, his smiling eyes crinkling, but he honored it.

He was forty-four and could not believe that I was about to turn sixty. We talked and laughed and smiled more. We ambled into the calm sea and swam and played like porpoises in the clear green water. We ran back to our towels and gave each other massages, embracing, kissing, laughing.

By the end of the day, I felt safe enough to let him drive me back to my apartment on the road behind the dunes and take me out to dinner in his village. However, I still had my city-dating survival instincts. I asked for his ID information to give to Dan and my landlady, Maria.

"Of course," he said, digging it out of the glove compartment and handing over his driver's license and some other ID. I copied down the numbers onto two of my business cards.

When we drove up to my apartment building, Maria was standing in an open doorway, supervising her cleaning staff. I pointed to Dmitri and said, "OK?" I felt about fifteen years old, asking my mother if I could go out with the cute guy I met on the beach. I didn't remember until later that I was almost sixty.

Maria recognized Dmitri and gave me a nod and one thumb up. I offered her the ID information, but she shook her head and said, "Not necessary!"

I could see that my precautions may have been a little over the top on this rural island of twenty thousand people where most knew each other. I slipped the info under Dan's door.

I brought Dmitri into my studio for a quick shower and change. We kept it on the light, playful level that we had developed on the beach—after all, we had been naked all day. Then he drove us about twenty-five minutes north, through the main island town, up the coast and then inland to his village. The main part of his town consisted of a row of whitewashed stucco buildings, where older men and women sat on their stoops and followed us with their eyes as we drove by.

His property contained several rough-hewn buildings rising along the side of a hill. The highest building held a big porch with a view down the valley to the sea. I asked if the structures came with the land. He held up a piece of rubble and said, "This is what came with the land!" He and his uncle and brother had been working on it for twenty-five years, having very little money to put into it. We climbed uneven stone steps up to the porch, where I gazed at the view and glanced at the other buildings. I wanted to see inside the house, but he had left the key in the car and was afraid the taverna where we planned to eat would soon be closing.

"You can see it after dinner," he said. I was excited but felt a tinge of worry about where it would lead if we returned to his house so late. I was leaving early in the morning and still had to pack, and it was a long drive back to my lodging.

He drove us to a village taverna run by an older stooped man with a weathered face who frowned the whole time. We were the lone patrons on his forty-table patio, as the tourist season had been slow to start. We accepted the only food offered, roast chicken and fried local potatoes, along with the most delectable Greek salad ever and some undrinkable white wine the owner had made himself. Apart from the wine, it was one of the most delicious dinners I'd ever tasted. In my best and only Greek, I thanked him: "*Efharisto!*" But the owner did not even glance at me. Dmitri shrugged it off. "He never smiles," he said.

Dmitri and I talked about his life on the island—very low income, but more peaceful than driving a taxi in Athens; the Greek economy—infuriating, because the austerity measures imposed by the European Union in exchange for the bailout loan had hurt many people he knew; and Greece's weather compared to California's—similar. I told him about my job, but downplayed my relatively comfortable life. We fed scraps of our chicken to waiting cats. I offered to pay for dinner, but he would not let me.

By then it was almost midnight, and he decided it was too late to go back to his house—a relief and a disappointment. He drove me back to my studio and I invited him in to say good night. But I couldn't just say good night. He was too adorable, and he'd been so sweet all day. I kissed him and he kissed back. I pulled him to me, letting him know I wanted more. After we had a quick safe sex talk, he produced a condom, and then he turned me on expertly with his fingers before slipping inside me and slowly moving in and out for a sexy few minutes. It was a satisfying end to our date. After all, Jay had encouraged me to enjoy him. So I did.

⊶————⊷

I stayed up until three in the morning packing and got up before six to catch a bus into town for the ferry to my last island. Sitting on a bench in the bow as the ferry chugged across the water all morning, I had time to muse about why I had changed my mind and ended up on a date and even in bed with Dmitri, when I was so in love with Jay.

As the hot sun poured down on my face, I felt flooded with warmth from the inside too. My freedom to have a date with Dimitri coexisted alongside my relationship with Jay. Phil had been right to question my ad—I didn't want monogamy. I wanted what Jay was offering—a close relationship with someone who matched me on many levels, a commitment to stay connected, and a freedom to be with others as a celebrated part of our relationship, not a threat to it. Like me, Jay was able to hold a vision of freedom and commitment at the same time. That warmth inside was my heart filling up with love for Jay.

I remembered how much my heart had longed for Timothy, Gregory, and even Rob. Now it was clear why I lingered with them and why we parted. Each had offered one or two aspects of my ideal partner—intelligence, spiritual awareness, emotional engagement, sexual passion, warm companionship, meaningful work, freedom to be with others—but not all of them. They were partial partners. Jay embodied all of these traits, so instead of feeling only partially met, I felt full and completely matched. On the fiftieth date, I knew I'd found the ideal partner in Jay.

When the ferry pulled into my island, I made my way from the main port to a quiet harbor, where the tiny balcony of my studio overlooked a narrow street. Strung out on three hours of sleep, I rested until dark, missing my first day there, but I didn't mind. Not only had the time spent with Dmitri been my fantasy day on a Greek island, it had ultimately helped me see more clearly what I loved about Jay. I sent a grateful *"Efharisto!"* to Dmitri for helping me finish the dating project in such a rewarding way.

SIXTIETH BIRTHDAY

~~~~~~~~~~

Two weeks later I was back in Oakland. It was almost 7:28 p.m. on Tuesday, June 14, 2011—the exact time I was born sixty years earlier. I was sitting on a chair looking out over the light-filled living room in Sarah's spacious apartment above Lake Merritt. Fifty of my favorite women and men were strewn about in chairs, on couches, and on the floor. Their talk died down as they looked at me expectantly. Feeling elegant in my white-and-black Aphrodite Greek dress, I felt as full of light as the sunbeams pouring through the windows. Jay was sitting next to me in a white poet's shirt and black pants. We matched. I glanced at him, met his eyes, reached for his hand, and squeezed it. He squeezed back.

I turned from Jay and gazed at my guests. "You are all my dearest friends," I said. "Thank you for being here for my birthday." We had spent the last two hours mingling in the high-ceilinged rooms of Sarah's elegant home, eating Mediterranean food and catching up with each other. I had gone through the crowd, enjoying seeing my friends dressed up, telling anyone I talked to how important they had been to me. I knew that if I missed someone, they would still get a personalized card from me. I'd written down what I appreciated about each person

291

there, along with a special memory of a time we spent together. Jay had helped me print the cards, as I was still writing up to the afternoon of the party. He had shown no impatience that I was doing all this at the last minute. Instead he pitched in, and because of that, we finished them in time to arrive early.

"As my friends," I continued, feeling sure of what I wanted to say, having practiced this speech on the way home from Greece and during the week leading up to my birthday, "you all know that I've been on a quest to find a partner. You supported me through the ups and downs of my dating project, and some of you were my dates." Smiles and murmurs spread through the group. At least ten of my dates were there—including Randy, Ben, Homer, Reed, Phil, Jules, and Jay. "You all know what I've been through, and I so appreciate your presence and support."

"After a long search, and a trip to Greece, I'm hereby declaring the dating project over," I said, pausing dramatically. "I've decided to choose Jay as my partner."

The cheers were immediate.

"I want to thank each of you for however you supported me, or Jay, in finding each other." I mentioned my close friends, my women's group, and my HAI community. I added a few more thank-yous, including to Sarah for having the party at her gorgeous place.

And then Jay said, "Lucky me to be chosen by this amazing woman!" A relieved chuckle ran through the room—he appreciated me. Most didn't know him as well as they knew me.

"And now, we're going to appreciate this incredible woman," Jay said. "I'll start." I had thought about how presumptuous it seemed to gather people for my birthday and ask them to all appreciate me in lieu of gifts. But almost all of these friends had been to HAI. They knew that appreciations were the best gift of all.

"I didn't know there was a woman in the world like you," Jay said. "One who was smart and sexy and funny and energetic and loving and creative and upbeat, and who wanted to be with me! I appreciate how you stay so connected and cocreate this amazing relationship with me. I want to continue to be with you and go deeper." As he gazed into my eyes, mine filled with tears, recognizing the commitment he was offering.

And then my friends added to what Jay said, calling out one by one from their seat or coming up to me and speaking into my eyes. They spoke of my positive energy, warmth, support for others, generosity, and determination and pluck to create the dating project. They were all the things I loved about myself, ways I'd been striving to become since my first HAI workshop. Homer walked right up to me. "I don't have any words," he said, "except that I love you." With that, he put his big black cowboy hat with the brown leather cord around it on my head. His love meant a lot, now that I'd gotten past the longing for him and saw him as a dear lover and friend. I felt even more elegant with his hat on—it looked oddly right with my dress.

My five lovers there—Homer, Ben, Phil, Reed, and Jay—were ready to love me up after the party, but after the appreciations, I was so full of everyone's love that I didn't need it. I had my friends, Jay as my lover and partner, and a future bright with love, sex, and intimacy.

Epilogue

WINTER SOLSTICE (2018)

'm standing in my living room by the fireplace, in front of my friends during this year's solstice ceremony. The fire that Jay made is blazing warmly behind me. It's my turn to say what I'm leaving behind in 2018. But I can't think of anything. There's my college job—I retired this year, but I let that go earlier. And I have a tiny personality flaw that I'd love to leave behind—impatience—but I've been working on that for a while. That's it. Everything else I want to keep.

At the three winter solstices of my dating project—2008, 2009, and 2010—I declared I would find a partner with whom I could share love, sex, joy, peace, creativity, and abundance. I just realized that I have all those things. I have the partner—Jay and I are celebrating our eighth anniversary next month on a naked cruise—and our life is full of those qualities, and more. We share love, sex, joy, and peace with each other on honeymoons and on adventures with friends—houseboats on the Delta, weekends in beach houses, Burning Man, clothing-optional resorts in Florida and Jamaica, visits to Jules and Tatiana in Mexico, three cruises (two of them naked), and a summer exploring Italy. We support each other's creativity—my writing and Jay's research. And we share an abundance of things we love, as shown in these glimpses of our life:

⟋————⟍

"Oh, sweetie!" I exclaim as Jay walks in holding a bouquet of irises. "These are beautiful!" Sometimes he brings a few red carnations, sometimes a bouquet with sunflowers and roses and our favorite, Peruvian lilies. Even though he brings me flowers every time he comes to Oakland—almost every weekend for the last eight years—I'm always touched. As if he'd walked out of the pages of date number 23, "Mr. Right," the one where Jules brought me flowers and was the perfect date. Now, all week I'll see the irises that the real Mr. Right brought.

⟋————⟍

We're getting dressed for the HAI holiday party, and I ask Jay, "Shall I wear the low-cut black slinky dress or the long black velvet one with silver sequins?"

"I love the one with sequins," he says. "But whatever you wear is fine. I'm just proud to be your partner at the party." I put on the sequin dress—it makes me feel festive. I add sparkly earrings and new strappy black heels that Jay helped me pick out. The old ones wore out.

"Let me take your picture," he says. Like the one Jules took of me putting on the original black heels the night of our date. By now, Jay and I have taken thousands of pictures of each other.

⟋————⟍

I walk into the holiday party at the community center while Jay parks the car, and friends start hugging me in greeting as soon as I walk in the door. "Where's Jay?" they ask. When he walks in the door, I smile and join him. I'm as proud to be with Jay as he is with me, and our faces show it. Could we be that shining couple walking into the party, as Reed and Olivia were ten years ago, my ideal couple from the "Ideal" chapter?

◦————◦

We wander around the holiday party, chatting with friends, remembering adventures we've shared with them in the last eight years. Jay starts talking to a man he's close to, and I spot a girlfriend I've not seen for years. Soon we're across the room from each other, but I feel an invisible thread connecting us. It's that connection I treasure. I know we will circle back to each other, in a close but spacious dance—the one that Ross and I savored in date number 30, "Balance," during the 2009 NYE party at the big house.

◦————◦

The next night, we're wending our way up the Oakland hills to Chandler's home for a sex party. A clingy black dress with a see-through back and high/low hem makes me feel sexy, and Jay has on one of his sparkly shirts.

"The most important thing for me," Jay is saying, "is for us to stay connected."

"Me too," I say, knowing that we will. It helps that we'll start out making love with each other before we consider being with anyone else. And it helps that we have a rule: if one of us is making love to someone else, the other can interrupt at any time for whatever reason. I interrupted Jay once at an early sex party, and he welcomed me into his embrace, giving me the reassurance I needed. I've not had to do that since, because I feel so secure with Jay.

Jay says that I wrecked his poly reputation because he only wants to be with me, emotionally. I feel his commitment to our relationship—he's the one who named us "C&J," started calling my house "C&J Central," and talks about doing things for C&J, like getting us early boarding tickets on airplanes, or making time to connect, or planning for our future. It's the commitment I wanted—to the relationship—with freedom to have sex with others. It's our own definition of polyamory: we don't have romantic relationships with others. As Jay says, we save the candlelight dinners for each other, but we snack on sex with our friends.

⊱————⊰

Jay and I are going on a Sunday hike in our favorite East Bay hills. We're training for the Tetons and need to get on the trail by three o'clock to hike eight miles before sunset. So we need to mobilize at two.

But we're running late. We had such a good plan. We spent the morning leisurely making love, had breakfast on the deck in the warm sun, and at noon agreed: two hours of work until the hike! We settle in—he in the study doing his mathematical modeling on his big computer, and me in the kitchen nook writing on my laptop. Only we get a little too settled. We know the deadline—stop at two. But neither of us stops at two. We enjoy our work, and we both have a hard time leaving one enjoyable activity to go on to the next.

Finally at two thirty, I say, "The hike! We have to get ready!"

"Right!" he calls from the study. "Just wrapping up."

I start cutting up fruit for snacks and gather my hiking clothes. He slowly puts on his hiking shorts and looks for his hat. I go down my list of hiking supplies, find them, and stuff them in my daypack. Finally I'm ready to go. By now it's after three.

"OK!" I say. "Ready?"

"Almost," he says from the study.

I frown. *We're already late. What's taking him so long?* I stand outside the study. "We're going to be late!" I whine.

He's going through his checklist. "Standing there won't make me go faster," he says.

I swallow my impatience. I smile to myself. I got what I asked for—someone who's not a stickler for time and who loves their work. I can't blame him—I'm like that too.

◦————◦

"I think we should visit your mother more often than twice a year," Jay said in 2015.

"Really?" I said. I call her every morning on my way to work, and we have short and sweet conversations, but I don't enjoy our visits—she still tends to criticize me.

"We don't know how much time we have with her," said Jay. "I'll buffer you."

And he did. We flew down to see her more often that year and the next, including every Thanksgiving, New Year's, and her ninety-second birthday in December 2016. On one visit, I snapped at her in response to her criticism. My mother later turned to Jay and said, "Why does she do that? How do you deal with it?"

"I just remind myself that she has a heart of gold," Jay said to her.

My mother smiled. "True," she said. "She does."

She loved our 2017 NYE party hats and horns. A selfie we took that night shows the three of us deliriously happy. Several weeks later, my mother passed away, sitting in her favorite chair, my sister and a caregiver nearby. I was so grateful to Jay for those visits.

◦————◦

Back at the sex party, we start out making love with each other, and then move into separate connections with others—me with Chandler, and Jay with our single friend Iris, first in separate rooms and then on the same bed. Eventually I'm on the big bed, and Jay has a vibrator against me, Chandler is stroking my legs and feet, and someone else is holding my arms down and kissing

299

me. I feel utterly taken and surrender into a yummy orgasm. I kiss Jay, Chandler, and the other guy, and then Jay enters me deeply and I feel him even more.

Driving home from the party, Jay and I debrief—did we each do what we wanted and stay connected? Yes, we decide. "There was no one else I wanted to go home with," Jay says. He always says that. "Me too," I say, knowing that there never is for me either.

At home, we make love again. After a sex party especially, we want to affirm that we are back with each other. In the morning, as I do each day, I get up early and meditate in my hot tub with my tea—the alone time Jay knows I need. This is the oasis of calm, warmth, and affection that I wanted, in the middle of an exciting life.

The vision of the relationship I wanted is still on my bathroom wall:

I am in a relationship
in which we adore and accept each other
and joyfully and creatively celebrate
our deep connections
of heart, spirit, body, and mind!

It must have worked.

NOTES

~~~

PART I: LETTING GO
The Plan
1. The *Human Awareness Institute (HAI)* can be found at: https
   ://www1.hai.org/

PART II: TOUCH
Waves
1. From "Magnificence," by Peter Makena. Used by permission
   from Peter Makena.
2. I use this Sanskrit word to refer to my vagina and vulva, as it
   has the connotation of sacred space.

PART IV: LONGING
Phone Dating
1. From "Mississippi" by Bob Dylan, © 1996 by Special Rider
   Music. Used by permission from Special Rider Music / Bob
   Dylan Music Company.

PART V: VISIONS
Relationship Class
1. *LoveWork*s can be found at: https://loveworkssolution.com/

ACKNOWLEDGMENTS

~~~~~~~~~~~~~~~

It took many years, many writing teachers, and a big Bay Area writing community to transform me from a social scientist report-writer into a writer of memoir. I'm grateful to all my writing teachers and writing companions for their honest feedback and generous encouragement as I turned my story into something others might want to read. I benefited greatly from the talented teachers in the Bay Area at the Writing Salon, Writer's Grotto, Writing Pad, and the Sonoma County Writer's Camp, and from those in NYC's Gotham online classes. Special appreciation for the substantial guidance, inspiration, and encouragement along the way from Alison Luterman, Andy Couturier, Brooke Warner, Jenny Bitner, Julia Scheeres, Rachel Howard, and Sasha Cagen.

Many appreciations to my friends and family for the support and encouragement you have given me in many big and little ways, from reading and listening enthusiastically to my stories, to welcoming me at our gatherings, to letting me disappear and miss out on being with you so I could write. I am so grateful for your presence in my life.

A huge gratitude to the Human Awareness Institute and everyone in that community, for teaching me everything I needed to know about relationships, listening to my stories during entertainment nights year after year, and allowing me to include part of a workshop in the book.

Appreciations to my fifty dates and the other men in this story for being so honest, real, and totally yourselves. Each of you taught me something about myself and the relationship I wanted. I hope you all find your special someone.

Big appreciations to Peter, the ideal ex-boyfriend and my ongoing friend, for being a fairy-tale start to the story and for allowing me to include him in it, and to Jim, for not only being a fairy-tale conclusion and continuation of the story but for being a loving and sexy companion and one of my favorite editors as I wrote it.

Special thanks to Catherine Rose, for saying, "You have to write these stories down!" To David Brownstein, who said, "Why don't you make writing your sabbatical project?" To Andy Couturier, who first asked, "How is the book going?" And to Nancy Barnes, who told me that while it may have been enjoyable for me to experience fifty dates, my readers did not need to go on all fifty with me.

Many thanks to the inspirational and courageous Brooke Warner for starting She Writes Press to empower and publish women's voices and for creating a community where women support each other through the highs and lows of the publishing process. I can't imagine publishing a book any other way. Thank you to Brooke and the many talented women on the staff of She Writes Press for taking such good care of me and my book.

And a deep gratefulness for all my sister She Writes Press authors for walking this path with me so bravely and generously. You are all amazing, and I'm proud to be among you.

ABOUT THE AUTHOR

C arolyn Lee Arnold drew upon her thirty years as a social
science researcher and ten years as a relationship workshop
assistant to create the dating project in *Fifty First Dates after Fifty*.
A native Californian from Los Angeles with a New England
education, Carolyn found her true home in the San Francisco
Bay Area, where she prepared for dating and life by attending
spiritual ceremonies, working in free clinics, leading women's
backpacking trips, hiking the local green hills, identifying as
a lesbian-feminist in the 1970s and '80s, and earning graduate
degrees in women's studies, statistics, and educational research.
Fifty First Dates after Fifty is her first book, and excerpts have
been published in *Persimmon Tree*, *Outside In Literary & Travel
Magazine*, and the Human Awareness Institute's *Enlighten
Journal*. An excerpt from her second memoir, about her lesbian-
feminist years, has been published in *Noyo River Review*. Still
a feminist, she lives in the Bay Area with her partner, one of her
fifty dates. For more information, including dating resources,
visit carolynleearnold.com.

Author photo © Andrea Scher

SELECTED TITLES FROM SHE WRITES PRESS

She Writes Press is an independent publishing
company founded to serve women writers everywhere.
Visit us at www.shewritespress.com.

Mating in Captivity: A Memoir by Helen Zuman. $16.95, 978-1-63152-337-3. A Harvard grad seeks a mate in a cult that forbids monogamy. To pursue love on her own terms, she must brave exile and learn self-trust.

Too Much of Not Enough: A Memoir by Jane Pollack. $16.95, 978-1-63152-527-8. After her husband drops the bomb that he's seeing someone else, Jane Pollak finds independence and self-acceptance by reviewing old lessons through a new lens of compassionate awareness and courageously pursuing exciting new unknowns—a journey that leads her to a reinvented, more authentic, life.

Insatiable: A Memoir of Love Addiction by Shary Hauer. $16.95, 978-1-63152-982-5. An intimate and illuminating account of corporate executive—and secret love addict—Shary Hauer's migration from destructive to healthy love.

Jumping Over Shadows: A Memoir by Annette Gendler. $16.95, 978-1-63152-170-6. Like her great-aunt Resi, Annette Gendler, a German, fell in love with a Jewish man—but unlike her aunt, whose marriage was destroyed by "the Nazi times," Gendler found a way to make her impossible love survive.

Big Wild Love: The Unstoppable Power of Letting Go by Jill Sherer Murray. $16.95, 978-1-63152-852-1. After staying in a dead-end relationship for twelve years, Jill Sherer Murray finally let go—and ultimately attracted the love she wanted. Here, she shares how, along with a process to help readers get unstuck and find their own big, wild love.

First Date Stories: Women's Romantic to Ridiculous Midlife Adventures by Jodi Klein. $16.95, 978-1-64742-185-4. A collection of hopeful, hilarious, and horrific tales—plus dating tips and inspirational quotes—designed to remind women in their mid-thirties and beyond that not all first dates are created equal, and sometimes they can be the beginning of something wonderful.